Microsoft®

Step by Step

MICROSOFT OFFICE
Microsoft®
OFFICE
USER SPECIALIST

APPROVED COURSEWARE

Microsoft®
Project 2000®

Microsoft Office Application

Carl S. Chatfield, PMP, and Timothy D. Johnson, MCP

PUBLISHED BY
Microsoft Press
A Division of Microsoft Corporation
One Microsoft Way
Redmond, Washington 98052-6399

Library of Congress Cataloging-in-Publication Data
Chatfield, Carl S., 1964-
    Microsoft Project 2000 Step by Step / Carl S. Chatfield, Timothy D. Johnson.
        p. cm.
    Includes index.
    ISBN 0-7356-0920-9
    1. Microsoft Project 2000.   2. Industrial project management--Computer programs. I.
Johnson, Timothy D., 1962- II. Title.

    HD69.P75 C465   2000
    005.369--dc21   99-086770

Printed and bound in the United States of America.

10 11 12 13 14 15   QWT   7 6 5 4 3 2

Distributed in Canada by H.B. Fenn and Company Ltd.

A CIP catalogue record for this book is available from the British Library.

Microsoft Press books are available through booksellers and distributors worldwide. For further information about international editions, contact your local Microsoft Corporation office or contact Microsoft Press International directly at fax (425) 936-7329. Visit our Web site at www.microsoft.com/mspress. Send comments to *mspinput@microsoft.com*.

Acquisitions Editor: Susanne Forderer
Project Editor: Kim Fryer

Part No. 097-000-7904

Acknowledgments

The authors wish to acknowledge the immeasurable contribution our reviewers made to the quality of this book. This book is a "from the ground up" (or "from the bottom up") effort, meaning that all of its content was created from scratch for Microsoft Project 2000. Our reviewers helped us develop what we hope is a realistic, informative, and technically accurate project management scenario used throughout the lessons of this book, as well as the descriptions of specific Microsoft Project features.

The "real-world" project managers and Microsoft Project users we'd like to thank include the following.

Rebecca Chatfield, Ph.D.: Database Designer

Darryl Chinn: Technical Writer

Kathleen Galvin: Senior Technical Writer, Excell Data, Inc.

John T. (JT) Harrison, PMP

Marcia R. Lombardi: The Boeing Company

Bruce Taylor, PMP: Project Managment Instructor and Consultant, Bluewater Project Management Services

John R. Spilker, PMP: Project Director

Susan Stainsby: Documentation Manager, Pacific Edge Software

Steve P. Wilhite, PMP: Project Management Consultant

The "insider" Microsoft Project technical experts we'd like to thank include the following.

Preethi Ramani, Program Manager, Microsoft Project
Adrian D. Jenkins, Microsoft Project PSS Lead
The Microsoft Project Support Team

v

Contents

Finding Your Best Starting Point

Microsoft Project 2000 is a powerful project management program you can use to help build project plans, track work completed, and account for variance from your baseline plan. With this book and its companion CD-ROM, you'll learn how to use Microsoft Project 2000 to manage your project's costs, schedule, and resources.

important

This book is designed for use with Microsoft Project 2000 for the Windows operating system. To find out which version of Microsoft Project you're running, you can check the product package or you can start the program, click the Help menu, and then click About Microsoft Project. If this book is not compatible with your software, a Step by Step book matching your software is probably available. Please visit the Microsoft Press World Wide Web site at http://mspress.microsoft.com or call 1-800-MSPRESS (1-800-677-7377) for more information.

Finding Your Best Starting Point in This Book

This book is designed for beginning users of project management software, as well as for those who are upgrading to Microsoft Project 2000 from an earlier version. Use the following table to find your best starting point in this book.

If you are	Follow these steps

New

To computers or
Microsoft Project

1 See Appendix A for an introduction to using Windows-based programs.

2 Install the practice files as described in the "Using the CD-ROM" section of this book.

3 Work through the book from start to finish. Earlier lessons describe how to set up a project, while later lessons explain how to track, manage, and communicate project information.

If you are	Follow these steps

Upgrading

from Microsoft Project 98

1 Learn about the new features of Microsoft Project 2000 that are covered in this book by reading through the following section, "New Features in Microsoft Project 2000."

2 Install the practice files as described in the "Using the CD-ROM" section of this book.

3 Complete the lessons that cover the topics you need. You can use the table of contents to find information about general topics. You can use the index to find information about a specific topic or feature.

If you are	Follow these steps

Setting up

a project plan,
but don't intend to track

work once the project
has started

1 Install the practice files as described in the "Using the CD-ROM" section of this book.

2 Complete the lessons in Parts 1, 2, and 3 only. These will help you set up, fine-tune, and print the plan.

If you are	Follow these steps
Referencing this book after working through the lessons	**1** Use the index to locate information about specific topics, and use the table of contents to locate information about general topics. **2** Read the Quick Reference at the end of each lesson for a brief review of the major tasks in the lesson. The Quick Reference topics appear in the same order as they occur in the lesson.

New Features in Microsoft Project 2000

Microsoft Project 2000 contains new and enhanced features that help you manage projects more effectively. One important area of improvement is in Web-based collaboration, so your entire team can record and share project information more easily. The PERT Chart in earlier versions of Microsoft Project has been redesigned from the ground up and renamed the Network Diagram. If you use Microsoft Office 2000, you might notice that it and Microsoft Project 2000 share more components and elements of the user interface than ever before.

The following table lists the features that are new or substantially changed in Microsoft Project 2000 and the lessons in which you can learn how to use them. You can also use the index to find information about a specific feature or a task you want to perform.

 The 2000 New! icon appears in the margin throughout this book next to information about these new features of Microsoft Project 2000.

To learn how to	See
Work with estimated durations and month durations	Lesson 3
Set up and work with material resources	Lessons 4, 8
Set a deadline for a task; create a task calendar	Lesson 6
View tasks or resources grouped by cost or other criteria	Lesson 9
Include summary project information in headers and footers	Lesson 10
Print graphic indicators of project status	Lesson 15
Use the redesigned online Help system in Microsoft Project to get a broad view of project management processes	Appendix A
Use Microsoft Project Central and decide whether your project team should use it; learn about improvements to integration with Microsoft Outlook	Appendix D

Corrections, Comments, and Help

Every effort has been made to ensure the accuracy of this book and the contents of the Microsoft Project 2000 Step by Step CD-ROM. Microsoft Press provides corrections and additional content for its book through the World Wide Web at: http://mspress.microsoft.com/support

If you have comments, questions, or ideas regarding this book or the CD-ROM, please send them to us.

Send e-mail to: mspinput@microsoft.com

Or send postal mail to:
Microsoft Press
Attn: Step by Step Editor
One Microsoft Way
Redmond, WA 98052-6399

Please note that support for the Microsoft Project 2000 product itself is not offered through the above addresses. For help using Microsoft Project 2000, visit the Microsoft Product Support Services Web site at the following location:
http://www.microsoft.com/support/

You can call Microsoft Project 2000 Technical Support at (425) 454-2030 Monday through Friday between 5 A.M. and 9 P.M. Pacific time and Saturday between 9 A.M. and 3 P.M. Pacific time, excluding holidays.

Visit Our World Wide Web Site

We invite you to visit the Microsoft Press World Wide Web site. You can visit us at the following location:

http://mspress.microsoft.com

You'll find descriptions of all of our books, information about ordering titles, notices of special features and events, additional content for Microsoft Press books, and much more.

You can also find out the latest in software developments and news from Microsoft Corporation by visiting the following World Wide Web site:

http://www.microsoft.com/

We look forward to your visit to the Web!

Using the Microsoft Project 2000 Step by Step CD-ROM

The CD-ROM inside the back cover of this book contains the practice files that you'll use as you perform the exercises in the book and multimedia files that demonstrate many features introduced in the exercises. By using the practice files, you won't waste time creating the samples used in the lessons—instead, you can concentrate on learning how to use Microsoft Project 2000. With the files and the step-by-step instructions in the lessons, you'll also learn by doing, which is an easy and effective way to acquire and remember new skills.

important

Before you break the seal on the practice CD-ROM package, be sure that this book matches your version of the software. This book is designed for use with Microsoft Project 2000 for the Windows operating system. To find out which version of Microsoft Project you are running, you can check the product package or you can start the software, click the Help menu, and then click About Microsoft Project. If your program is not compatible with this book, a Step by Step book matching your software is probably available. Please visit our World Wide Web site at http://mspress.microsoft.com or call 1-800-MSPRESS (1-800-677-7377) for more information.

If you have not yet purchased Microsoft Project 2000, you can use the evaluation version of Microsoft Project 2000 included on this book's CD-ROM to complete the exercises in this book. For more information, see "Installing the Evaluation Software" below.

Installing the Practice Files

Follow these steps to install the practice files on your computer's hard disk so that you can use them with the exercises in this book.

1   If your computer isn't on, turn it on now.

2   If you're using Windows NT or Windows 2000, press Ctrl+Alt+Del to display a dialog box asking for your user name and password. If you are using Windows 98, you will see this dialog box if your computer is connected to a network.

3   If necessary, type your user name and password into the appropriate boxes, and then click OK. If you see the Welcome dialog box, click the Close button.

4   Remove the CD-ROM from the package inside the back cover of this book and insert it in the CD-ROM drive of your computer.

5   Click the Install Practice Files option.

The setup program window appears with the recommended options preselected for you. For best results in using the practice files with this book, accept these preselected settings.

6   Follow the instructions on the screen.

7   When the files have been installed, remove the CD-ROM from your CD-ROM drive and replace it in the package inside the back cover of the book.

A folder called MS Project 2000 SBS Practice has been created on your hard disk, and within it the practice files have been placed in folders that correspond to the lesson numbers. A shortcut to the practice folder is placed on your desktop.

Using the Practice Files

Each lesson in this book explains when and how to use any practice files for that lesson. When a practice file is needed for a lesson, the book will list instructions on how to open the file. The lessons are built around a scenario that simulates a real project management environment, so you can easily apply the skills you learn to your own work. For the scenario in this book, you'll imagine that you are the project manager of Industrial Smoke and Mirrors, a small film production company. Your company recently installed Microsoft Project 2000, and you are eager to use it to manage a short film project that is getting underway.

The screen illustrations in this book might look different from what you see on your computer, depending on how your computer is set up. To help make your screen match the illustrations in this book, please follow the instructions in Appendix B, "Matching the Exercises."

For those of you who like to know all the details, here's a list of the practice files used in the lessons. For the convenience of readers who don't want to work from the beginning of each lesson, separate practice files are included.

The Part 1 folder contains

Lesson number and files	Description
Lesson01 (None)	This lesson does not require a file
Lesson02 (None)	In this lesson you create a new file for a short film project
Lesson03 03A.mpp	A copy of the file you created in Lesson 2
Lesson04 04A.mpp	A copy of the file you worked on in Lesson 3
Lesson05 05A.mpp	A copy of the file you worked on in Lesson 4

The Part 2 folder contains

Lesson number and files	Description
Lesson06 06A.mpp	A copy of the file you worked on in Lesson 5, with additional tasks, resources, and assignments
Lesson07 07A.mmp	A copy of the file you worked on in Lesson 6
Lesson08 08A.mpp	A copy of the file you worked on in Lesson 7
Review & Practice Part2A.mpp	Practice file for Part 2

The Part 3 folder contains

Lesson number and files	Description
Lesson09	
09A.mpp	A copy of the file you worked on in Lesson 8
Lesson10	
10A.mpp	A copy of the file you worked on in Lesson 9
Lesson11	
11A.mpp	A copy of the file you worked on in Lesson 10
Lesson12	
12A.mpp	A copy of the file you worked on in Lesson 11.
Letter To Client.rtf Sample Task List.xls	Files you use for importing and exporting information from Microsoft Project
Lesson13	
13B.mpp 13B.mpp	Two files you use to create a resource pool, consolidated file, and cross-project links
Review & Practice	
Part3A.mpp	
Part3B.mpp	
Commercial Part 3.mpp	
Promo Part 3.mpp	Practice files for Part 3

The Part 4 folder contains

Lesson number and files	Description
Lesson14	
14A.mpp	A copy of the file you worked on in Lesson 12
Lesson15	
15A.mpp	A copy of the file you worked on in Lesson 14
Lesson16	
16A.mpp	A copy of the file you worked on in Lesson 15
Review & Practice	
Part4A.mpp	Practice file for Part 4

Using the Multimedia Files

Throughout this book, you will see icons for multimedia files for particular exercises. Use the following steps to run the multimedia files.

1   Insert the CD in the CD-ROM drive of your computer.

2   Click the Browse CD option.

3   Double-click the Multimedia folder, and double-click the file you want to view.

Uninstalling the Practice Files

Use the following steps when you want to delete the practice files added to your hard disk by the Step by Step setup program.

1   On the Windows taskbar, click Start, point to Settings, and then click Control Panel.

2   Double-click the Add/Remove Programs icon.

    The Add/Remove Programs dialog box appears.

3   Choose one of the following:

    ● In Windows 98 or Windows NT: On the Install/Uninstall tab, select Microsoft Project 2000 SBS Practice from the list, and then click Add/Remove.

    ● In Windows 2000: Under Currently Installed Programs, select Microsoft Project 2000 SBS Practice from the list, and then click Change/Remove.

    A confirmation message appears.

4   Click Yes or OK.

    The practice files are uninstalled.

5   Click Close or OK to close the Add/Remove Programs dialog box.

6   Close the Control Panel window.

Need Help with the Practice Files?

Every effort has been made to ensure the accuracy of this book and the contents of the practice files CD-ROM. If you do run into a problem, Microsoft Press provides corrections for its books through the World Wide Web at:

http://mspress.microsoft.com/support/

We invite you to visit our main Web page at:

http://mspress.microsoft.com

You'll find descriptions of all of our books, information about ordering titles, notices of special features and events, additional content for Microsoft Press books, and much more.

Installing the Evaluation Software

The CD-ROM inside the back cover includes an evaluation version of Microsoft Project 2000. If you have not yet purchased Microsoft Project 2000, you can install the evaluation version to complete all of the exercises in this book, and for your own general evaluation and testing of Microsoft Project 2000.

The system requirements for the evaluation version are as follows:

- PC with a Pentium 75 MHz or higher processor

- Microsoft Windows 95 or later operating system, or Microsoft Windows NT Workstation operating system version 4.0 with Service Pack 3 or later, or Microsoft Windows 2000 Professional

- 20 MB of RAM for Windows 95 or later; 32 MB of RAM for Windows NT Workstation 4.0 or 64 MB of RAM for Windows 2000 Professional

- 100 MB available hard-disk space for typical installation

- CD-ROM drive

Please note the following prior to installing the evaluation version:

- If you have previously installed the full version of Microsoft Project 2000, do not install the trial version.

- If you have previously upgraded to or installed a Microsoft Project 2000 Beta version on your computer, uninstall it prior to installing the Microsoft Project 2000 trial version.

- If you have Microsoft Project 4.0, 4.1, or 98 installed on your computer, Setup will ask you if you want to remove these versions. Choose No when prompted.

- The trial version will stop functioning 60 days from the time you install it, regardless of how frequently you use it. The files you create or edit with the trial version are not affected once the trial version expires.

- Microsoft does not provide technical support for the evaluation version of Microsoft Project 2000. Should you have any questions about the trial software, visit the Microsoft Project newsgroup. To view or subscribe to this newsgroup, point your newsreader to news://msnews.microsoft.com/microsoft.public.project

Follow these steps to install the evaluation version of Microsoft Project 2000 on your computer's hard disk.

1   Remove the CD-ROM from the package inside the back cover of this book and insert it in the CD-ROM drive of your computer.

     A menu screen will appear. If the menu does not appear, double-click StartCD.exe in the root of the CD.

2   In the Microsoft Project 2000 CD-ROM dialog box, click Browse CD.

     The contents of the CD-ROM are displayed.

3   Open the Eval folder.

4   Double-click Setup.exe.

     The installation program starts.

     Follow the instructions that appear on your screen.

Introducing Project Management

After completing this lesson, you will be able to:

✔ *Understand what projects are and how they differ from ongoing operations.*

✔ *Define projects in terms of the project triangle.*

✔ *Apply the features of Microsoft Project 2000 to both the planning and the executing phases of projects.*

ESTIMATED TIME
15 min.

This lesson introduces project management. Although project management is a broad subject, this lesson focuses on the "project triangle" model. In this model, you work with projects in terms of time, cost, and scope.

Practice files for the lesson

To complete this lesson, you won't need to start Microsoft Project or open a project file. Just read on.

Understanding What Defines a Project

Succeeding as a project manager requires that you complete your projects on time, finish within budget, and make sure your customers are happy with what you deliver. That sounds simple enough, but how many projects have you heard of (or worked on) that were completed late or cost too much or didn't meet the needs of their customers?

For more information about the Project Management Institute and the PMBOK, see Appendix E, "What's Next?"

A Guide to the Project Management Body of Knowledge (referred to as the PMBOK—pronounced "pimbok") defines a **project** as "a temporary endeavor undertaken to create a unique product or service." Let's walk through this definition to clarify what a project is and is not.

First, a project is *temporary*. A project's duration might be just a week or it might go on for years, but every project has an end date. You might not know that end date when the project starts, but it's out there somewhere in the future. Projects are not the same as **ongoing operations**, although the two have a lot in common. Ongoing operations, as the name suggests, go on indefinitely; you don't establish an end date. Examples include most activities of accounting and human resources departments. People that run ongoing operations might also manage projects; for example, a manager of a human resources department for a large organization might plan a college recruiting fair. But projects are distinguished from ongoing operations by an expected end date, such as the date of the recruiting fair.

Next, a project is an *endeavor*. **Resources,** such as people and equipment, need to do work. The endeavor is *undertaken* by a team or an organization, so projects have a sense of being intentional, planned events. Successful projects don't happen spontaneously; some amount of preparation and planning happens first.

Finally, every project *creates a unique product or service*. This is the **deliverable** for the project, the reason that the project was undertaken. A refinery that produces gasoline does not produce a unique product. The whole idea, in this case, is to produce a standardized commodity; you usually don't want to buy gas from one station that is significantly different from gas at another station. On the other hand, commercial airplanes are unique products. Although all Boeing 777 airplanes might look about the same to most of us, each is, in fact, highly customized for the needs of its purchaser.

By now, you may be getting the idea that a lot of the work that goes on in the world is project work. If you schedule, track, or manage any of this work, then congratulations are in order: you are already doing some project management work!

Project management has been a recognized profession since about the 1950s, but project management work in some form has been going on as long as people have been doing complex work. When the Great Pyramids in Egypt were built, somebody somewhere was tracking resources, schedule, and the specifications for the final deliverable.

tip

Project management is now a well-recognized job in most industries. To learn more about organizations that train project managers and advance project management as a profession, see Appendix E, "What's Next?"

The Project Triangle: Seeing Projects in Terms of Time, Cost, and Scope

You can visualize project work in many ways, but our favorite is what's sometimes called the **project triangle:**

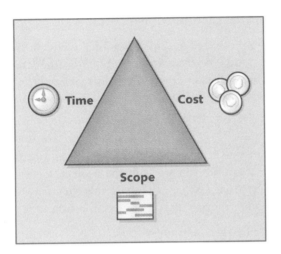

This theme has many variations, but the basic idea is that every project has some element of a time constraint, has some type of budget, and requires some amount of work to complete. (In other words, it has a defined scope.) The term *constraint* has a specific meaning in Microsoft Project, but here we're using the more general meaning of a limiting factor. Let's consider these constraints one at a time.

Time

Have you ever worked on a project that had a deadline? (Maybe we should ask, have you ever worked on a project that did not have a deadline?) Limited **time** is the one constraint of any project with which we are all probably most familiar. If you're working on a project right now, ask your team members what the project deadline is. They might not know the project budget or the scope of work in great detail, but chances are they all know the project deadline.

Here are some examples of time constraints:

- You're writing a paper for a class and the instructor has a "no late papers" policy.

- You're building a house and you must finish the roof before the rainy season arrives.

- You are assembling a large display booth for a trade show that starts in two months.

- You are developing a new inventory tracking system that must be tested and running by the start of the next fiscal year.

Most of us have been trained to understand time since we were children, and we carry wristwatches, paper and electronic organizers, and other tools to help us manage time. For many projects that create a product or result in an event, time is the most important constraint to manage.

Cost

You might think of cost just as dollars, but project cost has a broader meaning: costs are all the resources required to carry out the project. Cost includes the people and equipment who do the work, the materials they use, and all the other events and issues that require money or someone's attention in a project.

Here are some examples of cost constraints:

- You have signed a fixed-price contract to deliver an inventory-tracking software system to a client. If your costs exceed the agreed-upon price, your customer might be sympathetic but probably won't be willing to renegotiate the contract.

- The president of your organization has directed you to carry out a customer-research project using only the staff and equipment in your department.

- You have received a $5,000 grant to create a public art installation. You have no other funds.

For virtually all projects, cost is ultimately a limiting constraint; few projects could go over budget without eventually requiring corrective action.

Scope

You should consider two aspects of scope: product scope and project scope. Every successful project produces a unique product: a tangible item or a service. You might develop some products for one customer you know by name. You might develop other products for millions of potential customers waiting to buy them (you hope). Customers usually have some expectations about the features

For more information on determining project scope, see Lesson 3, "Entering and Organizing Tasks."

and functions of products they consider purchasing. **Product scope** describes the intended quality, features, and functions of the product—often in minute detail. Documents that outline this information are sometimes called product specifications. A service or an event usually has some expected features as well. We all have expectations about what we'll do or see at a party, a concert, or the Olympic Games.

Project scope, on the other hand, describes the work required to deliver a product or a service with the intended product scope. Although product scope focuses on the customer or the user of the product, project scope is mainly the concern of the people who will carry out the project. Project scope is usually measured in *tasks* and *phases*.

Here are some examples of scope constraints:

- Your organization won a contract to develop an automotive product that has exact requirements—for example, physical dimensions measured to .01 millimeters. This is a product scope constraint that will influence project scope plans.

- You are constructing a building on a lot that has a height restriction of 50 feet.

- You can use only internal services to develop part of your product, and those services follow a product development methodology that is different from what you had planned.

Product scope and project scope are closely related. The project manager who manages project scope well must also understand product scope or must know how to communicate with those who do.

Time, Cost, and Scope: Managing Project Constraints

Project management gets most interesting when you have to balance the time, cost, and scope constraints of your projects—"balance" as on a high wire. You could also think of juggling these constraints, or juggling them while on a high wire...well, you get the idea. Let's return to the project triangle model. The project triangle illustrates the process of balancing constraints because the three sides of the triangle are connected, and changing one side of a triangle affects at least one other side. (You can see this in action if you assemble a physical model with a rubber band or toothpicks.) Here are some examples of constraint balance:

- If the duration (**time**) of your project schedule decreases, you might need to increase budget (**cost**) because you must hire more resources to do the same work in less time. If you can't increase the budget, you might need to reduce the **scope** because the resources you have can't do all of the planned work in less time.

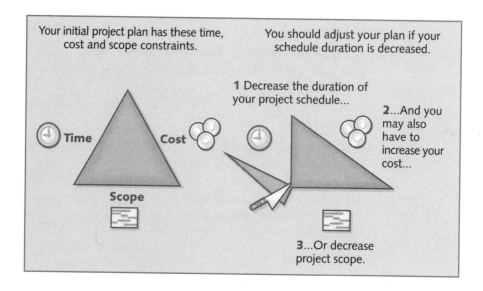

Your initial project plan has these time, cost and scope constraints.

You should adjust your plan if your schedule duration is decreased.

Time   Cost

Scope

1 Decrease the duration of your project schedule...

2...And you may also have to increase your cost...

3...Or decrease project scope.

If you must decrease a project's duration, make sure that overall project quality is not unintentionally lowered. For example, testing and quality control often occur last in a software development project; if the project duration is decreased late in the project, those tasks might be the ones cut back. You must weigh the benefits of decreasing the project duration against the potential downside of a deliverable with poorer quality.

- If the budget (*cost*) of your project decreases, you might need more *time* because you can't pay for as many resources or for resources of the same efficiency. If you can't increase the time, you might need to reduce project *scope* because fewer resources can't do all of the planned work in the time you have.

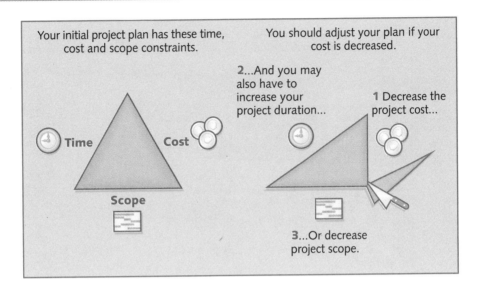

If you must decrease a project's budget, you should look at the **grades** of material resources for which you had budgeted. For example, did you plan to shoot a film in 35 mm when cheaper 16 mm film would do? A lower-grade material is not necessarily a lower-quality material. As long as the grade of material is appropriate for its intended use, it might still be of high quality. Another example: fast food and gourmet are two grades of restaurant food, but you may find high-quality and low-quality examples of each.

You should also look at the costs of the human and equipment resources you have planned to use. Can you hire less experienced people for less money to carry out simpler tasks? Reducing project costs can lead to a poorer quality deliverable, however. As a project manager, you must consider (or more likely communicate to the decision makers) the benefits versus the risks of reducing costs.

- If your project *scope* increases, you might need more *time* or more resources (*cost*) to do the additional work. If the project scope increases after the project has started, it's called **scope creep**. Changing project scope midway through a project is not necessarily a bad thing; for example, your intended customer might have changed and you need to deliver a different product to the new customer. Changing project scope is a bad thing only if the project manager doesn't recognize and plan for the new requirements—that is, when other constraints (cost, time) are not correspondingly examined and, if necessary, adjusted.

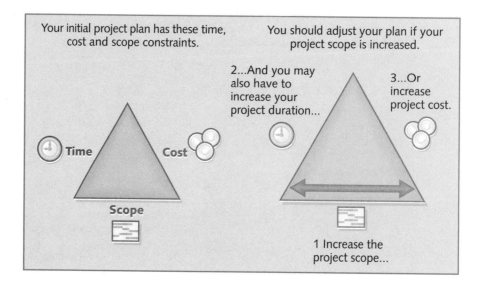

Time, cost, and scope are the three essential elements of any project. To succeed as a project manager, you'll have to know quite a bit about how all three of these constraints apply to your projects. You need a tool to help manage them.

Managing Your Projects with Microsoft Project

The best project management tool in the world can never replace your good judgment. However, the tool can and should help you accomplish the following while looking and feeling like other productivity programs you might use frequently:

- Track all the information you gather about the work, duration, and resource requirements for your project.

- Visualize your project plan in standard, well-defined formats.

- Schedule tasks and resources consistently and effectively.

- Exchange project information with all **stakeholders** over an intranet or the Internet.

- Communicate with resources and other stakeholders, while leaving ultimate control in the hands of the project manager.

You knew we'd bring up Microsoft Project somewhere in this lesson, didn't you? In the lessons that follow, you'll be introduced to the rich functionality of Microsoft Project in a realistic context: managing a project from conception to completion.

One Microsoft Project expert we know describes the program as "a database that knows about time."

One way to visualize the overall work required from a project manager is in terms of major areas of effort over time. Below, we've provided pointers to the relevant parts of this book for each phase of project management.

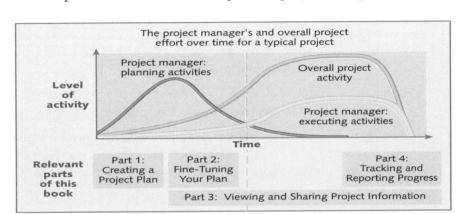

Parts 1 and 2 of this book describe how to plan a project. Part 3 describes communication activities you might perform at any point in a project's life cycle. Part 4 describes the how to track actual work against your project plan, and take corrective steps when necessary.

Not everything in this book will apply to your needs, and you'll probably have needs that this book won't address. But, after you complete this tutorial, you'll be off to a great start with Microsoft Project.

Glossary

Cost All the resources required to carry out the project, including people and equipment who complete the work and the materials they use as they complete the work. Cost is one side of the project triangle model.

Deliverable The final product or service you intend the project to create.

Grade A characterization of a resource that describes the appropriate functional use of the resource but not the quality of the resource.

Ongoing operations Activities that have no planned end date and are repetitive in nature. Examples include accounting, managing human resources, and some manufacturing.

Product scope The quality, features, and functions (often called specifications) of the deliverable of the project.

Project A temporary endeavor undertaken to create a unique product or service.

Project scope The work required to deliver a product with agreed-upon quality, features, and functions.

Project triangle A popular model of project management in which time, cost, and scope are represented as the three sides of a triangle. A change to one side will have some effect on at least one of the other two sides. This model has many variations.

Resources People, equipment, and material (and the associated costs of each) required to complete the work of a project.

Scope The products or services to be provided by a project and the work required to deliver them. For project planning, it's useful to distinguish between product scope and project scope. Scope is one side of the project triangle model.

Scope creep An increase in product scope after project planning has concluded and project execution has started. Scope creep can cripple a project if it is not recognized and responded to by the project manager.

Stakeholders All people or organizations that might be affected by project activities (those who "have a stake" in its success). These include those working on the project, as well as others (such as customers) external to the project work.

Time The scheduled durations of individual tasks and of the overall project; the schedule. Time is one side of the project triangle model.

2

Finding Your Way Around in Microsoft Project

ESTIMATED TIME
20 min.

After completing this lesson, you will be able to:

✔ *Start Microsoft Project and create a project file based on a template.*

✔ *Use and customize menus and toolbars.*

✔ *Display different views and tables.*

✔ *Create a project file and enter a project start date.*

✔ *Enter properties about the project file.*

✔ *Save a project file and set options about saving files.*

In this lesson, you will be introduced to the major parts of the Microsoft Project interface, and you will create the project file you will work with throughout the lessons in this book.

Microsoft Project is a member of the Microsoft Office family of desktop programs, so much of what you see in Microsoft Project is similar to what you see in Microsoft Word, Excel, and Access. The organization of the general menu bar and toolbar, for example, is very similar. You have access to the same online Help tools, such as the Office Assistant and ToolTips, throughout Microsoft Project. Much of what you do with Microsoft Project is distinct from what you do with other Office programs, however.

Getting Started with Microsoft Project

PROJ2000E-3-3

In this exercise, you start Microsoft Project, create a file based on a **template**, and see the major areas of the default Microsoft Project interface.

1   On the Windows taskbar, click the Start button.

The Start menu appears.

2   On the Start menu, point to Programs, and then click Microsoft Project.

Microsoft Project appears. Your screen should look similar to the following illustration.

When you initially start Microsoft Project, the following items appear in the application window:

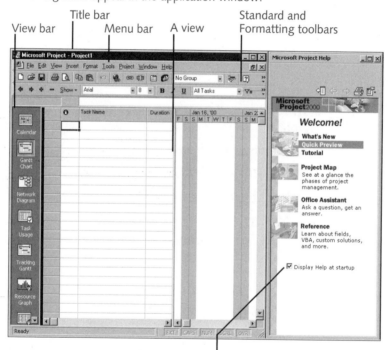

When you start Microsoft Project, Help appears in this window. To stop Help from appearing when you start Microsoft Project, click here. If you later change your mind about Help displaying on startup, on the Tools menu click Options, and then on the General tab click the Display Help On Startup box.

3 On the Microsoft Project Help title bar, click the Minimize button.

The Help window minimizes, and the Microsoft Project window expands to fill the screen. Next you will view the templates included with Microsoft Project and create a project file based on one of them.

4 On the File menu, click New.

The New dialog box appears.

2000 New! **5** Click the Project Templates tab.

Your screen should look similar to the following illustration.

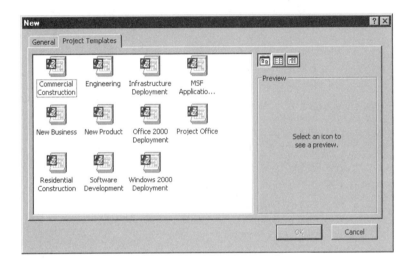

2000 New! All of the templates listed have been developed by project management professionals just for Microsoft Project 2000.

6 Select Residential Construction, and then click OK.

Microsoft Project creates a file based on the Residential Construction template, and the Project Information dialog box appears.

2

Finding Your Way Around

Every project is scheduled from either a start date or a finish date.

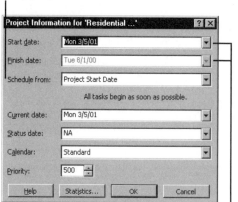

Once you choose how to schedule the project, you pick either the start date or the finish date. Most projects should be scheduled from the project start date.

Microsoft Project proposes the current date as the project start date.

7   Click OK.

Your screen should look similar to the following illustration, although the exact dates you see in the Gantt Chart probably differ.

Microsoft Project adjusts the initial tasks in the project to begin at the project start date you specified.

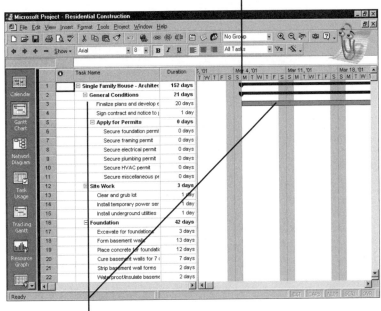

The Gantt Chart view is divided into a table on the left and a graphical chart on the right. The bars on the right correspond to tasks on the left.

tip

Most items you see in Microsoft Project support **ToolTips**. Point to the bars and dates in the Gantt Chart or to buttons on the toolbars to see some of the available ToolTips.

For the next few exercises in this lesson, you will use the sample data provided by the template to identify the major parts of the Microsoft Project interface.

Finding Your Way Around

2

tip

In addition to creating a file based on a template, you can save any Microsoft Project file as a template. When you do so, you can choose which information you want to exclude from the template, such as planned or actual schedules and cost information. For more information, ask the Office Assistant "How do I save a Project file as a template?"

Working with Menus and Toolbars

Most of the instructions you give to Microsoft Project are given through the Menu bar and toolbars. Initially, Microsoft Project displays the Menu bar and two of its 10 toolbars: Standard and Formatting.

Like other Microsoft Office 2000 applications, Microsoft Project customizes the menus and toolbars for you, based on how frequently you use specific commands or toolbar buttons. The most frequently used commands and buttons

Try out the Office Assistant

If you use such Microsoft Office programs as Excel and Word, you're probably familiar with the **Office Assistant**, a cartoon character that appears in the program's window. The primary purpose of the Office Assistant in Microsoft Project is to locate Help topics based on questions you ask. To try it, click the Office Assistant and in the What Would You Like To Do box, type **Tell me about Templates in Project,** and then click Search. The Office Assistant locates and displays the topics that are most closely related to the keywords or concepts in your question. Click the first topic listed, "Templates included with Microsoft Project." If you'd like to learn more about these templates, read the topic that appears in the Microsoft Project Help window. To close the list of found topics, click the Office Assistant.

If you prefer not to use the Office Assistant, you can still use the same underlying tools to get access to Help topics. In the Microsoft Project Help window, click the Show button to see the navigation tabs available with Help. Click the Answer Wizard tab. Type the same question again, and then click Search. You'll see similar results. The Answer Wizard tab is available whether or not the Office Assistant is displayed. To display Help without using the Office Assistant, open the Help menu, and click Contents And Index.

will remain visible on the menus and toolbars, while the commands and buttons you don't use will be temporarily hidden.

> ## tip
>
> Most items and screen regions you see in Microsoft Project support **shortcut menus**. To see some of the available shortcut menus, right-click items such as bars in the Gantt Chart or buttons on the toolbars.

In this exercise, you learn to customize the behavior of the menus and toolbars in Microsoft Project.

1 Click the Tools menu.

Microsoft Project initially displays only a portion of all commands on the Tools menu.

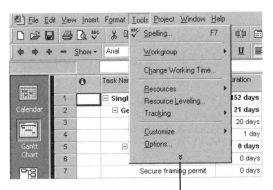

Initially, Microsoft Project displays only the most commonly used commands on a menu. Click the chevron here to see all commands.

2 Click the chevron at the bottom of the menu.

Microsoft Project expands the Tools menu to show all commands. The commands that initially were hidden now appear with a lighter gray background.

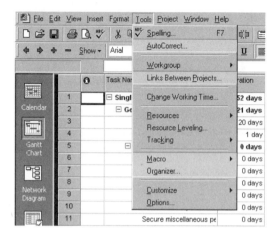

tip
To quickly expand a menu, you can double-click the menu name.

3   Point to Customize, and in the submenu that appears, click Toolbars.
Microsoft Project displays the Customize dialog box.

4   Click the Options tab.

To disable the personalized menu behavior, clear this box.

Here you can control the behavior of menus and toolbars in Microsoft
Project.

5   Select the Standard And Formatting Toolbars Share One Row check box, and then click Close.

Microsoft Project rearranges the Standard and Formatting toolbars so they appear side-by-side rather than stacked. Your screen should look similar to the following illustration.

When the toolbars are arranged side-by-side, there is more vertical space for the Microsoft Project data.

6   Click More Buttons on the Standard or the Formatting toolbar.

Microsoft Project displays the buttons that do not fit on the single row. As you use Microsoft Project, the program will show the buttons you use most often on the toolbar, but will hide those you do not use and place them in this secondary list.

7   On the Tools menu, point to Customize, and then click Toolbars.

8   Click the Options tab, clear the Standard And Formatting Toolbars Share One Row check box, and then click Close.

Microsoft Project rearranges the Standard and Formatting toolbars so they once again appear stacked.

Switching Between Views and Tables

The working space in Microsoft Project is called a **view**. Microsoft Project contains dozens of views, but you normally work with just one view (sometimes two) at a time. You use views to enter, edit, analyze, and display your project information. The default view, the one that you see when Microsoft Project starts, is the Gantt Chart view.

There are various ways to switch between views:

- ▓ Select from the most commonly used views on the View bar on the left edge of the Microsoft Project window.

- ▓ Select from the same set of views on the View menu.

- ▓ See all available views by selecting the More Views command on the View menu.

Finding Your Way Around

2

Each view focuses on **task, resource,** or **assignment** details. In most views, these details are organized into **tables.** For example, the default table you see in the Gantt Chart view is called Entry table, and it contains information about tasks. A table is a spreadsheet-like grid of data, organized into rows and columns. Each row contains information about a unique task or resource. Each column describes a unique value of that task or resource.

To change the table that appears in a view, on the View menu, point to Table, and then select the table you want. Switching tables changes which information you see in the view, but it never changes the information itself.

In general, the methods used to control what you see in Microsoft Project can be summarized as:

- Select the view that most broadly organizes and presents the task, resource, or assignment information the way you want.
- In the selected view, choose a table that contains the specific project details about a task or resource that you're interested in. (Note that not all views support tables.)
- Filter, sort, or otherwise organize the data to suit your needs.

In addition to using the built-in views and tables as they are, you can customize them or create your own. You will do this in Lesson 9, "Getting Project Information to Look the Way You Want."

In this exercise, you switch between different views and tables.

1   In the Gantt Chart view, notice the two horizontal scroll bars at the bottom of the window. Move the horizontal scroll bar in the table portion of the Gantt Chart view to the right to see more columns of information about the tasks in this project.

2   Move the horizontal scroll bar in the chart portion of the Gantt Chart view to the right to see more Gantt bars.

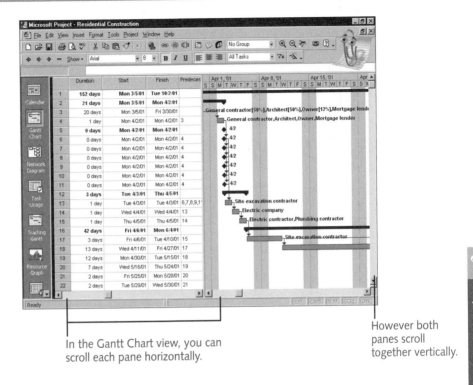

In the Gantt Chart view, you can scroll each pane horizontally.

However both panes scroll together vertically.

Next you switch to another view.

3 On the View menu, click Resource Sheet.

Microsoft Project switches to the Resource Sheet view. Your screen should look similar to the following illustration.

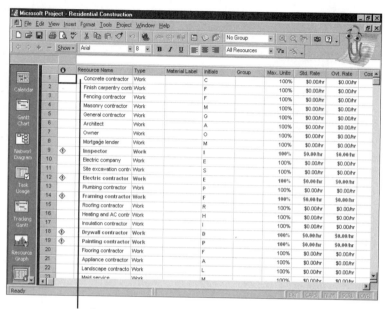

In the Resource Sheet view and other resource views, each row in the table contains information about one resource.

This view focuses on resource details. The default table in the Resource Sheet view is the Entry table. However, you can switch to another table to see different details about the resources.

4   On the View menu, point to Table: Entry and then click Work.

Microsoft Project displays the Work table in the Resource Sheet view.

To conclude this exercise, you will switch to a view that focuses on the assignments of resources to tasks.

5   On the View menu, click Task Usage.

Microsoft Project switches to the Task Usage view. Your screen should look similar to the following illustration.

In the Task Usage view and other task views, each row in the table contains information about one task or its assigned resources.

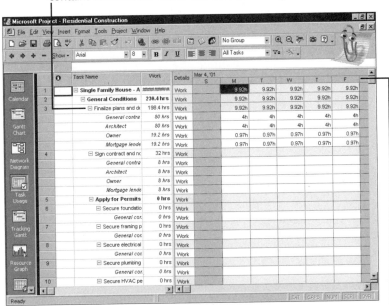

The timescale in a usage view shows work values on a daily or other basis.

In this view, you see tasks in the numbered rows on the left, and beneath them the resources assigned to each task. On the right side of the window, you see a **timescaled** grid that shows you daily work values per assignment. The Task Usage view, like the Gantt Chart and a few other views in Microsoft Project, is divided into two regions. Each region has its own horizontal scroll bar.

In later lessons, you will work more with these and other views and tables. For now, you are done with the Residential Construction file, and you are ready to create a Microsoft Project file that you will use throughout this book.

6   On the File menu, click Close.

7   When prompted to save changes to the Residential Construction file, click No.

Use combinations of views to see more details

You can display two views simultaneously in the Microsoft Project window. For example, you can display the Gantt Chart view in the upper pane and the Task Usage view in the lower pane of the window. With this arrangement, the task you select in the upper pane changes what you see in the lower pane. Likewise, scrolling the timescale grid in the lower pane adjusts the timescale grid in the Gantt Chart view in the upper pane.

The Resource Allocation and Task Entry views are both predefined split-screen or combination views. You can also display two views of your choice by clicking Split on the Window menu. Once the Microsoft Project window is split into two panes, click in the upper or lower pane, and then choose the view you want to appear there. To return to a single view, on the Window menu, click Remove Split.

Creating a Project File

PROJ2000-1-17

As mentioned in the introduction to this lesson, Microsoft Project focuses on time. Almost every project starts on one date and finishes on a later date. Sometimes you know the planned project start date, the planned project finish date, or both. However, when working with Microsoft Project you specify one date, not both: the project start date or the project finish date. Why? Because after you enter the project start or finish date and the **durations** of the tasks, Microsoft Project calculates the other date for you. Remember that Microsoft Project is not just a static repository of your project information; it is an active scheduling tool.

Most projects should be scheduled from a start date, even if you know that the project must end by a certain date. Scheduling from a start date causes all tasks to start as soon as possible, and it gives you the greatest scheduling flexibility. In later lessons, you will see this flexibility in action as we work with a project that is scheduled from a start date.

Now that you've had a brief look at the major parts of the Microsoft Project interface, you are ready to create the project plan you will use throughout this book. In this exercise, you create a file and specify the project's start date.

1   On the Standard toolbar, click New.

Microsoft Project creates a file, and the Project Information dialog box appears.

2   In the Start Date box, click the down arrow button.

A small monthly calendar appears. By default, Microsoft Project uses the current date as the project start date. However, in this exercise, you change the project start date to April 2, 2001.

3   Click the left or right arrow button until April 2001 is displayed.

4   Click April 2.

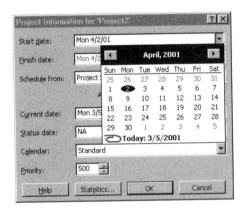

tip

You use this type of calendar in several places in Microsoft Project. Here is a handy shortcut for quickly picking a date with the calendar: click the name of the month to display a pop-up menu of all months, and then select the month you want. Next click the year to display up and down arrows, and then type or select the year you want.

The monthly calendar closes, and the Start Date box contains the date Mon 4/2/01.

5   Click OK to close the Project Information dialog box.

Entering Project Properties

Like other programs in the Office family, Microsoft Project keeps track of several file properties. Some of these properties are statistics, such as how many times the file has been revised. Other properties include information you might want to record about a project plan, such as the project manager's name or keywords to support a file search. Microsoft Project also uses properties in page headers and footers when printing.

In this exercise, you enter some properties that will be used later when printing project information and for other purposes.

1   On the File menu, click Properties.

The Properties dialog box appears.

2   Click the Summary tab.

3   In the Title box, type **Short Film Project**.

4   In the Subject box, type **Film Schedule**.

5   In the Author box, type your name.

6   In the Manager box, type your name, type your manager's name, or leave the box blank.

7   In the Company box, type **Industrial Smoke and Mirrors**.

8   In the Comments box, type **Includes pre-production, production, and post-production tasks**.

9   Select the Save Preview Picture check box.

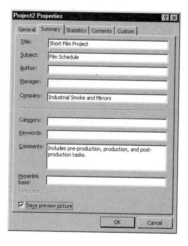

10   Click OK to close the dialog box.

Saving a Microsoft Project File

It's a good idea to save your work now. Because you have not previously saved this project file, you must specify a location and name for it.

tip
You can instruct Microsoft Project to automatically save the active file at a pre-defined interval, such as every 10 minutes. On the Tools menu, click Options. In the Options dialog box, click the Save tab, select the Save Every check box, and then specify the time interval you want. For more information, see "Customizing the Microsoft Project Environment" in Appendix C.

In this exercise, you name and save your project file.

1   On the Standard toolbar, click the Save button.

Because this project file has not previously been saved, the Save As dialog box appears.

2   Locate the Part 1 folder in the MS Project 2000 SBS Practice folder on your hard disk.

3   In the File Name box, type **Short Film Project 02**.

Tools ▾

4   Click the Tools button, and then click General Options.

The Save Options dialog box appears.

To protect a Microsoft Project file with a password, choose the options you want here.

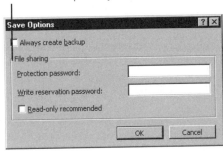

Here you can set options such as protecting Microsoft Project files with a password. You might never need to use the options in this dialog box, but it can be handy to know they're available.

5   Click Cancel to close the Save Options dialog box.

6   Click Save to close the Save As dialog box.

Microsoft Project saves the file as Short Film Project 02.

Finding Your Way Around

Lesson Wrap-Up

This lesson covered how to navigate in the Microsoft Project interface and create a project file.

If you are going on to other lessons:

1   On the Standard toolbar, click Save to save the changes you made to Short Film Project 02.

2   On the File menu, click Close to close the file.

If you aren't continuing to other lessons:

●   On the File menu, click Exit.

Glossary

Assignment The matching of a work resource (people or equipment) to a task to do work. A material resource may also be assigned to a task, but this type of assignment has no effect on the amount of work planned.

Duration The length of working time you expect it will take to complete a task.

Office Assistant The animated character that appears in Microsoft Project and other Office programs. You can use the Office Assistant to locate specific Help topics.

Resources People, equipment, and material (and the associated costs of each) required to carry out the work of a project.

Shortcut menu A menu you display by pointing to an item on the screen and then clicking the right mouse button. Shortcut menus contain only the commands that apply to the item to which you are pointing.

Table A spreadsheet-like presentation of project data, organized into vertical columns and horizontal rows. Each column represents one of the many fields in Microsoft Project, and each row represents a single task or resource.

Task A representation of the work required to complete some part of the project.

Template A Microsoft Project file format that lets you reuse existing project plans as the basis for new project plans. Microsoft Project includes several templates that relate to a variety of industries, and you can create your own templates.

Timescale The time period indicator that appears in the upper portion of some views, such as the Gantt Chart view. The timescale contains major and minor time indicators, such as weeks and days.

ToolTip A short description of an item on the screen, such as a toolbar, button or bar. To see a ToolTip, briefly point to an item.

View The format in which data is presented in Microsoft Project. There are three categories of views: charts, sheets, and forms.

Quick Reference

To start Microsoft Project

1   On the Windows taskbar, click the Start button.

2   On the Start menu, point to Programs, and then click Microsoft Project.

To create a project file based on a template

1   On the File menu, click New.

2   Click the appropriate tab.

3   Select the template you want, and click OK.

To customize the way toolbars are displayed

1   On the Tools menu, click Customize, and then select Toolbars.

2   Click the Options tab.

3   Select the options you want, and click Close.

To switch to a different view

●   On the View bar, click the view you want.

-Or-

●   On the View menu, click More Views, and then select the view you want.

To switch to a different table

●   On the View menu, click Table, and then select the table you want.

To create a project file and enter a start date

1   On the Standard toolbar, click New.

2   In the Start Date box, type or select the date you want.

To enter properties about a Microsoft Project file

1   On the File menu, click Properties.

2   Click the Summary tab, and then enter the information you want.

To save a Microsoft Project file

1   On the Standard toolbar, click the Save button.

2   If you have not previously saved the file, specify the file name and location you want.

3

Entering and Organizing Tasks

ESTIMATED TIME
45 min.

After completing this lesson, you will be able to:

✔ *Enter task information.*

✔ *Estimate how long each task should last, and enter task durations.*

✔ *Break a long task into tasks with shorter durations.*

✔ *Create task relationships by linking tasks.*

✔ *Find the project's duration.*

✔ *Add tasks to a task list.*

✔ *Delete tasks from a task list.*

✔ *Organize tasks into phases.*

✔ *Create a milestone to track an important event.*

In this lesson, you will work with **tasks**. Tasks are the most basic building blocks of any project—tasks represent the work to be done to accomplish the goals of the project. Tasks describe project work in terms of sequence, duration, and resource requirements. In this lesson, you will focus mainly on creating and arranging tasks in the right sequence and with the right durations.

Practice files for the lesson

To complete this lesson, you will use a file named Short Film Project 03. This file contains the project start date and properties you entered in Lesson 2. Before you begin this lesson, open the Part 1 folder in the MS Project 2000 SBS Practice folder on your hard disk. Open the file 03A, and save it with a baseline as Short Film Project 03 in the Part 1 folder.

Entering Tasks

In Microsoft Project, one place you enter tasks is in the Gantt Chart view. In the default Gantt Chart view, the bar chart appears in the right side, and a table appears in the left side of the view. (The **Entry table** appears by default, but you can display other tables as well.) Although the Entry table might look similar to a Microsoft Excel spreadsheet grid, it behaves more like a database table. Each row of the Entry table describes a single task, which is assigned a **task ID**. Task IDs appear on the left side of the task's row, and the column headings, such as Task Name and Duration, are field labels. The intersection of a row (or task) and a column is called a cell or **field**. In fact, the internal architecture of a file from Microsoft Project has much more in common with that of a file from a database program such as Microsoft Access than it does with that of a file from a spreadsheet program such as Excel.

In this exercise, you enter the first tasks required in the film project.

1   In the Entry table, click the cell directly below the Task Name column heading.

2   Type **Review script**, and then press Enter.

Your screen should look similar to the following illustration.

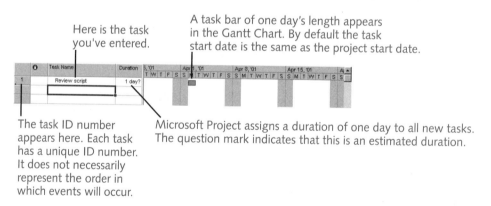

Here is the task you've entered.

A task bar of one day's length appears in the Gantt Chart. By default the task start date is the same as the project start date.

The task ID number appears here. Each task has a unique ID number. It does not necessarily represent the order in which events will occur.

Microsoft Project assigns a duration of one day to all new tasks. The question mark indicates that this is an estimated duration.

3   Enter the following task names below Review script, pressing Enter after each task name.

```
Develop script breakdown and schedule
Develop production boards
Pick locations
```

```
Hold auditions
Reserve camera equipment
Reserve sound equipment
```

Your screen should look similar to the following illustration.

Here are the additional tasks you entered.

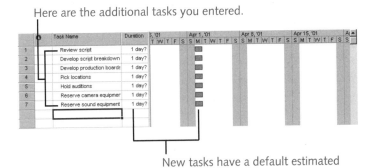

New tasks have a default estimated
duration of one day.

Project management focus: Defining the right tasks for the right deliverable

Every project has an ultimate goal or intent: the reason that the project was started. This is called the project **deliverable**. This deliverable is usually a product, such as a short film, or a service or event, such as a software training session. Defining the right tasks to create the right deliverable is an essential skill for a project manager. The task lists you create in Microsoft Project should describe all the work required, and only the work required, to complete the project successfully.

In developing your task lists, you might find it helpful to distinguish product scope from project scope. **Product scope** describes the quality, features, and functions of the deliverable of the project. In the scenario used in this book, for example, the deliverable is a short film, and the product scope might include length, subject, and audience. **Project scope**, on the other hand, describes the work required to deliver such a product or service. In our scenario, the project scope includes detailed pre-production, production, and post-production tasks relating to the creation of a short film.

The Project Management Institute's *A Guide to the Project Management Body of Knowledge* (PMBOK) describes task definition and sequencing in knowledge area 5, Project Scope Management, and knowledge area 6, Project Time Management.

Entering and Organizing Tasks 3

PROJ2000-1-5

Estimating Durations

A task's duration is the amount of time you expect it will take to complete the task. You determine the overall **duration** of a project by calculating the difference between the earliest start date and the latest finish date of the tasks that compose it. The project duration is also affected by other factors, such as task relationships, to be discussed in later lessons. Because Microsoft Project distinguishes between working and nonworking time, a task's duration doesn't necessarily correlate to elapsed time.

In Lesson 6, you will work more with the project calendar.

For example, a project might have a project calendar with working time defined as 9:00 A.M.–5:00 P.M. Monday through Friday, leaving non-working time defined as evenings and weekends. If you estimate that a task will take 16 hours of working time, you could enter its duration as **2d** to schedule work over two eight-hour workdays. You should then expect that starting the task at 9:00 A.M. on a Friday means that it wouldn't be completed until 5:00 P.M. on the following Monday. No work would be scheduled over the weekend, because Saturday and Sunday have been defined as nonworking time.

You can schedule tasks to occur over working and nonworking time, however. To do this, assign an **elapsed duration** to a task. For example, you might have the tasks "Pour foundation concrete" and "Remove foundation forms" in a construction project. If so, you might also want a task called "Wait for concrete to cure" because you don't want to remove the forms until the concrete has cured. The task "Wait for concrete to cure" should have an elapsed duration, because the concrete will cure over a contiguous range of days, whether they be working or nonworking days. If the concrete takes 48 hours to cure, you can enter the duration for that task as **2ed**, schedule the task to start on Friday at 9 A.M., and expect it to be complete by Sunday at 9 A.M. In most cases, however, you'll work with non-elapsed durations in Microsoft Project.

Microsoft Project can work with task durations that range from minutes to months. Depending on the scope of your project, you'll probably want to work with task durations on the scale of hours, days, and weeks. You should consider two general rules when estimating task durations:

- Project duration often correlates to task duration; long projects tend to have tasks with longer durations than short projects.

- If you track progress against your project plan (described in Part 4), you need to think about the level of detail you want to apply to your project's tasks. If you have a multi-year project, for example, it might not be practical or even possible to track tasks that are measured in minutes or hours. In general, you should measure task durations at the lowest level of detail or control you care about, but no lower.

tip

Although it's beyond the scope of this book, Program Evaluation and Review Technique (PERT) analysis can be a useful tool for estimating task durations. For more information, ask the Office Assistant in Microsoft Project how to "Estimate task durations by using PERT analysis."

How do you come up with accurate task durations?

For the project you work on in this book, the durations are supplied for you. For your real-world projects, you will often have to estimate task durations. Good sources of task duration estimates include

- Historical information from previous, similar projects.
- Estimates from the people who will complete the tasks.
- The expert judgment of people who have managed similar projects.
- Professional or industry organizations that relate to projects similar to yours.

For complex projects, you probably would combine these and other methods to estimate task durations. Because inaccurate task duration estimates are a major source of **risk** in any project, making good estimates is well worth the effort.

When working in Microsoft Project, you can use abbreviations for durations.

If you enter this abbreviation	It appears like this	And means
m	min	minute
h	hr	hour
d	day	day
w	wk	week
mo	mon	month
em	emin	elapsed minute
eh	ehr	elapsed hour
ed	eday	elapsed day
ew	ewk	elapsed week
emo	emon	elapsed month

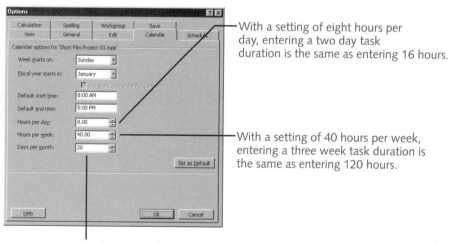

2000 New!

Microsoft Project 2000 supports entering month durations.

Microsoft Project uses standard values of minutes and hours for durations: one minute equals 60 seconds, and one hour equals 60 minutes. However, you can define the duration of days, weeks, and months for your project. To do this, you must first open the Tools menu, choose the Options command, and display the Calendar tab, illustrated below.

With a setting of eight hours per day, entering a two day task duration is the same as entering 16 hours.

With a setting of 40 hours per week, entering a three week task duration is the same as entering 120 hours.

With a setting of 20 days per month, entering a one month task duration is the same as entering 160 hours (eight hours per day x 20 days per month).

The exercises in this book require the default values: 8 hours per day, 40 hours per week, and 20 days per month.

In this exercise, you enter durations for the tasks you created earlier in the lesson. When you created those tasks, Microsoft Project entered an estimated duration of one day for each. (The question mark in the Duration field indicates that the duration is an explicit estimate, although really you should consider all task durations to be estimates until the task is completed.)

1   In the Entry table, click the cell directly below the Duration column heading.

   The Duration field for Task 1, "Review script," is selected.

2   Type **2w**, and then press Enter.

   The value 2 wks (short for two weeks) appears in the Duration field.

3   Enter the following durations for the remaining tasks.

Task ID	Task Name	Duration
2	Develop script breakdown and schedule	2w
3	Develop production boards	1mo
4	Pick locations	6w?
5	Hold auditions	1w
6	Reserve camera equipment	1w
7	Reserve sound equipment	5d

Your screen should look similar to the following illustration.

The question mark indicates
an explicit estimated duration.

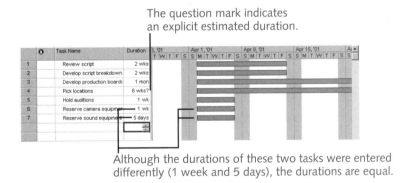

Although the durations of these two tasks were entered
differently (1 week and 5 days), the durations are equal.

You might recall from the discussion above that, by default, 1 week equals 40 hours, as does 5 days. You can see that the bar lengths of Task 6 (with a duration of one week) and Task 7 (with a duration of five days) are equal in the Gantt Chart.

tip
Typing a question mark after a duration (for example, **6w?**) is a good way to mark estimated durations that you might want to update after you know more about the scope of the task. You can later filter for tasks with estimated durations. On the Project menu, click Filtered For, and then click Tasks With Estimated Durations. For more information about filtering, see Lesson 9.

Breaking a Long Task into Shorter Tasks

Looking over the task durations, you can see that the estimated duration of Task 4, "Pick locations," is much longer than those of the other tasks. After thinking about the work required to complete this task, you decide to break it into two shorter, more manageable tasks.

In this exercise, you rename a task, shorten its duration, and insert a new task.

1   In the Entry table, click the name of Task 4, "Pick locations."

2   Click the text "Pick" so that the mouse pointer changes to an I-beam.

3   In the cell, highlight the word "Pick," type **Scout**, and then press Tab.
       The text is replaced, and the selection moves to the next field to the right, the duration of Task 4.

4   Click the down arrow button until the duration equals 4 wks, and press Enter.
       The selection moves down one row to Task 5. Next you will enter a new task.

5   On the Insert menu, click New Task.
       A new task appears directly below Task 4, and all subsequent task IDs are renumbered.

6   In the Task Name field for the new task, type **Select locations**, and then press Tab.

7   In the Duration field, type **2w**, and press Enter.

The new task, "Select locations," is given a task ID of 5 and a duration of two weeks. Your screen should look similar to the following illustration.

Here is the new task you inserted.

	0	Task Name	Duration
1		Review script	2 wks
2		Develop script breakdown	2 wks
3		Develop production boards	1 mon
4		Scout locations	4 wks
5		Select locations	2 wks
6		Hold auditions	1 wk
7		Reserve camera equipmen	1 wk
8		Reserve sound equipment	5 days

Linking Tasks

PROJ 2000-1-19

For a demonstration of various ways to link tasks, double-click the Link Tasks icon in the Multimedia folder on the Microsoft Project 2000 Step by Step CD-ROM.

Projects require tasks to be done in a specific order. For example, the task of filming a scene must be completed before the task of editing the filmed scene can occur. These two tasks have a finish-to-start **relationship**, which has two aspects.

■ The second task must occur after the first task; this is a **sequence**.

■ The second task can occur only if the first task is completed; this is a **dependency**.

In Microsoft Project, the first task ("Film the scene") is called the **predecessor** because it precedes tasks that depend on it. The second task ("Edit the filmed scene") is called the **successor** because it succeeds tasks on which it is dependent. Any task can be a predecessor for one or more successor tasks. Likewise, any task can be a successor to one or more predecessor tasks.

This might sound complicated, but it turns out tasks can have one of only four types of task relationships:

This task relationship	Means	Looks like this in the Gantt Chart	Example
Finish-to-start (FS)	The finish date of the predecessor task determines the start date of the successor task.		A film scene must be shot before it can be edited.
Start-to-start (SS)	The start date of the predecessor task determines the start date of the successor task.		Reviewing a script and developing the script breakdown and schedule are closely related, and they should occur simultaneously.

Entering and Organizing Tasks 3

This task relationship	Means	Looks like this in the Gantt Chart	Example
Finish-to-finish (FF)	The finish date of the predecessor task determines the finish date of the successor task.		Tasks that require specific equipment must end when the equipment rental ends.
Start-to-finish (SF)	The start date of the predecessor task determines finish date of the successor task.		Rarely used; has some application when tracking accounting tasks, for example.

Task relationships appear in several ways in Microsoft Project. The most common places to see task relationships are

█ In the Gantt Chart and Network Diagram views, task relationships appear as the lines connecting tasks.

█ In tables, such as the Entry table, task ID numbers of predecessor tasks appear in the Predecessor fields of successor tasks.

You create task relationships by creating **links** between tasks. In this exercise, you use different methods to create links between several tasks, creating finish-to-start relationships.

By default, the Standard toolbar appears directly below the menu bar. If you need help locating parts of the Microsoft Project interface, see Lesson 2.

1   On the Entry table, click the name of Task 1, "Review script," and then drag to the name of Task 2, "Develop script breakdown and schedule."

Tasks 1 and 2 are selected.

2   On the Standard toolbar, click the Link Tasks button.

Tasks 1 and 2 are linked with a finish-to-start relationship. Note that Microsoft Project changed the start date of Task 2 to the next working day following the completion of Task 1.

Clicking the Link Tasks button creates a finish-to-start (FS) task relationship. For instructions on creating other types of task relationships, see Lesson 6.

Your screen should look similar to the following illustration.

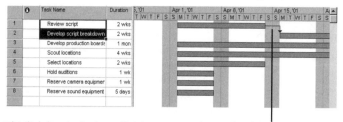

This link line indicates a finish-to-start relationship between these two tasks. Note that this link line extends over the weekend, which is nonworking time.

tip

To unlink tasks, select the tasks you want to unlink, and then click the Unlink Tasks button. If you unlink a single task that is part of a chain of linked tasks with finish-to-start relationships, Microsoft Project reestablishes links between the remaining tasks.

Next you will link two tasks in another way.

3 Select the name of Task 3, "Develop production boards."

4 On the Standard toolbar, click the Task Information button.

The Task Information dialog box appears.

5 Click the Predecessors tab.

6 Click the empty cell below the Task Name column heading, and then click the down arrow button that appears.

7 In the Task Name list, click Develop script breakdown and schedule, and press Enter. Your screen should look similar to the following illustration.

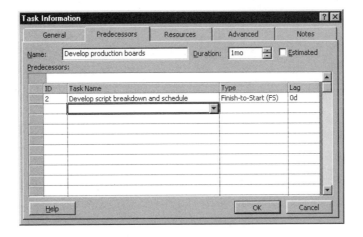

8 Click OK to close the Task Information dialog box.

Tasks 2 and 3 are linked with a finish-to-start relationship. Next you will verify this task relationship by viewing the Predecessors column.

9 At the bottom of the Entry table, drag the scroll box to the right until you can see the Predecessors column.

You can see Task 2 in the Predecessor field for Task 3. Your screen should look similar to the following illustration.

Entering and Organizing Tasks   3

The task IDs of predecessor tasks appear
in the Predecessors column

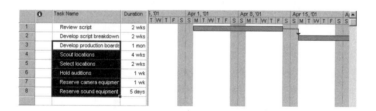

10   At the bottom of the Entry table, drag the scroll box to the left until the
leftmost column is visible again.

Next, you link the remaining tasks in a single step.

To select this
range of tasks,
first click the
name of Task
3, hold down
the Shift key,
and then click
the name of
Task 8.

tip

To see the complete name of a task or any other field that doesn't fit within the
width of a column, point to the cell for a moment. The full name will appear in
a tooltip.

11   Select Tasks 3 through 8.

12   On the Standard toolbar, click the Link Tasks button.

The remaining tasks are linked with finish-to-start relationships. Your screen
should look similar to the following illustration.

tip

You can also create a finish-to-start relationship between tasks right in the Gantt Chart. Point to the task bar of the predecessor task until the pointer changes to a four-pointed star. Then drag up or down to the task bar of the successor task.

Checking Project Duration

At this point, you might want to know the project duration. You haven't directly entered a total project duration, but Microsoft Project has calculated it, based on individual task durations and task relationships. An easy way to see the project's total duration is to check the Project Information dialog box. You can't edit the finish date directly because this project is set to schedule from the start date.

In this exercise, you see the current total duration of the project, based on the task durations and relationships you've entered.

1 On the Project menu, click Project Information.

Note the Finish date: 7/27/01.

Next let's look at the duration information in more detail.

2 Click the Statistics button.

The Project Statistics dialog box appears.

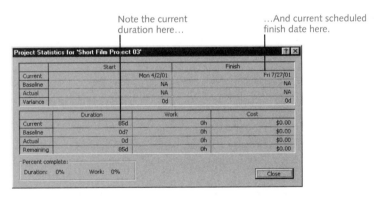

Note the current duration here...

...And current scheduled finish date here.

You don't need to pay attention to all these numbers yet, but the current finish date and the current duration are worth noting. You can visually verify these numbers right on the Gantt Chart.

3 Click the Close button to close the Project Statistics dialog box.

Next you will look at the complete project by changing the timescale in the Gantt Chart.

You can also click the Zoom In and Zoom Out buttons to change the timescale of the Gantt Chart.

4   On the View menu, click Zoom.

The Zoom dialog box appears.

5   Click Entire Project, and then click OK.

The entire project appears on the screen. Your screen should look similar to the following illustration.

To quickly change the timescale on the Gantt Chart...   ...click the Zoom In and Zoom Out buttons on the Standard toolbar.

You can see the project's overall duration in the Gantt Chart.

Inserting New Tasks

After looking over your initial plan, you remember that getting permits to film in public spaces can take some time and that you should apply for them early. You decide to add a task to track this.

In this exercise, you insert a new task.

1   On the Entry table, click the name of Task 6, "Hold auditions."

To insert a new task, you can also press the Insert key.

2   On the Insert menu, click New Task.

A blank row for a new task appears directly below Task 5.

3   In the Task Name field for the new task, type **Apply for filming permits** and then press Tab.

4   In the Duration field, type **1w** and press Enter.

Because you inserted a task between tasks that had a finish-to-start relationship, Microsoft Project linked the new task to the tasks above and below it. Your screen should look similar to the following illustration.

Here is the new task you inserted.   The new task is automatically linked to the adjacent tasks.

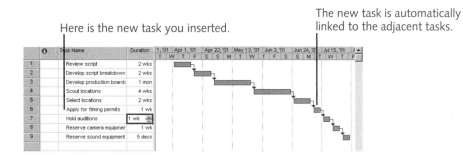

A couple of important things happened that you might not have noticed. First, after you inserted the new task, all subsequent task IDs were renumbered. Second, the task ID numbers of all predecessor tasks were changed.

Deleting Tasks

You might decide you need more information from the script about the acting talent needed for the film, so you decide to wait on holding auditions.

In this exercise, you delete a task.

1   On the Entry table, click the name of Task 7, "Hold auditions."

2   On the Edit menu, click Delete Task.

The task "Hold auditions" is deleted, and all subsequent task IDs are renumbered. Your screen should look similar to the following illustration.

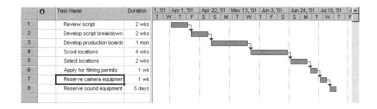

tip

You might have noticed on the Edit menu that the shortcut key for deleting a task is the Delete key. Pressing the Delete key in the Entry table deletes the entire task, not just the value in the active field. Should you ever inadvertently delete a task, click Undo Delete from the Edit menu before you perform another action. To delete just the value of the active cell, press Ctrl+Delete.

PROJ2000-1-14

Organizing Tasks into Phases

If you have a complex set of tasks, you should consider organizing them into **phases**, or groups of closely related tasks. In Microsoft Project, phases are represented by **summary tasks**.

A summary task behaves differently from other tasks. You can't edit its duration, start date, or other calculated values directly, because they are derived from the detail tasks. Summary tasks are useful for getting information about phases of project work. In Lesson 6, you will work with project outlines by reorganizing summary tasks and subtasks.

Project management focus: top-down and bottom-up planning

The two most common approaches to developing tasks and phases are **top-down** and **bottom-up planning**.

Top-down planning	Bottom-up planning
Identifies major phases or products of the project before filling in the tasks required to complete those phases. Complex projects may have several layers of phases.	Identifies as many of the bottom level detailed tasks as possible before organizing them into logical groups, called phases or summary tasks.
Works from general to specific	Works from specific to general

Project goals often flow from the top down, and project planning details tend to flow from the bottom up. Creating accurate tasks and phases for most complex projects requires a combination of top-down and bottom-

(continued)

continued

> up planning. For some project work, you will already know the low-level
> tasks; for others, you might initially know only the broader project goals.
>
> Microsoft Project Central, a companion product for Microsoft Project,
> enables bottom-up planning by allowing resources to create new tasks that
> can be added below summary tasks in Microsoft Project. For more infor-
> mation about Project Central, see Appendix D, "Introducing the
> Workgroup Features of Microsoft Project."

In this exercise, you create a summary task and insert additional tasks.

1   On the Entry table, click the name of Task 1, "Review script."

2   On the Insert menu, click New Task.

3   In the Task Name field for the new task, type **Pre-Production** and press
       Enter.

       You will next add two high-level activities, whose details you will fill in later.

4   Type the following task names below Task 9, "Reserve sound equipment,"
       pressing Enter after each task name.

       `Production`
       `Post-Production`

       Finally, you will make Task 1, "Pre-Production," a summary task by indent-
       ing the subtasks below it.

5   Select Tasks 2 through 9.

6   On the Formatting toolbar, click the Indent button.

       Task 1 becomes a summary task, and a summary task bar for it appears in
       the Gantt Chart. Your screen should look similar to the following illustration.

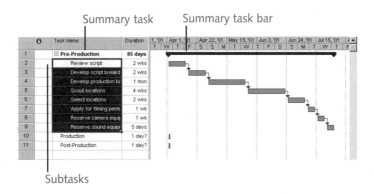

Summary task   Summary task bar

Subtasks

The duration for the Pre-Production summary task is 85 days. Microsoft Project calculated that duration based on the earliest start date and latest finish date of its subtasks.

> ## tip
> If your organization uses a work breakdown structure (WBS) process in the project planning phase, you may find it helpful to view WBS codes in Microsoft Project. For information about using WBS codes with Microsoft Project, ask the Office Assistant "View wbs codes."

Entering a Milestone

PROJ 2000-1-16

To wrap up your initial project planning, you might want to track an important event for your project, such as when the Pre-Production phase of the project will end. To do this, you will create a **milestone**.

Milestones are significant events that are either reached within the project (completion of a phase of work, for example) or imposed upon the project (a deadline by which to apply for funding, for example). Because the milestone itself doesn't normally include any work, milestones are represented as tasks with zero duration.

In this exercise, you create a milestone.

1   On the Entry table, click the name of Task 10, "Production."

2   On the Insert menu, click New Task.

3   Type **Pre-Production complete!** and then press Tab.

4   In the Duration field, type **0d** and then press Enter.

5   Select Tasks 9 and 10, and then click the Link Tasks button.
     The milestone is added to your file. Your screen should look similar to the following illustration.

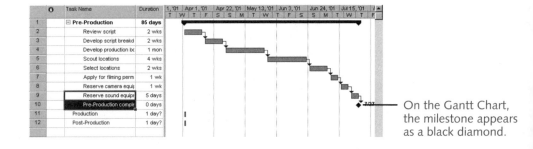

On the Gantt Chart, the milestone appears as a black diamond.

You can also filter for milestones. On the Project menu, click Filtered For, and then click Milestones.

tip

A milestone usually identifies a significant event or the completion of a phase of work. But the milestone itself requires no work, and it, therefore, has a duration of zero days. However, you can mark a task of any duration as a milestone if you want. Double-click the task name to display the Task Information dialog box, and then click the Advanced tab. Click Mark Task As Milestone.

Lesson Wrap-Up

This lesson covered how to enter tasks and durations, create task relationships, and create summary tasks.

If you are going on to other lessons:

1   On the Standard toolbar, click Save to save changes made to Short Film Project 03. Save the file without a baseline.

When you save the practice file, the Planning Wizard asks whether you want to save the file with or without a baseline. In Lesson 14, you will save a baseline plan with the project file. Until then, you will save the project files you use in the lessons of this book without a baseline.

2   On the File menu, click Close to close the file.

If you aren't continuing to other lessons:

●   On the File menu, click Exit.

Glossary

Baseline The original project plan, saved for later comparison. The baseline includes the planned start and finish dates of tasks and assignments, and their planned costs. Each Microsoft Project file can have at most one baseline.

Bottom-up planning Developing a project plan by starting with the lowest-level tasks before organizing them into broad phases.

Deliverable The final product, service, or event a project is intended to create.

Dependency A link between a predecessor task and a successor task. A dependency controls the start or finish of one task relative to the start or finish of the other task. The most common dependency is finish-to-start, in which the finish date of the predecessor task determines the start date of the successor task.

Duration The length of working time you expect it will take to complete a task.

Elapsed duration The total length of working and nonworking time you expect it will take to complete a task.

Entry table The grid in the left side of the default Gantt Chart view.

Field The lowest-level type of information about a task, resource, or assignment; also called a cell.

Link A logical relationship between tasks that controls sequence and dependency. In the Gantt Chart and Network Diagram views, links appear as lines between tasks.

Milestone A significant event that might be reached within the project or imposed upon the project. In Microsoft Project, milestones are normally represented as tasks with zero duration.

Phase A sequence of tasks that represent a major portion of the project's work. In Microsoft Project, phases are represented by summary tasks.

Planning Wizard An interactive tool from online Help that can walk you through some tasks, such as saving a baseline.

Predecessor A task whose start or end date determines the start or finish of another task or tasks, called successor tasks.

Product scope The quality, features, and functions (often called specifications) of the deliverable of the project.

Project scope The work required to produce a deliverable with agreed-upon quality, features, and functions.

Risk Any event that decreases the likelihood of completing the project on time, within budget, and to specification.

Relationship The type of dependency between two tasks, visually indicated by a link line. The types of relationships include finish-to-start, start-to-start, finish-to-finish, and start-to-finish.

Sequence The chronological order in which tasks occur. A sequence is ordered from left to right in most views that include a time scale, for example, the Gantt Chart view.

Successor A task whose start or finish date is determined by another task or tasks, called predecessor tasks.

Summary task A task that is made up of and summarizes the subtasks below it. In Microsoft Project, phases of project work are represented by summary tasks.

Task A representation of the work required to complete part of a project.

Task ID A unique number that Microsoft Project assigns to each task in a project. In the Entry table, the Task ID appears in the far left column.

Top-down planning Developing a project plan by identifying the highest-level phases or summary tasks before breaking them into lower-level components or subtasks.

Quick Reference

To enter tasks

1   In the Entry table, click a blank cell in the Task Name column.

2   Type the task name, and then press Enter.

To enter task durations

1   In the Entry table, click a cell in the Duration column.

2   Type the task duration, and then press Enter.

To rename a task

1   In the Entry table, click the task name.

2   Type the new name. To edit a portion of a name, click and then continue to point to the name you want to change. When the mouse pointer changes to an I-beam, select the portion of the name you want to replace, and type the new text.

To link tasks

1   On the Entry table, click the name of the predecessor task.

2   Hold down Ctrl, and click the successor task name.

3   On the Standard toolbar, click the Link Tasks button.

To display project duration and other statistics

1   On the Project menu, click Project Information.

2   Click the Statistics button.

To change a Gantt Chart's timescale to fit an entire project in the window

1   On the View menu, click Zoom.

2   Click Entire Project, and then click OK.

To insert a new task in a task list

1   On the Entry table, click the task name above which you want to insert a new task.

2   On the Insert menu, click New Task.

3   Click in the Task Name field for the new task, enter a name for it, and then press Enter.

To delete a task from a task list

1   On the Entry table, click the name of the task you want to delete.

2   On the Edit menu, click Delete Task.

To create a summary task

1   On the Entry table, click the name of the first subtask of the summary task you are creating.

2   On the Insert menu, click New Task.

3   Click in the Task Name field for the new task, type a name for it, and then press Enter.

4   Select the tasks that you want to make subtasks of the summary task you just created.

5   On the Formatting toolbar, click the Indent button.

To create a milestone

1   On the Entry table, enter a name for the milestone, and then press Tab.

2   In the Duration field, type **0d**, and press Enter.

3   If you want to specify a date for the milestone, select the Start field, type the date, and press Enter.

4   If you want to link a milestone to a task, select the task and click the Link Tasks button on the Standard toolbar.

4

Setting Up Resources

**ESTIMATED
TIME
40 min.**

After completing this lesson, you will be able to:

✔ *Enter basic resource information for the people who work on your projects.*

✔ *Enter basic resource information for the equipment that will be used in your projects.*

✔ *Enter basic resource information for the materials that will be consumed as your project progresses.*

✔ *Enter cost information for your resources.*

✔ *Associate resources with group names.*

✔ *Enter additional information about your resources in a text field.*

Resources are the people, equipment, and material needed to complete the project's tasks. Microsoft Project focuses on two aspects of resources: their availability and their costs. Availability determines when a specific resource can work on a task and how much work they can do, and costs refer to how much money will be required to pay for that resource.

In this lesson, you will set up some of the resources you need to complete the short film project. Managing resources effectively is one of the most powerful advantages of using Microsoft Project rather than task-focused planning tools, such as paper-based organizers. You don't need to set up resources and assign them to tasks in Microsoft Project; however, without this information, you might have less control over who does what work, when, and at what cost. Setting up resource information in Microsoft Project takes a little effort, but the time is well spent if your project is primarily driven by time or cost constraints. (And nearly all complex projects are driven by one, if not both, of these factors.)

Practice files for the lesson To complete this lesson, you will use a file named Short Film Project 04. This file contains the initial task list you developed in Lesson 3. Before you begin the lesson, open the Part 1 folder in the MS Project 2000 SBS Practice folder on your hard disk. Open the file 04A, and save it without a baseline as Short Film Project 04 in the Part 1 folder.

Setting Up People Resources

Microsoft Project works with two types of resources: work resources and material resources. **Work resources** are the people and equipment that do the work of the project. You will learn about material resources later in this lesson.

Here are some examples of work resources.

Work resource	Example
Individual people identified by name	John Thorson; Jan Miksovsky
Individual people identified by job title or function	Director; Camera operator
Groups of people who have common skills; when assigning such a resource to a task, you don't care who the individual resource is, as long as the resource has the right skills.	Electricians; Carpenters; Extras
Equipment	16 mm camera; 1,000 watt light

Equipment resources need not be portable; a fixed location or piece of machinery (for example, a film editing studio) can also be considered equipment.

All projects require some people resources, and some projects require only people resources. Although Microsoft Project isn't a complete resource or asset management system, it can help you make smarter decisions about how to manage work resources and at what financial cost.

In this exercise, you set up resource information for several people resources in the Resource Sheet view.

Resource Sheet

1   On the View Bar, click Resource Sheet.

2   On the Resource Sheet, click the cell directly below the Resource Name column heading.

3   Type **Clair Hector**, and press Tab.

4   In the Type field, make sure that Work is selected, and press Tab.
The two types of resources are work (people and equipment) and material. Because you're entering a work resource, you can skip the Material Label

tip

If you can't see the Resource Sheet button on the View bar, click the down arrow button at the bottom of the View bar until the Resource Sheet button appears.

Because you're entering a work resource, you can skip the Material Label field.

5 Press Tab again.

In the Initials field, Microsoft Project supplied the first initial from the resource name. But, for this project, you want to use at least two initials per resource.

6 In the Initials field, type **CH**, and press Tab.

7 Press Tab again to skip over the Group field for now.

8 In the Max. Units field, make sure that 100% is selected, and click the next empty cell in the Resource Name column. Your screen should look similar to the following illustration.

Here is the resource information you've entered.

	Resource Name	Type	Material Label	Initials	Group	Max. Units	Std. Rate	Ovt. Rate	Cos
1	Clair Hector	Work		CH		100%	$0.00/hr	$0.00/hr	

To see more buttons on the View bar, click this scroll button.

You'll work with cost information later in the lesson, but the **Max. Units** field merits some explanation now. This field represents the maximum capacity of a resource to accomplish any task. Specifying that Clair Hector has 100% maximum units means that 100% of Clair's time is available to work on the tasks to which you assign her. Microsoft Project will alert you if you assign Clair to more tasks than she can accomplish at 100% maximum units (or, in other words, if Clair becomes **overallocated**). You'll solve overallocation problems in Lesson 7.

tip

If you prefer, you can enter maximum units as partial or whole numbers (for example .5, 1, 2) rather than as percentages (50%, 100%, or 200%). To use this format, open the Tools menu, click Options, and then click the Schedule tab. In the Show Assignment Units As A box, click Decimal.

You can also have a resource that represents multiple people. Next you'll set up such a resource.

In lesson 5, you'll assign these resources to tasks.

9   In the Resource Name field below the first resource, type **Electrician**, and then press Tab.

10   In the Type field, make sure that Work is selected, and then press Tab twice.

11   In the Initials field, type **EL**, and then press Tab twice.

12   In the Max. Units field, type or select 200%, and then press Tab. Your screen should look similar to the following illustration.

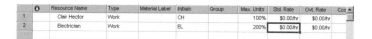

	0	Resource Name	Type	Material Label	Initials	Group	Max. Units	Std. Rate	Ovt. Rate	Cos ▲
1		Clair Hector	Work		CH		100%	$0.00/hr	$0.00/hr	
2		Electrician	Work		EL		200%	$0.00/hr	$0.00/hr	

The resource named Electrician doesn't represent a single person; instead, it represents a category of interchangeable people called electricians. Because the Electrician resource has maximum units set to 200%, you can plan on two electricians being available to work full time every workday. At this point in the planning phase, you don't know exactly who these electricians will be, and that's OK. You can still proceed with more general planning.

13   Enter the remaining resource information into the Resource Sheet. For each resource, make sure **Work** is selected in the Type field.

Resource Name	Initials	Max. Units
Jan Miksovsky	JM	100%
Scott Cooper	SC	100%
Jo Brown	JB	100%
Kim Yoshida	KY	100%
Peter Kelly	PK	100%
Jonathan Mollerup	JM	50%
John Thorson	JT	75%

Your screen should look similar to the following illustration.

When you create a new resource Microsoft Project assigns it 100% max. units by default. You change the resource's max. units here.

What's the best way to enter resource names?

In Microsoft Project, resource names can refer to specific people (for example, John Thorson or Jan Miksovsky) or to specific job titles (for example, Sound Technician or Director). Use whatever makes the most sense for your needs and for those who will see the project information you publish. The important questions to ask are, "Who will see these resource names?" and "How will they identify the resources?" This includes both working with resource names in Microsoft Project and viewing them in information published from Microsoft Project. For example, in the default Gantt Chart view, the resource's name, as you enter it in the Resource Name field, appears next to the bars of the tasks to which that resource is assigned.

A resource might be somebody already on staff or a position to be filled later. If you haven't yet filled all of the resource positions required, you won't necessarily have real people's names yet.

Setting Up Equipment Resources

You set up people and equipment resources in exactly the same way in Microsoft Project. However, you should be aware of important differences in how you can schedule those two types of resources. For example, most people resources have a working day of no more than 12 hours, but equipment resources might work around the clock. Moreover, people resources might be more flexible in the tasks they can perform, but equipment resources tend to be more specialized. For example, a director of photography for a film might also act as a camera operator in a pinch, but a movie camera can't replace an editing studio.

You don't need to track every piece of equipment that will be used in your project, but you might want to set up equipment resources when

■ Multiple teams or people might need a piece of equipment to do different tasks simultaneously, and the equipment might be overbooked.

■ You want to plan and track costs associated with the equipment.

In this exercise, you enter information about equipment resources in the Resource Information dialog box.

1   On the Resource Sheet, click the next empty cell in the Resource Name column.

2   On the Standard toolbar, click the Resource Information button.

The Resource Information dialog box appears.

You can also double-click a resource name or an empty cell in the Resource Name column to display the Resource

3   Click the General tab.

In the upper portion of the General tab, you might recognize the fields you saw in the Resource Sheet view. As with many types of information in Microsoft Project, you can usually work in at least two interfaces: a table and a dialog box.

4   In the Resource Name field, type **16 mm Camera**, and press Tab.

5   In the Resource Type field, select Work, and press Tab.

6   In the Initials field, type **16mm**. Your screen should look similar to the following illustration.

The Resource Information dialog box contains many of the same fields you see on the Resource Sheet view.

Resource Information	? X

General | Working Time | Costs | Notes

Resource name: 16 mm Camera   Initials: 16mm

Email: Group:

Workgroup: Default   Code:

Resource type: Work   Material label:

Windows Account...

Resource Availability

NA

Available From	Available To	Units
NA	NA	100%

Help   Details...   OK   Cancel

tip

The Resource Information dialog box contains a button labeled Details. If you have an e-mail program that complies with the Messaging Application Programming Interface (MAPI) and the program is installed on the same computer as Microsoft Project, you can click Details to see contact information about the selected resource. Examples of MAPI-compliant programs include Microsoft Outlook and Microsoft Exchange. For more information about e-mail integration, see Appendix D, "Introducing the Workgroup Features of Microsoft Project."

When creating a resource in the Resource Information dialog box, you can't enter a Max. Units value. However, you can edit this value in the dialog box, as well as on the Resource Sheet, after you create the resource.

7   Click OK to close the Resource Information dialog box and return to the Resource Sheet.

The Max. Units field shows 100% for this resource; next you'll change this.

8   In the Max. Units field for the 16 mm camera, type or select **300%**, and press Tab.

This means that you plan to have three 16 mm cameras available every workday.

9 Enter the remaining information about equipment resources in the Resource Information dialog box or directly in the Resource Sheet, whichever you prefer. In either case, make sure **Work** is selected in the Type field.

Resource Name	Initials	Max. Units
5000 Watt Light	5000WL	400%
Dolly	Dolly	200%
Crane	Crane	100%
Editing Lab	EL	100%

Your screen should look similar to the following illustration.

	❶	Resource Name	Type	Material Label	Initials	Group	Max. Units	Std. Rate	Ovt. Rate	Cos
1		Clair Hector	Work		CH		100%	$0.00/hr	$0.00/hr	
2		Electrician	Work		EL		200%	$0.00/hr	$0.00/hr	
3		Jan Miksovsky	Work		JM		100%	$0.00/hr	$0.00/hr	
4		Scott Cooper	Work		SC		100%	$0.00/hr	$0.00/hr	
5		Jo Brown	Work		JB		100%	$0.00/hr	$0.00/hr	
6		Kim Yoshida	Work		KY		100%	$0.00/hr	$0.00/hr	
7		Peter Kelly	Work		PK		100%	$0.00/hr	$0.00/hr	
8		Jonathan Mollerup	Work		JM		50%	$0.00/hr	$0.00/hr	
9		John Thorson	Work		JT		75%	$0.00/hr	$0.00/hr	
10		16 mm Camera	Work		16mm		300%	$0.00/hr	$0.00/hr	
11		5000 Watt Light	Work		5000WL		400%	$0.00/hr	$0.00/hr	
12		Dolly	Work		Dolly		200%	$0.00/hr	$0.00/hr	
13		Crane	Work		Crane		100%	$0.00/hr	$0.00/hr	
14		Editing Lab	Work		EL		100%	$0.00/hr	$0.00/hr	

Setting Up Material Resources

PROJ2000-1-8

Material resources are consumables that you use up as the project progresses. On a construction project, material resources might include nails, lumber, and concrete. On our project, film is the consumable resource that interests us most. You work with material resources in Microsoft Project mainly to track the rate of consumption and the associated cost. Although Microsoft Project isn't a complete system for tracking inventory, it can help you stay better informed about how quickly you are consuming your material resources.

In this exercise, you enter information about material resources.

1 On the Resource Sheet, click the next empty cell in the Resource Name column.

2 Type **16 mm Film**, and press Tab.

3 In the Type field, click Material, and press Tab.

4 In the Material Label field, type **Feet**, and press Tab.

Feet is the unit of measure you'll use to track film consumption during the project.

5   In the Initials field, type **Film**, and press Tab.

You will enter the cost of the material resource later. Your screen should look similar to the following illustration.

	ⓘ	Resource Name	Type	Material Label	Initials	Group	Max. Units	Std. Rate	Ovt. Rate	Cos ▲
1		Clair Hector	Work		CH		100%	$0.00/hr	$0.00/hr	
2		Electrician	Work		EL		200%	$0.00/hr	$0.00/hr	
3		Jan Miksovsky	Work		JM		100%	$0.00/hr	$0.00/hr	
4		Scott Cooper	Work		SC		100%	$0.00/hr	$0.00/hr	
5		Jo Brown	Work		JB		100%	$0.00/hr	$0.00/hr	
6		Kim Yoshida	Work		KY		100%	$0.00/hr	$0.00/hr	
7		Peter Kelly	Work		PK		100%	$0.00/hr	$0.00/hr	
8		Jonathan Mollerup	Work		JM		50%	$0.00/hr	$0.00/hr	
9		John Thorson	Work		JT		75%	$0.00/hr	$0.00/hr	
10		16 mm Camera	Work		16mm		300%	$0.00/hr	$0.00/hr	
11		5000 Watt Light	Work		5000WL		400%	$0.00/hr	$0.00/hr	
12		Dolly	Work		Dolly		200%	$0.00/hr	$0.00/hr	
13		Crane	Work		Crane		100%	$0.00/hr	$0.00/hr	
14		Editing Lab	Work		EL		100%	$0.00/hr	$0.00/hr	
15		16 mm Film	Material	Feet	Film			$0.00		

Here is the material resource you've entered.

The Material Label field only applies to material resources.

You will work more with material resources in Lesson 8.

Entering Resource Pay Rates

PROJ2000-1-9
PROJ2000E-1-1
PROJ2000E-3-1

You might recall from Lesson 1 that cost or budget is one side of the project triangle. Almost all projects have some financial aspect, and cost drives the project scope of many projects. Tracking and managing cost information allows the project manager to answer such important questions as:

▪ What is the expected total cost of the project, based on our task duration and resource estimates?

▪ Are we using expensive resources to do work that less expensive resources could do?

▪ How much money will a specific type of resource or task cost over the life of the project?

▪ Are we spending money at a rate that we can sustain for the planned duration of the project?

Work and material resources account for the majority of costs in many projects. To take full advantage of Microsoft Project's extensive cost management features, the project manager should know the costs associated with each work and material resource. For people resources, it may be difficult to get such information. In many organizations, only senior management and human resource specialists know the pay rates of all resources working on a project, and they might consider this information confidential. Depending on your organizational policies and project priorities, you might not be able to track resource pay rates. If you're unable to track this information, your effectiveness as a project manager might be reduced, and the **sponsors** of your projects should understand this.

For our filmmaking project, you have been entrusted with pay rate information for all people resources used in the project. In the information below, note that the fees for the camera, the lights, and the editing lab are rental fees. Because the Industrial Smoke and Mirrors film company already owns the dolly and crane, you won't bill yourself for them. The film rate requires additional explanation, however.

The purpose of assigning a standard pay rate to a material resource is to accurately predict (and later, track) the cost of materials against the project plan. For the material resource named 16 mm Film, you entered a unit of measure of feet in the Material Label field; next you'll enter a rate of 20 cents in the Std. Rate field. In other words, you'll assign a cost of 20 cents per foot to film. As you consume film over the course of the project, Microsoft Project will calculate the accrued cost of the film you consume. For example, if you shoot 12 minutes of film at 36 feet per minute, you will consume 432 feet of film. Entering that amount shows that you spent $86.40 (12 minutes × 36 feet × $0.20).

In this exercise, you enter cost information for each resource.

1   On the Resource Sheet, click the Std. Rate field for Resource 1, "Clair Hector."

2   Type **800/w**, and press Enter.

Clair's standard weekly rate appears in the Std. Rate column.

3   In the Std. Rate field for Resource 2, "Electrician," type **22/h**, and press Enter.

The electricians' standard hourly rate appears in the Std. Rate column. Your screen should look similar to the following illustration.

🛈	Resource Name	Type	Material Label	Initials	Group	Max. Units	Std. Rate	Ovt. Rate	Cos ▲
1	Clair Hector	Work		CH		100%	$800.00/wk	$0.00/hr	
2	Electrician	Work		EL		200%	$22.00/hr	$0.00/hr	
3	Jan Miksovsky	Work		JM		100%	$0.00/hr	$0.00/hr	
4	Scott Cooper	Work		SC		100%	$0.00/hr	$0.00/hr	
5	Jo Brown	Work		JB		100%	$0.00/hr	$0.00/hr	
6	Kim Yoshida	Work		KY		100%	$0.00/hr	$0.00/hr	
7	Peter Kelly	Work		PK		100%	$0.00/hr	$0.00/hr	
8	Jonathan Mollerup	Work		JM		50%	$0.00/hr	$0.00/hr	
9	John Thorson	Work		JT		75%	$0.00/hr	$0.00/hr	
10	16 mm Camera	Work		16mm		300%	$0.00/hr	$0.00/hr	
11	5000 Watt Light	Work		5000WL		400%	$0.00/hr	$0.00/hr	
12	Dolly	Work		Dolly		200%	$0.00/hr	$0.00/hr	
13	Crane	Work		Crane		100%	$0.00/hr	$0.00/hr	
14	Editing Lab	Work		EL		100%	$0.00/hr	$0.00/hr	
15	16 mm Film	Material	Feet	Film			$0.00		

4   Enter the following standard pay rates for these resources.

Resource name	Standard rate
Jan Miksovsky	18.75/h
Scott Cooper	775/w
Jo Brown	18.75/h
Kim Yoshida	9.40/h
Peter Kelly	16.75/h
Jonathan Mollerup	10/h
John Thorson	15.50/h
16 mm Camera	250/w
5000 Watt Light	100/w
Dolly	0/h
Crane	0/h
Editing Lab	200/d
16 mm Film	.20

Not all resources are paid a straight standard rate. Some resources require overtime pay for working more than a certain numbers of hours over a certain period of time.

5   On the Resource Sheet, click the Ovt. Rate field for Resource 2, "Electrician."

6   Type **33/h**, and press Enter.

Some resources require you to pay a price each time you use them. For example, a consultant or a piece of equipment might have a per-use fee in addition to or instead of an hourly rate. In our project, the Editing Lab has a $25 charge for setting it up and cleaning it every time you use it. You will enter this fee next.

To see the Cost/Use field, you might need to scroll right.

7   On the Resource Sheet, scroll to the right, and click the Cost/Use field for Resource 14, "Editing Lab."

8   Type **25**, and then press Enter.

Not all resources accrue cost in the same way. For example, a piece of rented equipment might require payment of a rental fee as soon as you rent the equipment, but employees usually accrue pay as time progresses. In the Accrue At field, you specify how Microsoft Project should handle a resource's cost accrual.

9   On the Resource Sheet, scroll further to the right, and click the Accrue At field for Resource 10, "16 mm Camera."

Rental fees for the 16 mm cameras must be paid before you use the equipment. To reflect this in your file, you want Microsoft Project to accrue the resource's cost as soon as the task starts.

To see the Accrue At field, you might need to scroll right.

10   In the Accrue At field, click Start.

Your screen should look similar to the following illustration.

	Type	Material Label	Initials	Group	Max. Units	Std. Rate	Ovt. Rate	Cost/Use	Accrue At	Base Calend
1	Work		CH		100%	$800.00/wk	$0.00/hr	$0.00	Prorated	Standard
2	Work		EL		200%	$22.00/hr	$33.00/hr	$0.00	Prorated	Standard
3	Work		JM		100%	$18.75/hr	$0.00/hr	$0.00	Prorated	Standard
4	Work		SC		100%	$775.00/wk	$0.00/hr	$0.00	Prorated	Standard
5	Work		JB		100%	$18.75/hr	$0.00/hr	$0.00	Prorated	Standard
6	Work		KY		100%	$9.40/hr	$0.00/hr	$0.00	Prorated	Standard
7	Work		PK		100%	$16.75/hr	$0.00/hr	$0.00	Prorated	Standard
8	Work		JM		50%	$10.00/hr	$0.00/hr	$0.00	Prorated	Standard
9	Work		JT		75%	$15.50/hr	$0.00/hr	$0.00	Prorated	Standard
10	Work		16mm		300%	$250.00/hr	$0.00/hr	$0.00	Start	Standard
11	Work		5000WL		400%	$100.00/wk	$0.00/hr	$0.00	Prorated	Standard
12	Work		Dolly		200%	$0.00/hr	$0.00/hr	$0.00	Prorated	Standard
13	Work		Crane		100%	$0.00/hr	$0.00/hr	$0.00	Prorated	Standard
14	Work		EL		100%	$200.00/day	$0.00/hr	$25.00	Prorated	Standard
15	Material	Feet	Film			$0.20		$0.00	Prorated	

Organizing Resources into Groups

In most projects, work resources fall into logical **groups**. Some examples of groups are shown in the table below.

Type of group	Example
Department	Director's Unit; Art Department
Functional	Technical; Artistic
Time sequence	Pre-production staff; Post-production staff
Employment status	Permanent employees; Contractors; Vendors

Once your project's work resources have been organized into groups, you can sort, filter, or group resources by resource group. In this exercise, you assign resources to groups.

1   On the Resource Sheet, scroll back to the left, and click the Group field for Resource 1, "Clair Hector."

2   Type **Producer's Unit**, and then press Enter.

3   Enter the following group names for these resources.

Resource name	Group
Electrician	Crew
Jan Miksovsky	Production
Scott Cooper	Director's Unit

The next several resources belong to the same group, so you will enter this information in one action.

4   In the Group field for Resource 5, "Jo Brown," type **Production**, and then press Enter.

5   Click Jo Brown's Group field again.

6   In the lower right corner of the cell, drag the fill handle down through the Group field of Resource 9, "John Thorson."

Microsoft Project fills the Group fields with the value "Production." (If you've used the fill handle in Microsoft Excel 2000, you might recognize this way of entering information.)

7   In the Group field for Resource 10, "16 mm Camera," type **Equipment** and press Enter.

8   Select Equipment, and then using the fill handle, copy the Equipment value down through Resource 14, "Editing Lab." Your screen should look similar to the following illustration.

	ⓘ	Resource Name	Type	Material Label	Initials	Group	Max. Units	Std. Rate	Ovt. Rate	Cos
1		Clair Hector	Work		CH	Producer's U	100%	$800.00/wk	$0.00/hr	
2		Electrician	Work		EL	Crew	200%	$22.00/hr	$33.00/hr	
3		Jan Miksovsky	Work		JM	Production	100%	$18.75/hr	$0.00/hr	
4		Scott Cooper	Work		SC	Director's Ui	100%	$775.00/wk	$0.00/hr	
5		Jo Brown	Work		JB	Production	100%	$18.75/hr	$0.00/hr	
6		Kim Yoshida	Work		KY	Production	100%	$9.40/hr	$0.00/hr	
7		Peter Kelly	Work		PK	Production	100%	$16.75/hr	$0.00/hr	
8		Jonathan Mollerup	Work		JM	Production	50%	$10.00/hr	$0.00/hr	
9		John Thorson	Work		JT	Production	75%	$15.50/hr	$0.00/hr	
10		16 mm Camera	Work		16mm	Equipment	300%	$250.00/hr	$0.00/hr	
11		5000 Watt Light	Work		5000WL	Equipment	400%	$100.00/wk	$0.00/hr	
12		Dolly	Work		Dolly	Equipment	200%	$0.00/hr	$0.00/hr	
13		Crane	Work		Crane	Equipment	100%	$0.00/hr	$0.00/hr	
14		Editing Lab	Work		EL	Equipment	100%	$200.00/day	$0.00/hr	
15		16 mm Film	Material	Feet	Film			$0.20		

After you associate each resource with a group name, you can sort and filter resources by group.

PROJ2000-5-13

Entering Additional Resource Information in a Text Field

You can display fields other than those that appear by default in the Entry table on the Resource Sheet. Some of these other fields, such as the Email Address field, have specific uses. Others are general purpose, and you can customize them to suit your needs. For example, job titles are so important in the film industry that film credits are organized by job titles. To record the resources' job titles, you will enter them into a **text field**. You can add whatever information you want in as many as 30 text fields for each of your resources.

The default resource fields describe many aspects of your resources, but you might have additional needs. In this exercise, you will insert a column into the Resource Sheet, and you will enter people's job titles.

1   On the Resource Sheet, click the Type column heading.

To insert a column, you can also se- lect a column heading and press Insert.

2   On the Insert menu, click Column.

The Column Definition dialog box appears. Here you choose the field you want to display and how you want it to appear.

3   In the Field Name list, click **Text1**.

tip

Type a letter to scroll to the field names that start with that letter in the Field Name list. In this case, typing **t** scrolls the field name list to Text1, which is the first item in the list that starts with "t."

4   In the Title box, enter **Title**.

Because the Title field will contain text, you'll align it to the left to match the other text fields in the Resource Sheet.

5   In the Align Title and Align Data lists, click Left.

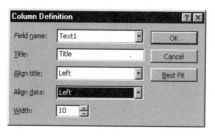

6 Click OK to close the Column Definition dialog box and return to the Resource Sheet.

7 Enter the following titles for these resources in the Title field.

Resource name	Title
Clair Hector	Producer
Electrician	(leave blank)
Jan Miksovsky	Director of photography
Scott Cooper	Director
Jo Brown	Production manager
Kim Yoshida	Production assistant
Peter Kelly	Sound technician
Jonathan Mollerup	2nd Assistant director
John Thorson	1st Assistant director

Your screen should look similar to the following illustration.

Here is the resource text field you've inserted and named "Title." Text fields are useful for any type of information you want to record about resources that are not addressed by the default fields.

	❶	Resource Name	Title	Type	Material Label	Initials	Group	Max. Units	Std. Rate	Ovt.
1		Clair Hector	Producer	Work		CH	Producer's	100%	$800.00/wk	$0
2		Electrician		Work		EL	Crew	200%	$22.00/hr	$33
3		Jan Miksovsky	Director of p	Work		JM	Production	100%	$18.75/hr	$0
4		Scott Cooper	Director	Work		SC	Director's U	100%	$775.00/wk	$0
5		Jo Brown	Production r	Work		JB	Production	100%	$18.75/hr	$0
6		Kim Yoshida	Production a	Work		KY	Production	100%	$9.40/hr	$0
7		Peter Kelly	Sound techr	Work		PK	Production	100%	$16.75/hr	$0
8		Jonathan Mollerup	2nd Assista	Work		JM	Production	50%	$10.00/hr	$0
9		John Thorson	1st Assistar	Work		JT	Production	75%	$15.50/hr	$0
10		16 mm Camera		Work		16mm	Equipment	300%	$250.00/hr	$0
11		5000 Watt Light		Work		5000WL	Equipment	400%	$100.00/wk	$0
12		Dolly		Work		Dolly	Equipment	200%	$0.00/hr	$0
13		Crane		Work		Crane	Equipment	100%	$0.00/hr	$0
14		Editing Lab		Work		EL	Equipment	100%	$200.00/day	$0
15		16 mm Film		Material	Feet	Film			$0.20	

In the next lesson, you will assign these resources to tasks.

Lesson Wrap-Up

This lesson covered how to set up work and material resources, as well as how to record other details, such as cost information.

If you are going on to other lessons:

1   On the Standard toolbar, click Save to save the changes you made to Short Film Project 04. Save the file without a baseline.

2   On the File menu, click Close to close the file.

If you aren't continuing to other lessons:

●   On the File menu, click Exit.

Glossary

Group A field in which you can specify a group name (such as a department) with which you want to associate a resource. If you organize resources into groups, you can then sort, filter, or group resources by group.

Material resources Consumables that are used up as the project progresses. As with work resources, you assign material resources to tasks. Unlike work resources, material resources have no effect on the total amount of work scheduled to be performed on a task.

Max. Units The maximum capacity of a resource to accomplish tasks. A resource that is available to work full time has a maximum units value of 100% or 1.0.

Overallocated The state of a resource that you have assigned to do more work than the resource can do within its normal work capacity. In Microsoft Project, you measure a single resource's work capacity in units. One full-time resource has 100% units, which you record in the Max. Units field.

Resources People, equipment, and material (and the associated costs of each) required to complete the work of a project.

Sponsor An individual or organization that provides financial support and champions the project team within the larger organization.

Text fields Columns or fields in forms in which you can enter any information you want about a resource. Microsoft Project allows up to 30 text fields for each resource.

Work resources The people and equipment that do the work of the project.

Quick Reference

To enter names and other details about work resources (people or equipment)

1   On the View bar, click Resource Sheet.

2   In the Resource Name field, enter the resource's name.

3   In the Type field, click Work.

4   In the Max. Units field, type or select the maximum capacity of this resource to accomplish any task.

5   Enter whatever other resource information would be useful for your project.

6   Repeat steps 2 through 5 for each resource.

To enter names and other details about material resources

1   On the View bar, click Resource Sheet.

2   In the Resource Name field, enter the material resource's name.

3   In the Type field, click Material.

4   In the Material Label field, enter the unit of measure you want to use for this resource. For example, you might measure cement in pounds or tons.

5   In the Std. Rate field, enter the cost per unit of measure for this material resource.

6   Enter whatever other resource information would be useful for your project.

7   Repeat steps 2 through 6 for each resource.

To enter cost rates for work resources (people or equipment)

1   On the View bar, click Resource Sheet.

2   In the Std. Rate field, enter the resource's pay rate, including the duration of a pay period.

3   If the resource should accrue overtime pay, enter its overtime pay rate in the Ovt. Rate field.

4   If the resource accrues a per-use cost, enter that amount in the Cost/Use field.

5 In the Accrue At field, click the method by which the resource accrues cost.

6 Repeat steps 2 through 6 for each resource.

To organize resources into groups

1 On the View bar, click Resource Sheet.

2 In the Group field for a resource, type the name of the group with which you want to associate the resource.

3 Repeat step 2 for each resource.

To display a text field

1 On the View bar, click Resource Sheet.

2 Click the column heading to the right of where you want to insert a text field.

3 On the Insert menu, click Column.

The Column Definition dialog box appears.

4 In the Field Name list, click one of the text fields named Text1 through Text30.

5 In the Title box, type the name you want to appear in the column heading for this field.

6 Enter whatever other options you want, and then click OK.

5

Assigning Resources to Tasks

ESTIMATED
TIME
40 min.

After completing this lesson, you will be able to:

✔ *Assign a resource to a task.*

✔ *Display duration, unit, and work values simultaneously.*

✔ *Assign multiple resources to a task.*

✔ *Turn off effort-driven scheduling for a task, and assign resources.*

✔ *Remove a resource assignment from a task.*

✔ *Assign a material resource to a task.*

✔ *Create resources in the Assign Resources dialog box, and assign them to tasks.*

In Lesson 3, you created tasks, and, in Lesson 4, you created resources. Now you are ready to assign resources to tasks. An **assignment** is the matching of a resource to a task to do **work**. From the perspective of tasks, you might call this a task assignment; from the perspective of resources, you might call it a resource assignment. It's the same thing either way: a task plus a resource equals an assignment.

You don't have to assign resources to tasks in Microsoft Project; you could just work with tasks. But there are several good reasons to assign resources in your project plan. If you assign resources to tasks, you can answer questions such as:

▪ Who should be working on what tasks, and when?

▪ Do you have the right number of resources to do the scope of work your project requires?

- Are you expecting a resource to work on a task at a time when that resource will not be available to work (for example, when the resource will be on vacation)?

- Have you assigned a resource to so many tasks that you've exceeded the resource's capacity to work—in other words, have you overallocated the resource?

- Are you evaluating the resource's performance against a pre-established plan? A resource that appears to be very busy but takes twice as long to complete a task as does another resource might not be as productive as he or she appears.

In this lesson, you use a variety of methods to assign resources to tasks. You assign work resources (people and equipment) and material resources to tasks, and you see where resource assignments should affect task duration and where they should not.

To complete this lesson, you will use a file named Short Film Project 05. This file contains the initial task list you developed in Lesson 3, plus the resource information you entered in Lesson 4. Before you begin this lesson, open the Part 1 folder in the MS Project SBS 2000 Practice folder on your hard disk. Open the file 05A, and save it without a baseline as Short Film Project 05 in the Part 1 folder.

Assigning a Single Resource to a Task

PROJ2000-1-18

Assigning a resource to a task allows you to track the resource's progress in working on the task. Microsoft Project also calculates resource and task costs for you, if you enter cost information.

You might recall from Lesson 4 that a resource's capacity to work is measured in **units** and recorded in the Max. Units field. It's easy to overallocate a resource: just assign a resource to one task with more units than the resource has available, or assign it to multiple tasks with schedules that overlap and with combined units that exceed those of the resource. Unless you specify otherwise, Microsoft Project assigns 100% of the resource's units to the task. If the resource has less than 100% maximum units, Microsoft Project assigns the resource's maximum units value.

The View bar appears on the left side of the Microsoft Project window. If you want help locating parts of the Microsoft Project interface, see Lesson 2.

In this exercise, you assign individual resources to tasks.

1   On the View bar, click Gantt Chart.

2   On the Standard toolbar, click Assign Resources.

The Assign Resources dialog box appears. In it, you see the resource names you entered in Lesson 4. If the Assign Resources dialog box obscures the Entry table, drag the dialog box out of the way, to the lower right corner of the screen.

3   In the Task Name column in the Entry table, click Task 8, "Reserve camera equipment."

4   In the Name column in the Assign Resources dialog box, select Jan Miksovsky, and then click Assign.

A check mark appears next to Jan Miksovsky's name, indicating that you have assigned her to the task of reserving camera equipment. In the Units column, you can see that she is assigned at 100%.

tip
You can also assign one or more resources to a task by using the mouse. First, select the resource or resources in the Assign Resources dialog box. To select multiple resources, click the first resource name, hold down Ctrl, and click the additional resource names. Point to the column to the left of the resource name. When the mouse pointer changes to a resource icon, drag the resource icon to the task name in the Entry table.

Next you assign other resources to tasks.

5   In the Entry table, click the name of Task 7, "Apply for filming permits."

6   In the Assign Resources dialog box, select Kim Yoshida, and click Assign.

A check mark appears next to Kim Yoshida's name, indicating that you have assigned her to the task you selected.

7   In the Entry table, click the name of Task 9, "Reserve sound equipment."

8   In the Assign Resources dialog box, select Peter Kelly, and then click Assign.

The names of assigned
resources appear next
to the Gantt bars.

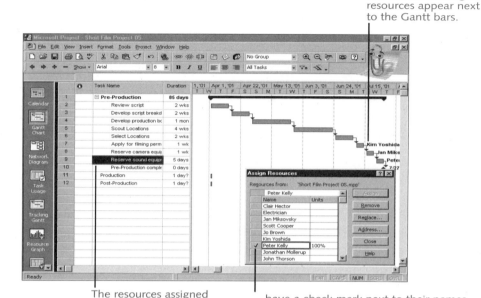

The resources assigned
to the selected task...

...have a check mark next to their names
in the Assign Resources dialog box.

9   Click Close to close the Assign Resources dialog box.

The Scheduling Formula: Viewing Duration, Units, and Work

PROJ2000-4-2

After you create a task but before you assign a resource to it, the task has **duration** but no work associated with it. Why no work? Work represents the amount of time a resource or resources will spend to complete a task. If you have one person working full time, the amount of time measured as work is the same as the amount of time measured as **duration**. The amount of work differs from the duration only if you assign more than one resource to a task or the one resource you assign isn't working full time.

Microsoft Project calculates work using what is sometimes called the **scheduling formula**:

$$\text{Duration} \times \text{Units} = \text{Work}$$

Let's look at an example. The duration of Task 8 is one week. For our Short Film project, a week equals 40 hours. (You can see how many hours constitute a week by opening the Tools menu, choosing the Options command, and clicking the Calendar tab.) When you assigned Jan Miksovsky to Task 8, Microsoft

Project applied 100% of Jan's working time to this task. The scheduling formula for Task 8 looks like this:

40 hours task duration × 100% resource units = 40 hours work

In other words, with Jan assigned to Task 8 at 100% units, the task should require 40 hours of work. You can verify this in Microsoft Project by displaying the Task Form in the Task Entry view.

In this exercise, you display the project in Task Entry view.

1   In the Gantt Chart, click the name of Task 8, "Reserve camera equipment."

2   On the View menu, click More Views.

3   In the Views box, click Task Entry, and then click Apply.

The Task Form appears in the lower pane of the Microsoft Project window.

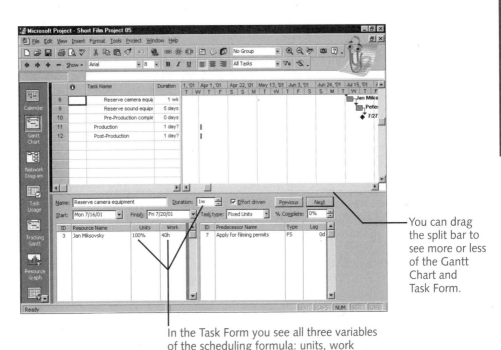

You can drag the split bar to see more or less of the Gantt Chart and Task Form.

In the Task Form you see all three variables of the scheduling formula: units, work and duration.

tip

To quickly display the Task Form below the Gantt Chart, you can also click Split on the Window menu.

The Task Entry view displays the Gantt Chart view in the upper pane of the Microsoft Project window and the Task Form view in the lower pane. The Task Form shows all three variables of the scheduling formula at once: the task's duration in the Duration field, the resource's units in the Units column, and the resulting work value for the task assignment in the Work column. We'll refer to these values frequently in this lesson so that you'll understand how Microsoft Project generates the values it does.

Assigning Multiple Resources to a Task

PROJ 2000-1-11

Now you will assign two resources to a single task to see the effect on the task's overall duration. By default, Microsoft Project uses a scheduling method called **effort-driven scheduling**. This means that a task's work remains constant regardless of the number of resources you assign. Microsoft Project applies effort-driven scheduling only when you assign resources to or remove resources from tasks.

As you saw above, you define the amount of work a task represents when you initially assign a resource or resources to it. If you later add additional resources to that task, the amount of work doesn't change, but the task's duration automatically decreases. Conversely, you might initially assign more than one resource to a task and later remove one of those resources from the task. If you do this with effort-driven scheduling on, the amount of work for the task stays constant, but the duration, or time it takes the remaining resource to complete that task, increases.

The following example illustrates the effect of effort-driven scheduling on a task as you assign resources to it. We've inserted the Work column in the Entry table, and we will focus on the Duration and Work columns in that table, as well as the individual resource's Units and Work columns in the Task Form.

Let's start with a task that has a 24-hour (3-day) duration, to which we've not yet assigned any resources. We want the duration of this task to decrease as we add additional resources to it (after the initial assignment), so we leave effort-driven scheduling on for the task.

Initially this task has a duration of 24 hours...

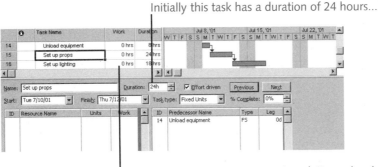

...but since no resources are assigned, its work value is 0.

Next we'll make the initial assignment: one resource at 100% units. You might recall from above that a task has a work value only after you initially assign a resource to the task. After we make the initial resource assignment, the task's duration and work value are both 24 hours.

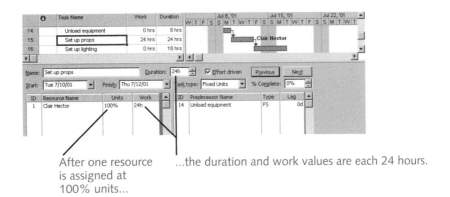

After one resource is assigned at 100% units...

...the duration and work values are each 24 hours.

tip

If you initially assign two resources to a task with a duration of 24 hours, Microsoft Project schedules each resource to work 24 hours, for a total of 48 hours of work on the task. However, if you initially assign one resource to a task with a duration of 24 hours and you later add a second resource, effort-driven scheduling will cause Microsoft Project to schedule each resource to work 12 hours in parallel, for a total of 24 hours of work on the task. Remember that effort-driven scheduling adjusts task duration only if you add or delete resources from a task.

Next we make the second resource assignment. We'll also assign that resource at 100% units. Because effort-driven scheduling is turned on, the task's work remains at 24 hours, but that work is distributed between the two resources. The task's duration is, therefore, reduced from 24 hours to 12.

After a second resource is assigned, total work remains 24 hours but the task's duration has decreased to 12 hours.

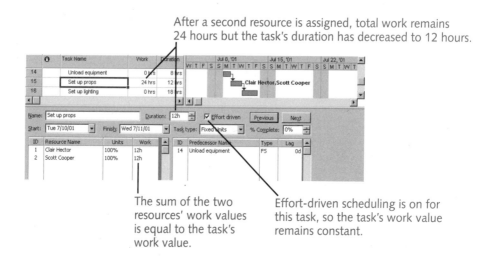

The sum of the two resources' work values is equal to the task's work value.

Effort-driven scheduling is on for this task, so the task's work value remains constant.

The resource unit values determine how Microsoft Project distributes the work between resources. In this example, we've assigned both resources at 100% units, so they share the work equally. If we had assigned either resource at anything other than 100%, the work would be distributed between them proportionally. For example, let's say that we initially assigned Clair Hector to a 24-hour task at 100% units. If we later added Scott Cooper at 50%, we would expect Clair to spend 16 hours on that task and Scott to spend only eight hours on that task.

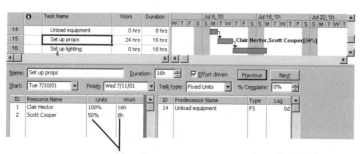

Here two resources are assigned at different units, so their individual work values differ as well.

You don't need to display the Work column or the Task Form for effort-driven scheduling to take effect; we displayed them here to help illustrate the scheduling calculations. By default, effort-driven scheduling is turned on in Microsoft Project, but you can turn it off for individual tasks or for all new tasks entered in a project.

In this exercise, you assign multiple resources to individual tasks and see how this affects task durations.

1   In the Entry table, click the name of Task 2, "Review script."

2   In the Resource Name column in the Task Form, click directly below the Resource Name column heading. Then click the small down arrow that appears there.

3   In the Resource Name list, click Scott Cooper, and click OK in the upper-right corner of the Task Form.

Scott Cooper is assigned to Task 2. A quick check of the scheduling formula looks like this:

$$80 \text{ hours (same as 2 weeks) task duration} \times 100\% \text{ resource units} = 80 \text{ hours work}$$

Next you'll assign a second resource to the task in the Task Form.

4   In the Resource Name column in the Task Form, click directly below Scott Cooper's name, and then click the small down arrow that appears there.

5   Click Clair Hector, and then click OK.

Clair Hector is also assigned to Task 2. Your screen should look similar to the following illustration.

The duration of this task decreases as
additional resources are assigned to it.

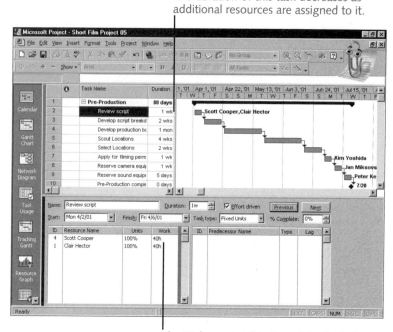

The 80 hours total task work is divided
between the two assigned resources.

As you can see in the Duration field and in the Gantt Chart, Microsoft Project reduced the duration of Task 2 from two weeks to one week.

The total work required is still 80 hours, as it was when just Scott was assigned to the task, but now the work is distributed evenly between Scott and Clair. This shows how effort-driven scheduling works. If, after an initial assignment, you add resources to a task, the total work remains constant but is distributed among the assigned resources. Further, the task's duration decreases accordingly. In the Task Form, the check mark in the Effort Driven check box tells you that effort-driven scheduling is turned on for Task 2.

The scheduling formula now looks like this:

$$40 \text{ hours (same as 1 week) task duration} \times 200\% \text{ resource units} = 80 \text{ hours work}$$

The 200% resource units is the sum of Scott's 100% plus Clair's 100%, and the 80 work hours is the sum of Scott's 40 hours plus Clair's 40 hours.

The other important effect of reducing the duration of Task 2 is that the start dates of all successor tasks changed as well. In Lesson 3, you created start-to-finish task relationships for these tasks. In this example, you see the benefit of creating task relationships rather than entering fixed start and finish dates. Microsoft Project adjusts the start dates of successor tasks that are not **constrained** by a fixed start date or finish date.

Next you assign multiple resources to Task 3.

6   In the Gantt Chart, click the name of Task 3, "Develop script breakdown and schedule."

7   Click the first row in the Resource Name column in the Task Form. Select Scott Cooper from the list, and click OK.

8   Click directly below Scott Cooper's name.

9   Click John Thorson, and then click OK.

Microsoft Project reduces the duration of Task 3 from 2 weeks to just over 1 week, and it adjusts the start dates of all successor tasks.

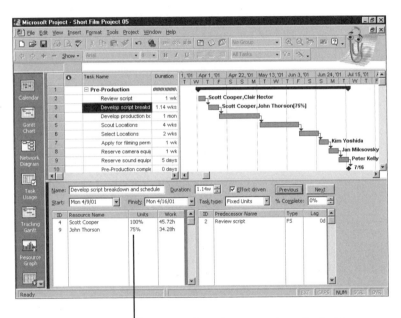

The Units values determines how the task's
work is divided among the assigned resources.

Because the values of the scheduling formula are not whole numbers in this case, let's look at how Microsoft Project came up with these values.

- The task duration of 45.7 hours (same as 1.14 weeks) is the result of dividing 80 hours of work by 175% units.

- Scott's work value of 45.7 hours represents 100% units times 45.7 hours task duration.

■   John's work value of 34.28 hours represents 75% units times 45.7 hours task duration.

Is Scott really going to work on this task exactly 45.7 hours, and John 34.28 hours? Probably not. Microsoft Project can produce numbers such as these that, while mathematically accurate, might be too precise to be practical. That's OK; the important thing is that you understand how the numbers were generated.

To finish this exercise, assign multiple resources to a task with the Assign Resources dialog box.

10   In the Gantt Chart, click the name of Task 5, "Scout locations."

11   On the Standard toolbar, click Assign Resources.

The Assign Resources dialog box appears.

12   In the Name column of the Assign Resources dialog box, select Jo Brown, and click Assign.

A check mark appears next to Jo Brown's name, indicating that you have initially assigned her to the task you selected.

13   In the Name column, select Jan Miksovsky, and click Assign.

The duration of Task 5 is reduced, and the start dates of all successor tasks are adjusted accordingly.

When should effort-driven scheduling apply?

You should think through the extent to which effort-driven scheduling should apply to the tasks in your projects. For example, if one resource should take 10 hours to complete a task, could 10 resources complete the task in one hour? How about 20 resources in 30 minutes? Probably not; the resources would likely get in each other's way and require additional coordination to complete the task. If the task is very complicated, it might require significant training before a resource could contribute fully. Overall productivity might even decrease if you assign more resources to the task. No single rule exists about when you should apply effort-driven scheduling and when you shouldn't. As the project manager, you should analyze the nature of the work required by each task in your project and use your best judgment.

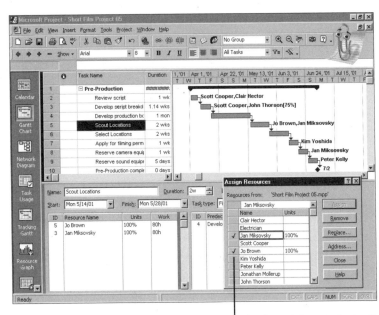

A check mark here indicates that the
resource is assigned to the selected task.

14 Click Close to close the Assign Resources dialog box.

Assigning Resources with Effort-Driven Scheduling Off

PROJ2000-1-10

Effort-driven scheduling might not apply to all tasks in a project, and you can turn it off when necessary. For example, let's say you have a task of monitoring wine as it ferments. Regardless of how many resources you assign to that task, it will still take the same amount of time. If you add more resources to a task with effort-driven scheduling turned off, the duration of the task will remain constant and the total work for the task will increase. Why is this? Let's look again at the scheduling formula:

$$\text{Duration} \times \text{Units} = \text{Work}$$

If the task's duration should not be affected by the number of resources as-signed, adding more resource units to a task must increase the total work. For example, the task of building a brick wall should see its duration decrease if a second bricklayer is assigned to help the initial bricklayer (effort-driven schedul-ing on). However the task's duration should not decrease if a foreman is also assigned to the task (effort-driven scheduling off). The foreman is working, but his or her work does not directly assist the two bricklayers.

In this exercise, you turn off effort-driven scheduling for a task and assign multiple resources to the task.

1 In the Entry table, click the name of Task 4, "Develop production boards."

2 In the Task Form, clear the Effort Driven check box.

3 Click the first row in the Resource Name column in the Task Form. Select Scott Cooper from the list, and then click OK.

4 Directly below Scott Cooper's name, click John Thorson, and then click OK.

5 Directly below John Thorson's name, click Kim Yoshida, and then click OK.

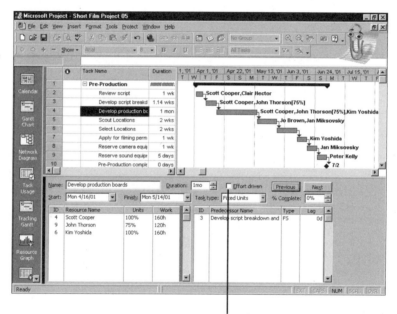

Effort-driven scheduling is off for this task, so the task's duration is not affected and work increases as resources are assigned.

As you can see, the task's duration remains the same regardless of how many resources you assign to it. Microsoft Project allocates each resource its own work amount, which increases the total amount of work on the task. The scheduling formula now looks like this:

160 hours (same as 20 days) task duration × 275% resource units
= 440 hours work

■ The 275% resource units is the sum of Scott's 100% plus John's 75% plus Kim's 100%.

■ The 440 work hours is the sum of Scott's 160 hours plus John's 120 hours plus Kim's 160 hours.

To finish this exercise, turn off effort-driven scheduling and assign multiple resources to a task in the Task Information dialog box.

6 In the Entry table, click the name of Task 6, "Select locations."

7 On the Standard toolbar, click the Task Information button.

The Task Information dialog box appears.

8 Click the Advanced tab.

9 Clear the Effort Driven check box, and then click the Resources tab.

10 Click directly below the Resource Name column heading.

11 In the Resource Name list, click Jo Brown.

12 In the Resource Name column, click directly below Jo Brown's name, and then click Scott Cooper.

13 In the Resource Name column, click directly below Scott Cooper's name, click Clair Hector, and then press Enter.

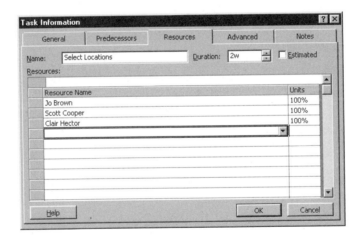

14 Click OK to close the Task Information dialog box.

In the Gantt Chart and Task Form, you can see that you have assigned these three resources to Task 6, for which effort-driven scheduling has been turned off.

Turning off effort-driven scheduling and assigning resources in the Task Information dialog box is another example of how you can accomplish the same task in different ways in Microsoft Project, depending on your preference.

Removing a Resource Assignment

You can remove a resource from a task at any time. You might want to do this for a variety of reasons:

- You realize the resource is not needed to complete the task.

- A resource will be unavailable (for example, on vacation) when a task must be worked on, and you need to assign a different resource to the task.

- An equipment resource breaks down and you need to substitute a different piece of equipment.

If effort-driven scheduling is turned on for the task, removing a resource increases the task's duration and redistributes the work between the remaining resources. If effort-driven scheduling is turned off, removing a resource decreases the task's total work but does not change the duration.

Effort-driven scheduling is turned off for Task 6. The scheduling formula for Task 6 prior to removing a resource assignment looks like this:

$$\text{80 hours (same as 2 weeks) task duration} \times 300\% \text{ resource units} = 240 \text{ hours work}$$

In this exercise, you remove a resource assignment from a task.

1   In the Task Form, click Jo Brown.

2   Press the Delete key, and then click OK in the upper right corner of the Task Form.

   Jo Brown is removed from the task.

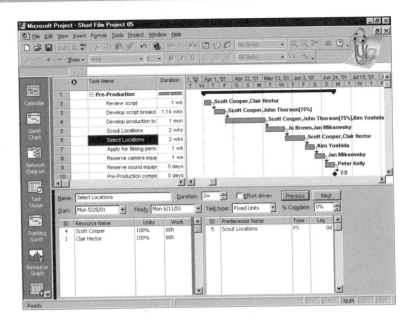

The scheduling formula for Task 6 now looks like this:

80 hours (same as 2 weeks) task duration × 200% resource units
= 160 hours work

The total work decreased when the resource was removed from the task. Next you will hide the Task Form.

3 On the Window menu, click Remove Split.

Assigning Material Resources to Tasks

In Lesson 4, you created the material resource named "16 mm film." In our film project, we're interested in tracking the use of film and its cost. When assigning a material resource, you can handle cost in one of two ways:

For a demonstration of various ways to assign resouces to tasks, double-click the Assign Resources icon in the Multimedia folder on the Microsoft Project 2000 Step by Step CD-ROM.

■ Assign a fixed unit quantity of the resource to the task. Microsoft Project will multiply the unit cost of this resource by the number of units you consume to determine the total cost.

■ Assign a variable rate quantity of the resource to the task. Microsoft Project will adjust the quantity and cost of the resource as the duration of the task changes.

In this exercise, you assign the material resource "16 mm film" to a task and enter a fixed unit quantity of consumption. In Lesson 8, you will work with variable rates of material resources.

1   On the Standard toolbar, click Assign Resources.

    The Assign Resources dialog box appears. You plan to shoot 60 minutes of film while scouting locations. Because 16 mm film is shot at a rate of 36 feet per minute, 60 minutes equals 2,160 feet of film.

2   In the Gantt Chart, click the name of Task 5, "Scout locations."

3   In the Assign Resources dialog box, scroll down the list of material resources until the 16 mm film resource appears, and select the Units field for that resource.

4   Type **2160**, and then click Assign.

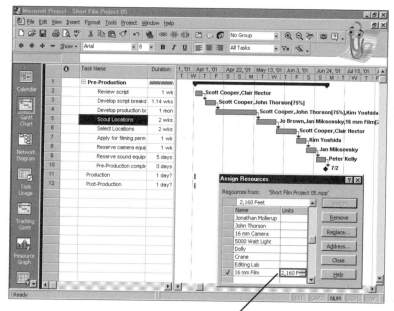

When entering units for a material resource assignment, rather than a percentage you enter a rate of consumption or (in this case) a fixed quantity.

Because 16 mm film is a material resource, it cannot do work. Therefore, assigning that resource does not affect the task's duration.

Creating a New Resource and Assigning It to a Task

At this point, you've created resources and assigned them to tasks by performing two separate actions. In the Assign Resources dialog box, you can do both in one action.

In this exercise, you create resources and assign them to a task in the Assign Resources dialog box.

1   In the Assign Resources dialog box, click the first empty cell in the Name column, type **Megan Sherman**, and then press Enter.

2   Select Megan Sherman's name, and then click Assign.

Megan Sherman is a new camera assistant you're adding to the project's resource list.

Next you'll enter her cost information.

3   Double-click Megan Sherman's name.

The Resource Information dialog box appears.

4   Click the Costs tab.

5   In the Standard Rate field, type **18/h**, and then press Enter.

6   Click OK to close the Resource Information dialog box.

7   Click Close to close the Assign Resources dialog box.

Megan has her own 16 mm camera, which you want to use while scouting locations. However, you don't want the assignment of the camera to affect the task's duration; it's not doing the same type of work as the people resources are. Next you'll turn off effort-driven scheduling for Task 5 and enter the camera resource information.

8   On the Standard toolbar, click the Task Information button.

9   Click the Advanced tab, and then clear the Effort Driven check box.

10   Click the Resources tab.

11   In the Resource Name column, click the first empty cell, type **Megan's 16 mm camera** and press Enter.

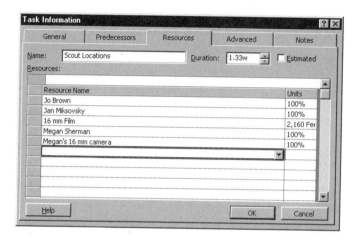

12 Click OK to close the Task Information dialog box.

Megan and her 16 mm camera are assigned to task 5. Because Megan was assigned when effort-driven scheduling was turned on, she decreased the overall task duration. However, Megan's 16 mm camera has no effect on task duration.

tip
You can create resources in many of the places in Microsoft Project where you can assign resources (such as the Task Form and the Assign Resources dialog box).

This exercise concludes the initial planning work for the short film project. In the next several lessons, you will refine the task, resource, and assignment details.

Lesson Wrap-Up

This lesson covered how to assign resources to tasks and explained how effort-driven scheduling affects task duration based on the number of resources you add or delete from a task.

If you are going on to other lessons:

1 On the Standard toolbar, click Save to save changes made to Short Film Project 05. Save the file without a baseline.

2 On the File menu, click Close to close the file.

If you aren't continuing to other lessons:

●   On the File menu, click Exit.

Glossary

Assignment   The matching of a work resource (people or equipment) to a task to do work. You can also assign a material resource to a task, but those resources have no effect on work or duration.

Constraint   A restriction placed upon a task's start or finish date, such as "must start on" or "start no earlier than."

Duration   The total span of working time for a task, measured from the task start date to task finish date. Duration is one variable in the scheduling formula: Duration × Units = Work.

Effort-driven scheduling   A scheduling method in which a task's work remains constant regardless of the number of resources assigned. If you add resources to a task, its duration decreases, but the work remains the same and is distributed among the assigned resources. Effort-driven scheduling is on by default in Microsoft Project, but you can turn it off for any task.

Scheduling formula   The concept behind how Microsoft Project calculates work, based on a task's duration and the resource units you assign to it. The scheduling formula is Duration × Units = Work.

Units   A standard way of measuring a resource's capacity to work when you assign it to a task in Microsoft Project. Units is one variable in the scheduling formula: Duration × Units = Work.

Work   The total amount of effort required to accomplish a task. Work is measured in person-hours and might not match the duration of the task. Work is one variable in the scheduling formula: Duration × Units = Work.

Quick Reference

To assign a resource to a task with the Assign Resources dialog box

1   On the View bar, click Gantt Chart.

2   On the Standard toolbar, click Assign Resources.

3   In the Entry table, select the name of the task to which you want to assign a resource.

4   In the Name column of the Assign Resources dialog box, select a resource, and then click Assign.

Assigning Resources to Tasks **5**

Gantt
Chart

To display the Task Form beneath the Gantt Chart

1   On the View bar, click Gantt Chart.

2   On the View menu, click More Views.

3   In the Views box, click Task Entry, and then click Apply.

To hide the Task Form with the Gantt Chart showing

●   On the Window menu, click Remove Split.

To assign a resource to a task in the Task Form

1   In the Entry table, select the name of the task to which you want to assign a resource.

2   In the Task Form, click directly below the Resource Name column heading.

3   In the Resource Name list, click the name of the resource you want, and then click OK in the upper-right corner of the Task Form.

To turn off effort-driven scheduling for a selected task

●   In the Task Form, clear the Effort Driven check box.

—Or—

1   On the Standard toolbar, click the Task Information button.

2   Click the Advanced tab.

3   Clear the Effort Driven check box.

To remove a resource assignment in the Task Form

1   In the Entry table, click the name of task from which you want to remove the resource assignment.

2   In the Task Form, click the name of the resource, press the Delete key, and then click OK in the upper right corner of the Task Form.

To assign a fixed amount of a material resource to a task with the Assign Resources dialog box

1   On the Standard toolbar, click Assign Resources.

2   In the Entry table, click the name of the task to which you want to assign a material resource.

3   In the Units column of the Assign Resources dialog box, enter the number of units of the material resource you want to assign, and then click the Assign button.

To create a resource and assign it to a task with the Assign Resources dialog box

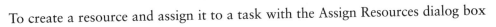

1   On the Standard toolbar, click Assign Resources.

2   In the Entry table, click the name of the task to which you want to assign a resource.

3   In the Assign Resources dialog, click the first empty cell in the Name column. Type the name of the new resource, and then press Enter.

4   Double-click the name of the new resource, and in the Assign Resources dialog box enter the information you want and click OK.

5   In the Assign Resources dialog box, click Assign.

Review & Practice

**ESTIMATED
TIME
10 min.**

You will review and practice how to:

✔ *Create task names and durations in the Gantt Chart view, and then link the tasks.*

✔ *Enter resource names and max. units.*

✔ *Assign resources to tasks, and specify the units values for each assignment.*

✔ *Zoom the Gantt Chart so the entire project is visible on your screen.*

Before you move on to Part 2, which covers fine-tuning task, resource, and assignment details, you can practice the skills you learned in Part 1 by working through this Review & Practice section.

Scenario

Leonard Zuvela is the manager of an up-and-coming band named Fourth Coffee. Leonard has seen other films your company, Industrial Smoke and Mirrors, has produced, and likes what he's seen. In fact, Leonard would like your crew to produce Fourth Coffee's next music video. He's asked you to put together a "quick and dirty" schedule for a music video project. You have a short time in which to produce the project plan and decide to deliver a Gantt Chart with tasks, durations, and resource assignments as part of your proposal. If you get the job, you'll fine-tune the plan later.

For a demonstration of how to complete this step, double-click Part 1 Step 1 in the Multimedia folder on the Microsoft Project 2000 Step by Step CD-ROM.

You must complete the exercises in steps 1 through 4 sequentially.

Step 1: Set Up Tasks

Producing a music video follows a sequence of activities similar to other film projects you've worked on. Based on your conversations with Leonard, you realize that he doesn't know much about project management terminology or processes, so you decide a simple Gantt Chart with high-level tasks would be most appropriate.

1   Start Microsoft Project, and create a new Microsoft Project file.

2   Enter a project start date of May 7, 2001.

3   Save it in the MS Project 2000 SBS Practice Part 1 folder without a baseline as Music Video Project 1.

4   Enter the following task list:

Task ID	Task Name	Duration
1	Pre-Production	(leave at 1d? duration)
2	Develop script breakdown	2w
3	Develop choreography	3w
4	Production	(leave at 1d? duration)
5	Rehearsal	3d
6	Shoot	2d
7	Post-Production	(leave at 1d? duration)
8	Fine cut edit	1w
9	Add final music	1w
10	Clone dubbing master	1d
11	Hand off final video	0d

5   Make Tasks 1, 4, and 7 summary tasks.

6   Select and link Tasks 1 through 11 with finish-to-start relationships.

7   Turn off effort-driven scheduling for all tasks.

For more information about	See
Setting the project start date	Lesson 2
Entering task information	Lesson 3
Creating summary tasks	Lesson 3
Linking tasks	Lesson 3
Effort-driven scheduling	Lesson 5

For a demonstration, double-click Part 1 Step 2 in the Multimedia folder.

Step 2: Set Up Resources

Leonard is very interested in the resources scheduled to work on the music video project and has suggested some specific people he's worked with before. However, to keep the initial project plan simple, you'll enter types of jobs rather than specific names of people as resources for the project plan. The resource named "Talent" represents the eight members of Fourth Coffee; you don't need to list them separately.

1 Switch to the Resource Sheet view.

2 Enter the following resource information.

Resource ID	Resource Name	Max. Units
1	Camera Operator	300%
2	Choreographer	100%
3	Director	100%
4	Editor	100%
5	Producer	100%
6	Production Staff	400%
7	Sound Engineer	300%
8	Talent	800%

For more information about	See
Switching to different views	Lesson 2
Entering resource information	Lesson 4

Step 3: Assign Resources to Tasks

For a demonstration, double-click Part 1 Step 3 in the Multimedia folder.

The music video project is more time-constrained than cost-constrained at this point, so producing the schedule has taken priority over producing a detailed budget. However, in anticipation of working out a detailed budget later, you make an initial pass at assigning resources to tasks and specifying the assignment units per task for each resource.

1 Switch to the Gantt Chart view.

2 Display the Assign Resources dialog box.

3 Assign resources to tasks as shown in the following table. Assign all resources at the units values shown below.

Task ID, Name	Resource Name (Units)
2, Develop script breakdown	Choreographer (100%), Director (100%), Editor (100%), Producer (100%)
3, Develop choreography	Camera Operator (100%), Choreographer (100%), Talent (800%)
5, Rehearsal	Camera Operator (100%), Choreographer (100%), Director (100%), Production Staff (200%), Sound Engineer (100%), Talent (800%)
6, Shoot	Camera Operator (300%), Choreographer (100%), Director (100%), Producer (100%), Production Staff (400%), Sound Engineer (100%), Talent (800%)
8, Fine cut edit	Director (100%), Editor (100%), Producer (100%)
9, Add final music	Director (100%), Editor (100%), Sound Engineer (100%)
10, Clone dubbing master	Sound Engineer (100%)
11, Hand off final video	Producer (100%)

4   Close the Assign Resources dialog box.

For more information about	See
Assigning resources to tasks	Lesson 5

Step 4: View the Entire Project in the Gantt Chart

For a demonstration, double-click Part 1 Step 4 in the Multimedia folder.

One easy way to see the entire project on a single screen is to change the timescale of the Gantt Chart. This also will work well later when you're ready to print the Gantt Chart.

●   Change the zoom level to view the entire project.

For more information about	See
Changing the zoom level of the Gantt Chart	Lesson 3

Finish the Review & Practice

If you are going on to Part 2:

1   On the Standard toolbar, click Save to save changes made to Music Project Video 1. Save the file without a baseline.

2   On the File menu, click Close to close the file.

If you aren't continuing to Part 2:

●   On the File menu, click Exit.

LESSON

6

Fine-Tuning Task Details

**ESTIMATED TIME
60 min.**

After completing this lesson, you will be able to:

✔ *Change the working time for the project and make holidays nonworking time.*

✔ *Create a task calendar and apply it to tasks.*

✔ *Enter lead and lag time and change task relationships.*

✔ *Change a task type and see the effects this has on how Microsoft Project schedules tasks.*

✔ *Split a task to record an interruption in work.*

✔ *Enter a fixed cost and specify how it should accrue.*

✔ *Set up a recurring task in the project schedule.*

✔ *Apply a constraint to a task.*

✔ *Reorder tasks.*

✔ *Record deadlines for tasks.*

✔ *Identify the tasks on the critical path.*

✔ *Record task details in notes and insert a hyperlink to content on the World Wide Web.*

In Part 1, you created an initial task list and made resource assignments for the short film project. In the lessons in this part, you refine the project plan, starting with task details.

To complete this lesson, you will use a file named Short Film Project 06. This project file contains the fully developed project plan you started in Part 1, with additional tasks, resources, and assignments. Before you begin this lesson, open the Part 2 folder in the MS Project 2000 SBS Practice folder on your hard disk. Open the file 6A, and save it without a baseline as Short Film Project 06 in the Part 2 folder.

Adjusting Working Time for the Project

PROJ2000E-3-4

Calendars define the working time for the entire project, for individual resources, and for tasks. Microsoft Project uses calendars, as well as task relationships and other information, to build a schedule for the project.

There are two types of calendars: **base calendars** and resource calendars. You use base calendars to:

- Serve as the calendar for the entire project. When used this way, it's called the **project calendar.** The project calendar defines working and nonworking time for tasks that do not have resources assigned and for fixed-duration tasks.

- Serve as the calendar for a specific task. When used this way, it's called a **task calendar.** A task calendar defines working and nonworking times for a specific task, regardless of the project calendar. You will create a task calendar in the next section.

- Supply the default working times for resources. In Lesson 7, you will update resource calendars.

The three base calendars included with Microsoft Project are:

- Standard: covers the traditional working day, Monday through Friday from 8:00 A.M. to 5:00 P.M., with an hour off for lunch.
- 24 Hours: has no nonworking time.
- Night Shift: covers a "graveyard" shift schedule of Monday night through Saturday morning, 11:00 P.M. to 8:00 A.M., with a one-hour break.

You specify which base calendar to use as a project calendar in the Project Information dialog box. (You open this dialog box by clicking the Project Information command on the Project menu.) By default, Microsoft Project uses the Standard base calendar as the project calendar.

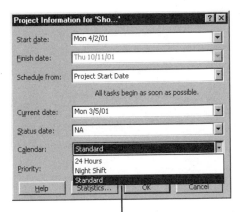

Microsoft Project includes three base calendars that cover most scheduling needs. You can also create your own custom calendar.

You can customize the working times of any base calendar in the Change Working Time dialog box. (You can open this dialog box by clicking the Change Working Time command from the Tools menu.) You can also create a new base calendar if none of the built-in base calendars fits your project's needs.

In this exercise, you change the working time for the project calendar and make some holidays nonworking times for the entire project.

1   On the Tools menu, click Change Working Time.

The Change Working Time dialog box appears. Except for special tasks that you will address in the next section, the normal daily working schedule for the film project will be 10:00 A.M. through 7:00 P.M. Monday through Friday, with a lunch break at 1:00 P.M.

To select these calendar column headings with your mouse, drag from the M column heading to the F column heading.

2   Make sure that Standard (Project Calendar) appears in the For box. In the calendar below the Select Date(s) label, select the Monday through Friday column headings.

3   In the From and To boxes, enter the time values shown in the illustration on the next page (note that the exact month you see might differ).

tip
Press the Tab key to easily move between the From and To boxes.

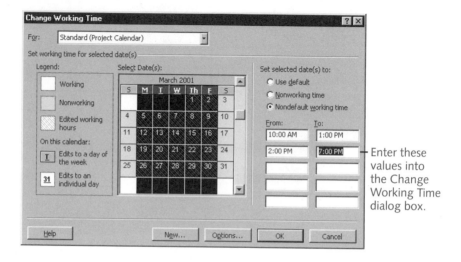

Enter these values into the Change Working Time dialog box.

Now the project calendar and all resource calendars will use these times as their default working day.

While you're in the Change Working Time dialog box, you'll mark some holidays as nonworking time for the project calendar.

4 In the calendar below the Select Date(s) label, scroll up or down to November 2001.

5 Select the dates November 22 and 23.

6 Under Set Selected Date(s) To, click Nonworking Time.

7 Scroll down to December 2001.

8 Select the dates December 24 and 25.

9 Under Set Selected Date(s) To, click Nonworking Time.

These holidays are now nonworking time for the entire project.

There is one other set of time-related settings to adjust: the default start and end times, which Microsoft Project will apply if you enter a task's start or end date but do not specify a time.

10 In the Change Working Time dialog box, click Options.

The Options dialog box appears, with only the Calendar tab active. This is the same dialog box you would see if you clicked the Options command on the Tools menu.

11 In the Default Start Time box, enter **10:00 AM**.

12 In the Default End Time box, enter **7:00 PM**.

tip

These default time settings have no effect on the working or nonworking times of calendars.

13   Click OK to close the Options dialog box, and then click OK again to close the Change Working Time dialog box.

Adjusting Working Time for Individual Tasks

**PROJ2000-1-7
AND
PROJ2000-1-12**

Sometimes you want specific tasks to occur at times that are outside of the project calendar's working time. To accomplish this, you apply a task calendar to these tasks. You specify which base calendar to use as a task calendar. You need a task calendar only when you want a task to have different working and nonworking times from the project calendar. Here are some examples of when you might need a task calendar:

■ You are using the Standard base calendar as your project calendar, and you have a task that must run overnight.

■ You have a task that must occur over the weekend.

Unlike with resources and resource calendars, Microsoft Project does not automatically create task calendars as you create tasks. When you need a custom task calendar, you assign one of the base calendars provided with Microsoft Project (or more likely a new base calendar you've created) to the task. You specify a task calendar on the Advanced tab in the Task Information dialog box. (You can open this dialog box by clicking the Task Information command on the Project menu.)

For example, if you assign the 24 Hours base calendar to a task, Microsoft Project will schedule that task according to a 24-hour workday rather than the working time specified in the project calendar.

tip

When you assign a base calendar to a task, you can choose to ignore resource calendars for all resources assigned to the task. Doing so causes Microsoft Project to schedule the resources to work on the task according to the task calendar and not their own resource calendars (for example, to work 24 hours per day). If this would result in resources working in what would otherwise be their nonworking time, you might want to first discuss this with the affected resources.

In the film project, a few of the scenes must be filmed at night. However, the project calendar does not include working time late enough to cover the filming of these scenes. Because these tasks are really exceptions to the project's normal working time, you don't want to change the project calendar. In this exercise, you create a new base calendar, and you apply it to the appropriate tasks.

1   On the Tools menu, click Change Working Time.

2   In the Change Working Time dialog box, click the New button.

      The Create New Base Calendar dialog box appears.

3   In the Name box, type **Evening Shoot**.

4   In the Make A Copy Of box, make sure Standard is selected, and then click OK.

5   In the calendar below the Select Date(s) label, select the column headings for Monday through Friday.

6   In the upper row of the From and To boxes, enter **7:00 PM** and **12:00 AM**, and then delete the values in the second row. Your Change Working Time dialog box should look like this:

This custom base calendar contains unique working
times not available in the built-in base calendars.

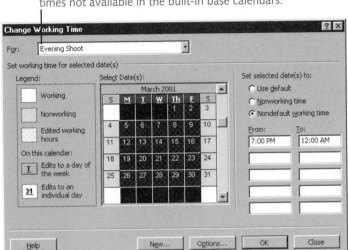

7   Click OK to close the dialog box.

Next you will apply the Evening Shoot calendar to two tasks.

8   Select the name of Task 22, "Scene 2 shoot." While holding down the Ctrl
key, select the name of Task 34, "Scene 4 shoot." Both scenes must be
filmed at night.

9   On the Standard toolbar, click the Task Information button.

The Task Information dialog box appears. The title of the dialog box reads
"Multiple Task Information," indicating that you have selected more than
one task and that the options you choose will apply to all selected tasks.

10   Click the Advanced tab.

11   In the Calendar box, select Evening Shoot from the list.

12   Click the Scheduling Ignores Resource Calendars box twice so that a check
mark appears in it. Then click OK to close the dialog box.

Microsoft Project applies the Evening Shoot calendar to Tasks 22 and 34. A
calendar icon appears in the Indicators column, reminding you that these
tasks have task calendars applied to them. Your screen should look similar to
the following illustration:

This icon tells you which tasks have task calendars applied to them. These tasks may be scheduled outside of the normal working time of the project calendar.

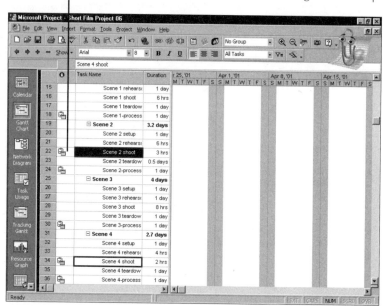

Because you chose to ignore resource calendars in the previous step, the resources assigned to these tasks will be scheduled at times that would otherwise be nonworking times for them.

You might notice that other tasks have calendars applied to them as well. Use task calendars whenever you want to allow exceptions to the project calendars' normal working time and you don't want to redefine working time for the entire project.

Adjusting Task Relationships

PROJ2000-2-11

You might recall from Lesson 3 that there are four types of task dependencies, or **relationships**:

- Finish-to-start (FS): The finish date of the **predecessor** task determines the start date of the **successor** task.

- Start-to-start (SS): The start date of the predecessor task determines the start date of the successor task.

- Finish-to-finish (FF): The finish date of the predecessor task determines the finish date of the successor task.

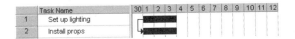

Start-to-finish (SF): The start date of the predecessor task determines the finish date of the successor task.

When you enter tasks in Microsoft Project and link them by clicking the Link Tasks button on the Standard toolbar, the tasks are given a finish-to-start (FS) relationship. This might be fine for most tasks, but you will probably want to change some task relationships. Here are some examples of tasks that require relationships other than finish-to-start:

You can start setting up the lighting for a film scene as soon as you start setting up the props (start-to-start relationship). This reduces the overall time required to complete the two tasks, as they are completed in parallel.

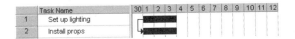

Planning the scene filming sequence can begin before the script is complete, but it can't finish until after the script is complete. You want the two tasks to finish at about the same time (finish-to-finish relationship).

Task relationships should reflect the sequence in which work should be done. Once you've established the correct task relationships, you can fine-tune your schedule by entering overlap (called **lead time**) or delay (called **lag time**) between the finish or start dates of predecessor and successor tasks.

Assuming two tasks have a finish-to-start relationship:

Lead time causes the successor task to begin before its predecessor task concludes.

Lag time causes the successor task to begin some time after its predecessor task concludes.

Here's an illustration of how lead and lag time affect task relationships. Let's say you initially planned the following three tasks using finish-to-start relationships:

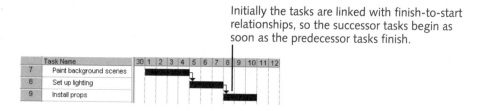

Initially the tasks are linked with finish-to-start relationships, so the successor tasks begin as soon as the predecessor tasks finish.

Before Task 8 can start, you need to allow an extra day for the paint applied in Task 7 to dry. You don't want to add a day to Task 7's duration, because no real work will occur on that day. Instead, you enter a one-day lag between Tasks 7 and 8:

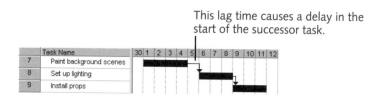

This lag time causes a delay in the start of the successor task.

However, Task 9 can start as soon as Task 8 is halfway completed; to make this happen, you enter a 50% lead time between Tasks 8 and 9:

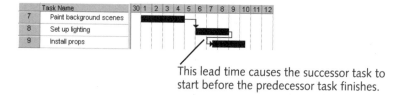

This lead time causes the successor task to start before the predecessor task finishes.

You can enter lead and lag time as units of time (for example, 2 days) or as a percentage of the duration of the predecessor task (for example, 50%). Lag time is entered in positive units, lead time in negative units (for example, –2 days or –50%). You can apply lead or lag time to any type of task relationship: finish-to-start, start-to-start, and so on. Some places you can enter lead or lag time are in the Task Information dialog box or in the Predecessors column in the Entry Table.

In this exercise, you change task relationships and enter lead and lag time between predecessor and successor tasks.

Double-click-
ing a task
name displays
the Task Infor-
mation dialog
box.

1 In the Entry table, double-click the name of Task 8, "Apply for filming permits."

The Task Information dialog box appears.

2 Click the Predecessors tab.

3 In the Lag field for predecessor Task 7, type **-50%**, and press Enter.

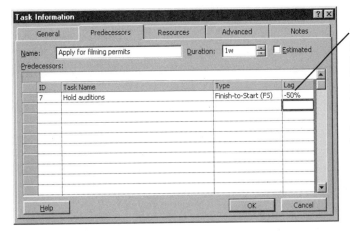

To enter lead
time against a
predecessor
task, enter it as
negative lag
time either in
units of time
such as days,
or as a per-
centage of the
duration of the
predecessor
task.

Entering lag time as a negative value produces lead time.

4 Click OK to close the Task Information dialog box.

5 To see how the lag time affects the scheduling of the successor task, on the
Standard toolbar, click the Go To Selected Task button.

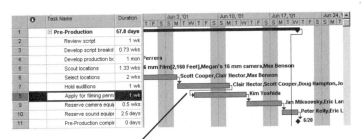

Lead time causes the successor task to start before
the predecessor task has finished, although the
two tasks still have a finish-to-start relationship.

Microsoft Project scrolls the Gantt Chart to display Task 8's Gantt bar. Task 8
is now scheduled to start when Task 7 is 50% complete. Should the duration
of Task 7 change, Microsoft Project will reschedule the start of Task 8.

Next you will change the task relationship between two tasks.

6   In the Entry table, double-click the name of Task 10, "Reserve sound equipment."

The Task Information dialog box appears.

7   Click in the Type field for predecessor Task 9. Select Start-to-Start (SS), and click OK.

Microsoft Project changes the task relationship between Tasks 9 and 10 to start-to-start.

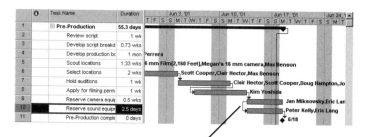

The start-to-start task relationship causes the two tasks to start at the same time. Should the start of the predecessor task change, the start of the successor task would change as well.

8   Using the Predecessors tab in the Task Information dialog box, change the following relationship details.

Task	Change
65, "Rough cut edit"	Enter a 5-day lead time against the predecessor Task 64. (Remember to enter lead time as a negative number: -5d.)
70, "Add final music"	Change the task relationship type with predecessor Task 69 to start-to-start.

9   On the Standard toolbar, click the Go To Selected Task button.

When you are done, your screen should look similar to the following illustration:

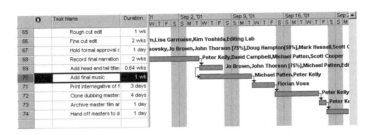

Assigning tasks start-to-start relationships or entering lead times where appropriate are both excellent techniques to shorten overall project duration. Microsoft Project cannot automatically make such schedule adjustments for you, however. As project manager, you must analyze your task's sequences and relationships and make those adjustments where appropriate.

Changing Task Types

PROJ2000-1-13

You might recall from Lesson 5 that Microsoft Project uses the following formula, called the **scheduling formula**, to calculate a task's work value:

$$\text{Work} = \text{Duration} \times \text{Units}$$

Each value in the scheduling formula corresponds to a **task type**. A task type determines which of the three scheduling formula values remains fixed if the other two values change.

The default task type is **fixed units**: when you change a task's duration, Microsoft Project recalculates work. Likewise, if you change a task's work, Microsoft Project recalculates the task's duration. In either case, the units value is unchanged. The two other task types are fixed duration and fixed work.

For a **fixed duration** task, you can change the task's units or work value, and Microsoft Project will recalculate the other value. For a **fixed work** task, you can change the task's units or duration value, and Microsoft Project will recalculate the other value. Note that you cannot turn off effort-driven scheduling for this task type.

Which is the right task type to apply to each of your tasks? It depends on how you want Microsoft Project to schedule that task. The following table summarizes the effects of changing any value for any task type. (You read it like a multiplication table.)

Fine-Tuning Task Details

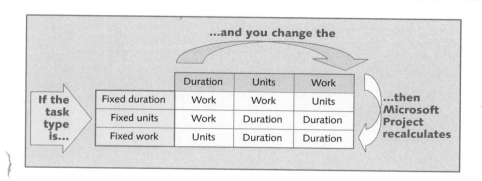

If the task type is...	...and you change the		
	Duration	Units	Work
Fixed duration	Work	Work	Units
Fixed units	Work	Duration	Duration
Fixed work	Units	Duration	Duration

...then Microsoft Project recalculates

To see the selected task's task type, on the Standard toolbar, click the Task Information button, and then click the Advanced tab. You can also see the task type in the Task Form. (When in the Gantt Chart view, you can display the Task Form by opening the Window menu and clicking the Split command.) You can change a task type at any time. Note that characterizing a task type as "fixed" doesn't mean that its duration, units, or work values are unchangeable. You can change any value for any task type.

In this exercise, you change the task types of two tasks.

1   In the Entry table, select the name of Task 2, "Review script."

2   On the Window menu, click Split.

The Task Form appears in the lower pane of the window. In it, you can see that Task 2 is a Fixed Units task with a total work value of 80 hours (that is, 40 hours each for two resources), resource units of 100% each, and a one-week duration. Next you will change the task's duration to see the effects on the other values.

3   In the Duration field in the Task Form, type or select **2w**, and then click OK in the upper-right corner of the Task Form.

As we'd expect, the units value remains fixed at 100% for each resource and the total work value increases to 160 hours (80 hours each).

Task types and effort-driven scheduling

A lot of people misunderstand task types and effort-driven scheduling and conclude that these two issues are more closely related than they really are. Both settings affect work, duration, and units values. However, effort-driven scheduling affects your schedule only when assigning or removing resources from tasks, while changing a task type affects only the resources currently assigned to the task. For more information about effort-driven scheduling, see "Assigning Multiple Resources to a Task" in Lesson 5.

4   On the Edit menu, click Undo Entry.

Microsoft Project resets Task 2's duration to 1 week.

After a discussion among all the resources who will review the script, all agree that the task's duration should double but the work required to complete the task should remain the same. Next you change the task's type from fixed units to fixed work, and you increase the task's duration.

5   In the Task Type box in the Task Form, select Fixed Work, and click OK.

Microsoft Project changes the task type of Task 2 to fixed work. Next you will change the task's duration to see the effects on the other values.

6   In the Duration field in the Task Form, type or select **2w**, and click OK.

Each resource's units value decreases to 50%, and the total work remains fixed at 80 hours (40 hours each).

Changing the duration of a fixed work task causes Microsoft Project to recalculate resource units.

Increasing the duration of a fixed work task decreases the level of effort (measured as units) that resources will apply to the task. Put another way, the resources will put in the same overall effort (measured as work) over a longer time period.

Next you change a task type using the Task Information dialog box.

7   In the Entry table in the top pane of the window, select the name of Task 67, "Hold formal approval showing."

tip
Rather than scrolling through the Entry Table, click anywhere in the Entry Table, press Ctrl+G (or click Go To on the Edit menu) to display the Go To dialog box, enter **67** in the ID box, and then click OK.

8   On the Standard toolbar, click the Task Information button.

The Task Information dialog box appears.

9   Click the Advanced tab.

The selected task describes the formal screening of the film for the financial backers of the project. The task is scheduled for a full day, although a few of the assigned resources will work for the equivalent of a half day. To reflect this (and properly manage resource costs for the task), you will make this a fixed duration task and adjust the work values for some of the assigned resources.

10 In the Task Type box, select Fixed Duration.

11 Click the Resources tab.

12 In the Units column, set the Units values for Jan Miksovsky and David Campbell to 50% each.

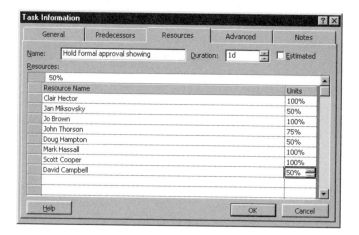

13 Click OK to close the Task Information dialog box.

You can see the two resources' updated work values in the Task Form in the lower pane.

The units values you entered for these resources in the Task
Information dialog box are reflected in the Task Form as well.

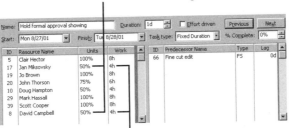

Since the task type is fixed duration and you changed
the units values, Microsoft Project recalculated these
work values.

In fact, you could have performed this entire exercise in either the Task Form
or the Task Information dialog box, depending on your preference.

14 On the Window menu, click Remove Split.

tip

A summary task always has a fixed-duration task type, and you can't change
it. Because a summary task is based on the earliest start date and the latest finish date of its subtasks, its duration is calculated based on its subtasks and is not
directly editable. If you wish to confirm this, double-click Summary Task 61, "Post-
Production," and view the Advanced tab in the Task Information dialog box.

PROJ2000-1-4

*For a demonstra-
tion of how to
split tasks, in the
Multimedia
folder on the MS
Project 2000 SBS
CD-Rom,
double-click
SplitTasks.avi.*

Interrupting Work on a Task

When initially planning project tasks, you might know that work on a certain
task will be interrupted. You can **split** the task to indicate times when the work
will be interrupted and when it can resume. Here are some reasons why you
might want to split a task:

▪ There is an *anticipated* interruption in a task. For example, a
   resource might be assigned to a week-long task but need to attend
   an event on Wednesday that is unrelated to the task.

▪ There is an *unanticipated* interruption in a task. Once a task is
   underway, a resource might have to stop work on the task because
   another task has taken priority. Once the second task is completed,
   the resource can resume work on the first task.

Fine-Tuning Task Details

6

> **tip**
>
> In either case, it's a good idea to document in a task note why a task was split. This helps if you —or anyone else—later refers back to the task. For more information about task notes, see "Documenting Task Details with Notes and Hyperlinks" later in this lesson.

In this exercise, you split a task.

1   In the Entry table, select the name of Task 4, "Develop production boards."

You know that work on this task will be interrupted for three days starting May 1.

> **tip**
>
> The **timescale** is divided into a **major** and a **minor** scale. Adjusting the minor scale is important for splitting tasks: the precision of the minor scale determines the smallest time increment into which you can split a task. With the timescale set at the Days level, you must split a task by at least a day. If you wanted to split a task at the hourly level, you'd have to adjust the minor timescale further (via the Timescale command on the Format menu).

2   To see Task 4's Gantt bar, on the Standard toolbar, click the Go To Selected Task button.

The timescale is divided into major units (on top) and minor units (below). The fineness of the minor scale determines how you can split tasks. In this example, you can split tasks into one-day increments.

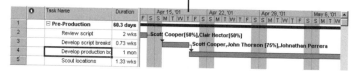

3   On the Standard toolbar, click the Split Task button.

A ToolTip appears, and the mouse pointer changes.

4   Move the mouse pointer over the Gantt bar of Task 4.

Use this ToolTip to help you accurately split tasks.

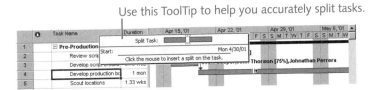

This ToolTip is essential for accurately splitting a task; it contains the date at which you'd start the second segment of the task if you dragged the mouse pointer from its current location on the Gantt bar. As you move the mouse pointer along the Gantt bar, you see the start date in the ToolTip change.

5 Move the mouse pointer until the start date of Tue 5/1/01 appears in the ToolTip.

6 Drag to the right until the start date of Fri 5/4/01 appears in the ToolTip, and then release the mouse button.

Microsoft Project inserts a task split, represented in the Gantt Chart as a dotted line, between the two segments of the task.

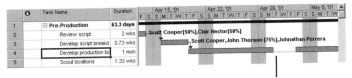

The split appears as a dotted line connecting the segments of the task.

Here are a few more things to keep in mind when splitting tasks:

- You can split a task into as many segments as you wish.
- You can drag a segment of a split task left or right to change the duration of the split.
- The time of the task split itself (represented by the dotted line) is not counted in the duration of the task (unless the task is fixed duration), because no work occurs during the split.
- If the duration of a split task changes, the last segment of the task is increased or decreased.
- If a split task is rescheduled (for example, if its start date changes), the entire task, splits and all, is rescheduled. The task keeps the same pattern of segments and splits.

6

Fine-Tuning Task Details

- To rejoin two segments of a split task, drag one segment of the task until it touches another segment.

- If you do not want to display splits as a dotted line, on the Format menu, click Layout, and then clear the Show Bar Splits check box.

Other activities might introduce task splits, including adjusting resource assignments and resource leveling. For more information about adjusting resource assignments, see Lesson 8. For more information about resource leveling, see Lesson 7.

Entering Fixed Costs

For most projects, most financial costs are derived from work or material resource costs. In Lesson 4, you entered hourly and weekly cost rates for resources. However, in addition to (or sometimes instead of) the resource costs associated with a task, a task might have a **fixed cost**. A fixed cost is a specific monetary amount budgeted for a task. These costs remain the same regardless of how much time or effort resources expend to complete the task. Here are some common examples of fixed costs in projects:

- Travel expenses for a consultant, paid in addition to an hourly or a daily fee.

- A setup fee, charged in addition to a per-day rental fee, for a piece of equipment.

- A permit to film in a public location.

If you enter both resource costs and fixed costs for a task, Microsoft Project adds the two to determine the task's total cost. If you do not enter resource cost information into a project plan (perhaps because you do not know how much your resources will be paid), you can still gain some control over the project's total cost by entering fixed costs per task.

You can specify when fixed costs should **accrue**:

- Start. The entire fixed cost is scheduled for the start of the task. When tracking progress, the entire fixed cost of the task is incurred as soon as the task starts.

- End. The entire fixed cost is scheduled for the end of the task. When tracking progress, the entire fixed cost of the task is incurred only after the task is completed.

■ Prorated. The fixed cost is distributed evenly over the duration of the task. When tracking progress, the project incurs the cost of the task at the rate at which the task is completed. For example, if a task has a $100 fixed cost and is 75% complete, the project has incurred $75 against that task.

When planning a project, the accrual method you choose for fixed costs determines how these costs are scheduled over time. This can be important in anticipating budget and cash-flow needs. By default, Microsoft Project assigns the prorated accrual method for fixed costs, but you can change that in order, for example, to match your organization's cost accounting practices.

For the film project, you know from experience that the filming permits will cost $500, payable when you apply for the permits. In this exercise, you assign a fixed cost to a task and specify its accrual time.

1   On the View menu, point to Table: Entry, and click Cost.

The Cost table appears, replacing the Entry table.

2   In the Fixed Cost field for Task 8, "Apply for filming permits," type or select **500**, and press Tab.

3   In the Fixed Cost Accrual field, select **Start**, and press Enter.

A fixed cost value is accrued at the start or finish of a task, or prorated over the duration of the task, depending on the option you choose.

	Task Name	Fixed Cost	Fixed Cost Accrual	Total Cost
1	⊟ Pre-Production	$0.00	Prorated	$26,683.80
2	Review script	$0.00	Prorated	$1,575.00
3	Develop script breakd	$0.00	Prorated	$1,541.80
4	Develop production bc	$0.00	Prorated	$9,984.00
5	Scout locations	$0.00	Prorated	$3,712.00
6	Select locations	$0.00	Prorated	$5,070.00
7	Hold auditions	$0.00	Prorated	$2,595.00
8	Apply for filming perm	$500.00	Start	$876.00
9	Reserve camera equi	$0.00	Prorated ▼	$685.00
10	Reserve sound equipr	$0.00	Prorated	$645.00

4   On the View menu, point to Table: Cost, and click Entry.

Microsoft Project returns to the Entry table.

Now, Microsoft Project will schedule a $500 cost against the task "Apply for film permits" at the task's start date, and the project will incur this cost when the task starts. This cost is independent of the task's duration or of the costs of resources assigned to it.

Fine-Tuning Task Details

6

PROJ2000-1-3

Setting up a Recurring Task

Most projects require repetitive tasks, such as staff meetings, creating and publishing status reports, or quality inspections. Although it's easy to overlook the scheduling of such events, you should account for them in your project plan. After all, staff meetings and similar events that indirectly support the project require time from resources, and that's time diverted from their other assignments.

To help account for such events in your project plan, create a **recurring task**. As the name suggests, a recurring task repeats at a specified frequency, such as daily, weekly, monthly, or yearly. When you create a recurring task, Microsoft Project creates a series of tasks with "start no earlier than" **constraints**, no task relationships, and effort-driven scheduling turned off.

In this exercise, you create a recurring task.

1   In the Entry table, select the name of Task 12, "Production."

You want the recurring tasks to be inserted into the project as the last items in the Pre-Production phase, directly above Task 12.

2   On the Insert menu, click Recurring Task.

The Recurring Task Information dialog box appears.

3   In the Task Name box, type **Staff planning meeting**.

4   In the Duration box, type **2h**.

5   Under Recurrence Pattern, make sure Weekly is selected, and then select the Friday check box.

Next you specify the date of its first occurrence; by default, it's the project start date.

6   In the Start box, type **4/6/01 5:00 PM**.

Next you specify the number of recurrences. You do this by entering either an exact number of recurrences or a date by which the task should end.

7   Select End After, and then type or select **10** occurrences.

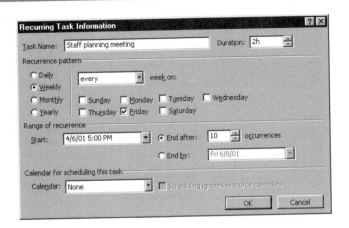

8   Click OK to create the recurring task.

Microsoft Project inserts the recurring tasks, nested within the Pre-Production phase. Initially the summary task is collapsed. A recurring task icon appears in the Indicators column.

Unlike other summary tasks, the summary recurring task shows only the individual recurrences of the task.

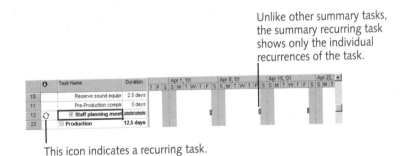

This icon indicates a recurring task.

Note that the summary Gantt bar for the recurring task does not look like the other summary Gantt bars in the Gantt Chart. A summary recurring task's Gantt bar shows only the occurrences or "roll-ups" of the individual occurrences of the task.

Next you assign resources to the recurring task.

9   On the Standard toolbar, click Assign Resources.

10   In the Assign Resources dialog box, select Clair Hector. Then hold down the Ctrl key while selecting Jo Brown, Johnathan Perrera, Kim Yoshida, and Scott Cooper.

11   Click Assign, and then click Close.

The Assign Resources dialog box closes, and Microsoft Project assigns the selected resources to the recurring task. Next you will view the individual occurrences of the recurring task.

12 Click the plus sign next to the summary recurring task's title "Staff planning meeting." Your screen should look similar to the following illustration:

Recurring tasks are automatically numbered sequentially. You can also see resource assignments for the individual tasks.

As you can see, each occurrence of the summary task is sequentially numbered, and the resource assignments appear for the subtasks.

13 Click the minus sign next to the summary recurring task's title, "Staff planning meeting," to hide the subtasks.

Here are a few more things to keep in mind when creating recurring tasks:

■ When you schedule a recurring task to end on a specific date, Microsoft Project suggests the current project end date. If you use this date and the project end date later changes, however, you must manually change the date at which the recurring task should end.

■ Microsoft Project alerts you if you create a recurring task that would occur during nonworking time (a holiday, for example). You then have the options of not creating that occurrence or scheduling it for the next working day.

■ You should always assign resources to recurring tasks with the Assign Resources dialog box. Entering resource names in the Resource Name field of the summary recurring task assigns the resources only to the summary task, not to the individual occurrences.

Setting Task Constraints

PROJ2000-1-15
AND
PROJ2000E-2-7

Every task you enter into Microsoft Project has some type of **constraint** applied to it. A constraint controls the start or finish date of a task and the degree to which that task can be rescheduled. There are three categories of constraints:

- **Flexible constraints.** Microsoft Project can change the start and finish dates of a task, but it cannot change its duration. For example, the task "Selecting locations to film" can start as soon as possible. There is no constraint date associated with flexible constraints.

- **Semi-flexible constraints.** A task has a start or finish date boundary. However, within that boundary, Microsoft Project has the scheduling flexibility to change start and finish dates (but not the duration) of a task. For example, the task "Install props" must finish no later than 3/26/01. However, it could finish before this date. Semi-flexible constraints are sometimes called soft constraints.

- **Inflexible constraints.** A task must begin or end on a certain date. For example, the task "Set up lighting" must end on 4/10/01. Inflexible constraints are sometimes called hard constraints.

In all, there are eight types of task constraints.

This constraint type	Means
As Soon As Possible (ASAP)	Microsoft Project will schedule a task to occur as soon as it can occur. This is the default constraint type applied to all new tasks when scheduling from the project start date. This is a flexible constraint.
As Late As Possible (ALAP)	Microsoft Project will schedule a task to occur as late as it can occur without delaying successor tasks or changing the project finish date. This is the default constraint type applied to all new tasks when scheduling from the project finish date. This is a flexible constraint.
Start No Earlier Than (SNET)	Microsoft Project will schedule a task to start on or after the constraint date you specify. Use this constraint type to ensure that a task will not start before a specific date. This is a semi-flexible constraint.

6

Fine-Tuning Task Details

This constraint type	Means
Start No Later Than (SNLT)	Microsoft Project will schedule a task to start on or before the constraint date you specify. Use this constraint type to ensure that a task will not start after a specific date. This is a semi-flexible constraint.
Finish No Earlier Than (FNET)	Microsoft Project will schedule a task to finish on or after the constraint date you specify. Use this constraint type to ensure that a task will not finish before a specific date. This is a semi-flexible constraint.
Finish No Later Than (FNLT)	Microsoft Project will schedule a task to finish on or before the constraint date you specify. Use this constraint type to ensure that a task will not finish after a specific date. This is a semi-flexible constraint.
Must Start On (MSO)	Microsoft Project will schedule a task to start on the constraint date you specify. Use this constraint type to ensure that a task will start on an exact date. This is an inflexible constraint.
Must Finish On (MFO)	Microsoft Project will schedule a task to finish on the constraint date you specify. Use this constraint type to ensure that a task will finish on an exact date. This is an inflexible constraint.

These eight types of constraints have very different effects on the scheduling of tasks:

- Flexible constraints, such as As Soon As Possible, allow tasks to be scheduled without any limitations other than their predecessor and successor relationships. There are no fixed start or end dates imposed by these constraint types. Use these constraint types whenever possible.

■ Semi-flexible constraints, such as Start No Earlier Than or Start No Later Than, limit the rescheduling of a task within the date boundary you specify.

Constraint date

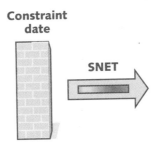

■ Inflexible constraints, such as Must Start On, completely prevent the rescheduling of a task. Use these constraint types only when absolutely necessary.

The type of constraint you apply to the tasks in your projects depends on what you need from Microsoft Project. You should use inflexible constraints only if the start or finish date of a task is fixed by factors beyond the control of the project team. Examples of such tasks include handoffs to clients and the end of a funding period. For tasks without such limitations, you should use flexible constraints. Flexible constraints give you the most discretion in adjusting start and finish dates, and they allow Microsoft Project to adjust dates automatically if your project plan changes. For example, if you've used ASAP constraints and the duration of a predecessor task changes from 4 days to 2 days, Microsoft Project adjusts or "pulls in" the start and finish dates of all successor tasks. However, if a successor task had an inflexible constraint applied, Microsoft Project could not adjust its start or finish dates.

In this exercise, you apply a Start No Earlier Than constraint to a task.

1 In the Entry table, select the name of Task 37, "Scene 3 setup."

This scene must be shot at a location that is not available to the film crew until July 5, 2001.

2 Drag the vertical divider bar to the right to show the Start column.

tip

If the Start column displays only pound signs (####), the column is too narrow to display its contents. To widen the column, move the mouse pointer to the divider between the Start and Finish columns.

When the mouse pointer changes to a two-headed arrow, double-click the divider. Microsoft Project widens the column to fit the content.

3 Select the Start field for Task 37, and then click the down arrow button to display the calendar box.

4 Click the right arrow button to display July 2001 in the calendar box, and then click July 5.

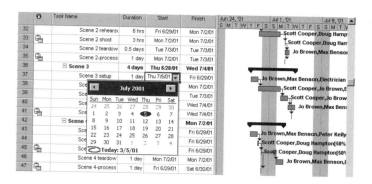

Microsoft Project applies a Start No Earlier Than constraint to the task, and a constraint icon appears in the Indicators column. You can point to the icon to see the constraint details in a ToolTip.

Point your mouse at a constraint indicator (or any icon in the Indicators column) to see more details.

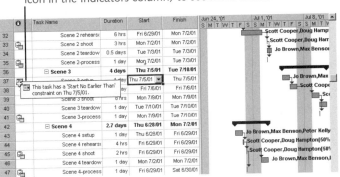

5   Drag the vertical divider bar back to the right edge of the Duration column.

All tasks that depend on Task 37 are also rescheduled. In a later section, you will document this constraint so that you have a good history of why you applied it.

Here are a few more things to keep in mind when applying constraints to tasks:

■   Selecting a date in the Finish column applies a Finish No Earlier Than (FNET) constraint.

■   You can create a Start No Earlier Than (SNET) constraint by dragging a Gantt bar directly on the Gantt Chart.

■   To remove a constraint, open the Project menu, click Task Information, and then click the Advanced tab. In the Constraint Type box, select As Soon As Possible or (if scheduling from the project finish date) As Late As Possible.

■   If you need to apply semi-flexible or inflexible constraints to tasks in addition to task relationships, you might create what's called negative slack. For example, you can create a finish-to-start relationship before applying a Must Start On constraint that forces the successor task to start before the predecessor task has finished. This would result in negative slack and a scheduling conflict. By default, the constraint date applied to the successor task will override the relationship. However, if you prefer, you can set Microsoft Project to honor relationships over constraints. On the Tools menu, click Option, and then click the Schedule tab. Clear the Tasks Will Always Honor Their Constraint Dates check box. This setting applies only to the current project file.

■   If you must schedule a project from a finish date rather than a start date, some constraint behaviors change. For example, the ALAP (rather than the ASAP) constraint type becomes the default for new tasks. You should pay close attention to constraints when scheduling from a finish date to make sure they have the effects you intend.

Reorganizing Phases and Tasks

*For a demonstra-
tion of how to
move and reor-
ganize tasks, in
the Multimedia
folder on the MS
Project 2000 SBS
CD-ROM,
double-click
MoveTasks.avi*

*You can also
open the Go
To dialog box
by pressing
the shortcut
key Ctrl+G.*

You might recall from Lesson 3 that summary tasks are useful for organizing tasks into phases and that they result in an **outline**. Outlines help you see the structure of your project at a higher level than the level of individual tasks. You work with phases in Microsoft Project by using the Show Subtasks, Hide Subtasks, and other buttons on the Formatting toolbar. You can also reorganize phases by cutting and pasting or dragging and dropping in a table.

In this exercise, you reorder the scene summary tasks to reflect the filming sequence, and then you link the scenes with finish-to-start relationships.

1 On the Edit menu, select Go To.

2 In the ID box, type **23**, and click OK.

Microsoft Project scrolls to Task 23, the Production summary task.

3 On the Formatting toolbar, click the Show button, and then click Outline Level 2. Microsoft Project collapses the Scene 1 through Scene 8 summary tasks.

	❶	Task Name	Duration	Jun 24, '01	Jul 1, '01	Jul 8, '01	Jul 15, '01
23		⊟ Production	12.5 days				
24		⊞ Scene 1	5.75 days				
30		⊞ Scene 2	3.2 days				
36		⊞ Scene 3	4 days				
42		⊞ Scene 4	2.7 days				
48		⊞ Scene 5	5.5 days				
54		⊞ Scene 6	12.5 days				
60		⊞ Scene 7	3.75 days				
66		⊞ Scene 8	6.5 days				

At this point, there are no links between the scene summary tasks, and Scene 3 starts later than the other tasks because of its Start No Earlier Than constraint.

It rarely happens in the making of any film that the scenes are shot in the order in which they appear in the film. The first scene is almost never shot first, nor the last scene last. Now you will reorder the scenes to reflect the order in which they are to be shot.

4 Click the task ID number for Task 60, "Scene 7."

Microsoft Project selects the entire row for Task 60. With the row selected, you can drag the summary task where you want it.

As you drag the selected task, an insertion bar appears on the Entry Table, indicating where you can drop the selected task.

5 Drag the task ID for Scene 7 up until it appears above Scene 1.

Microsoft Project inserts the Scene 7 summary task above Scene 1, and all subsequent task Ids are renumbered.

6 Click the task ID number for Scene 3, and drag the task until it appears above Scene 1.

7 Click the task ID number for Scene 5, and drag the task until it appears above Scene 4.

8 Click the task ID number for Scene 6, and drag the task until it appears above Scene 4.

9 Click the task ID number for Scene 8, and drag the task until it appears it above Scene 4.

Now the scenes appear in the order in which they will be shot.

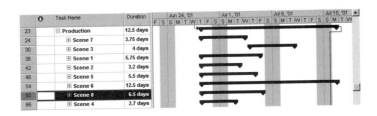

Next you will link the scenes.

10 Select the summary task names of Scene 7 through Scene 4.

11 On the Standard toolbar, click the Link Tasks button.

Microsoft Project links the Scene summary tasks with finish-to-start relationships.

12 On the Formatting toolbar, click Show Subtasks.

13 Scroll the Gantt Chart to the right to see the full sequence of the Production tasks.

Fine-Tuning Task Details

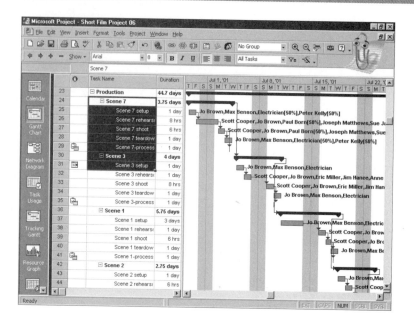

Now the Gantt Chart looks like the traditional "stair step" sequence of linked tasks. Note that Microsoft Project does not require that the order in which tasks are listed in the Entry table match the order of their start dates. If you wish, the first task of the project could appear in the last row of the Entry table. By tradition, however, Gantt Charts are usually organized in this top-to-bottom, first-to-last order.

Entering Deadline Dates

PROJ2000E-3-6

One common mistake new Microsoft Project users make is to place semi-flexible or inflexible constraints on too many tasks in their projects. As we noted above, such constraints severely limit your scheduling flexibility.

Yet if you know that a specific task must be completed by a certain date, why not enter a Must Finish On constraint? Here's why: let's say you have a five-day task that you want to see completed by Oct. 12, 2001, and today is Oct. 1 of that year. If you enter the Must Finish On October 12 constraint on the task, Microsoft Project will move it out so it will, indeed, end on October 12.

This task has a "must finish on" constraint applied, so Microsoft Project schedules it to finish on the specified date, but no earlier.

Now, even if the task could be completed earlier, Microsoft Project will not re-schedule it to start earlier. In fact, by applying that constraint, you've increased the **risk** for this task. If the task is delayed for even one day for any reason (a required resource is out sick, for example), the task will miss its planned finish date.

A better approach to scheduling this task is to assign it an As Soon As Possible (ASAP) constraint and enter a **deadline** of October 12. A deadline is a date value you enter for a task that indicates the latest date by which you want the task to be completed, but the deadline date itself does not constrain the task. Entering a deadline date causes Microsoft Project to display a deadline marker on the Gantt Chart, and you will be alerted if the task's finish date moves past its deadline.

With an ASAP constraint applied, the task starts earlier and leaves slack between the finish date and the deadline.

The deadline marker appears in the Gantt Chart. Should the scheduled finish date extend beyond the deadline date, Microsoft Project will alert you with an indicator in the Indicators column.

Now the task has the greatest scheduling flexibility. It might be completed well before its deadline, depending on resource availability, predecessor tasks, or whatever other scheduling issues apply.

In this exercise, you enter deadline dates for some tasks.

1   On the Edit menu, select Go To.

2   In the ID box, type **11** and click OK.

3   In the Entry table, double-click the name of Task 11, "Pre-Production Complete!"

Fine-Tuning Task Details

This task is a milestone marking the scheduled finish date of the pre-production phase of the project. As you want to make sure the pre-production tasks conclude by 7/13/01, you'll enter a deadline date for this milestone.

4 Click the Advanced tab.

5 In the Deadline box, type or select 7/13/01, and then click OK.

The Task Information dialog box closes, and Microsoft Project inserts a deadline date marker on the Gantt Chart.

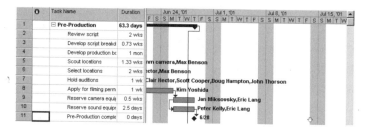

Now you can see at a glance how close the pre-production phase is to meeting or missing its deadline. Should the scheduled completion of the pre-production phase move past 7/13/01, Microsoft Project would display an alert indicator in the Indicators column.

Next you enter deadline dates for a summary task.

6 In the Entry table, double-click the name of Task 23, "Production."

This task is the Production Summary task. You want to conclude filming by the end of September.

7 In the Deadline box, type or select 9/28/01, and then click OK.

Except for one situation, entering a deadline date has no effect on the scheduling of a summary or subtask. However, a deadline date will cause Microsoft Project to alert you if the scheduled completion of a task exceeds its deadline date.

The one situation where the deadline date can affect the scheduling of a summary task (or any task) involves slack. When a task is given a deadline date, its slack does not extend beyond the deadline date.

Viewing the Project's Critical Path

A **critical path** is the series of tasks that will push out the project's end date if they are delayed. The word "critical" has nothing to do with how important these tasks are to the overall project. The word refers only to how their scheduling will affect the project's finish date. However, the project finish date is of great importance in most projects. If you want to shorten the duration of a project to bring in the finish date, you must begin by shortening the critical path.

*For a demon-
stration of
how to view
the critical
path, in the
Multimedia
folder on the
Microsoft
Project 2000
Step by Step
CD-ROM,
double-click
View Critical
Path.avi.*

Over the life of a project, the project's critical path is likely to change from time to time as tasks are completed ahead of or behind schedule. Schedule changes, such as assigning resources to tasks, can also change the critical path. After a task on the critical path is completed, it is no longer critical, because it cannot affect the project finish date. Microsoft Project constantly recalculates the critical path, even if you never see it.

A key to understanding the critical path is to understand **slack,** also known as float. There are two types of slack: free and total. **Free slack** is the amount of time a task can be delayed before it delays another task. **Total slack** is the amount of time a task can be delayed before it delays the finish of the project. A task is on the critical path if its total slack is less than a certain amount—normally, if it's zero.

In contrast, **noncritical tasks** have slack, meaning they can start or finish earlier or later within their slack time without affecting the project's completion date.

In this exercise, you view the project's critical path.

1   On the View menu, select More Views.

2   In the More Views dialog box, select Detail Gantt, and then click Apply.

     The project appears in the Detail Gantt view.

3   On the Edit menu, select Go to.

4   In the ID box, type **66**, and then click OK.

     Microsoft Project displays Task 66, the "Scene 4" summary task.

Noncritical tasks have free slack, displayed here.

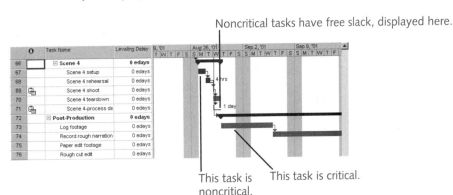

This task is   This task is critical.
noncritical.

Fine-Tuning Task Details

The Post-Production phase of the project contains most of the project's critical tasks. In the Detail Gantt view, Microsoft Project distinguishes between critical and noncritical tasks. Critical task bars are red, but noncritical task bars are blue. In this view, you can also see tasks with free slack.

You can also open the Go To dialog box by pressing the keyboard shortcut Ctrl+G.

5 On the Edit menu, select Go To.

6 In the ID box, type **59**, and then click OK.

Task 59, "Scene 6—process dailies," appears.

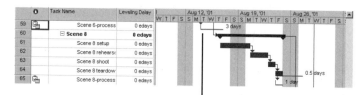

Slack is represented in the Gantt Chart as a thin teal-colored line following the Gantt bar. The numeric value of the task's free slack appears on the Gantt Chart as well—in this case, 3 days.

The blue bar represents the duration of the task. The thin teal line and the number next to it represent free slack for this task. As you can see, this particular task has quite a bit of free slack and is, therefore, a noncritical task. (Remember that the term "critical" in this sense has nothing to do with how important the task is compared to other tasks, only with how much or little total slack the task has.)

7 On the View menu, select Gantt Chart.

To conclude this exercise, you will view critical tasks in another way.

8 On the Project menu, point to Filtered For: All Tasks, and then click Critical.

Only the critical tasks appear in the Gantt Chart view.

9 On the View menu, click Zoom.

10 In the Zoom dialog box, click Entire Project, and then click OK.

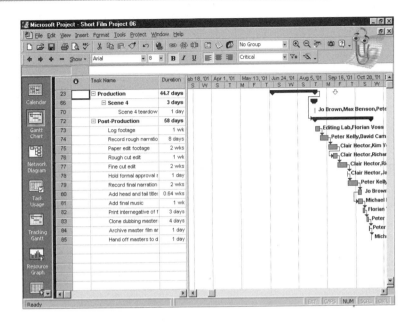

Microsoft Project changes the timescale in the Gantt Chart to display the full duration of all critical tasks in the project.

11   On the Project menu, point to Filtered for: Critical, and then click All Tasks.

Working with the critical path is the most important way to manage a project's overall duration. In later lessons, you will level resources and make other adjustments that might extend the project's duration. Checking the project's critical path and, when necessary, shortening the overall project duration is an important project management skill.

tip

In projects with more than one network or chain of linked tasks, each chain has its own critical path. However, by default, Microsoft Project displays only the critical path that determines the project finish date. To see all critical paths in a project, on the Tools menu, click Options, and then click the Calculation tab. Click the Calculate Multiple Critical Paths box, and then click OK.

Fine-Tuning Task Details

Documenting Task Details with Notes and Hyperlinks

You can record any additional information about a task that you want in a **note**. For example, if a task was delayed or split, it's a good idea to record the reason in a note. That way, the information resides in the Microsoft Project file and can be easily viewed or printed.

PROJ2000-3-2
PROJ2000-1-20

There are three types of notes: task notes, resource notes, and assignment notes. Task notes appear on the Notes tab in the Task Information dialog box. (You can open the Task Information dialog box by selecting the Task Information command from the Project menu.) Notes in Microsoft Project support a wide range of text formatting options; you can even link to or store graphic images and other types of files in Microsoft Project notes.

Hyperlinks allow you to connect a specific task to another file, a specific location in a file, a page on the World Wide Web, or a page on an intranet.

In this exercise, you enter task notes and hyperlinks to document important information about some tasks. You will work with resource notes in Lesson 7 and with assignment notes in Lesson 8.

1   Select the name of Task 31, "Scene 3 setup."

Earlier in this lesson, you applied a Start No Earlier Than constraint to this task.

2   On the Standard toolbar, click the Task Notes button.

Microsoft Project displays the Task Information dialog box with the Notes tab visible.

3   In the Notes box, type **This scene must be shot no earlier than July 5 due to limited access to site**, and click OK.

A note icon appears in the Indicators column.

4   Point to the note icon.

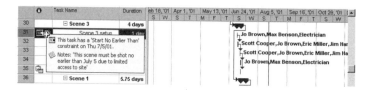

The note appears in a ToolTip. For notes that are too long to appear in a ToolTip, you can click the note icon to display the full text of the note.

To conclude this exercise, you create a hyperlink.

5   Select the name of Task 9, "Reserve camera equipment."

6   On the Standard toolbar, click the Insert Hyperlink button.

The Insert Hyperlink dialog box appears.

7   In the Text To Display box, type **Website of good camera rental company**.

8   In the Type The File Or Web Page Name box, type **http://www.rental101-inc.com**, and click OK.

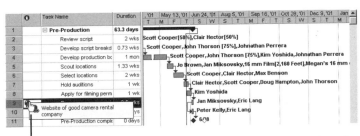

Point to a hyperlink indicator, and Microsoft Project displays the text you entered when you created the hyperlink.

A hyperlink icon appears in the Indicators column. Pointing to the icon displays the descriptive text you typed above. Clicking the icon opens the Web page in your browser.

Lesson Wrap-Up

This lesson covered how to apply a variety of important task-related tools after creating your project plan but before tracking actual work.

If you are going on to other lessons:

1   On the Standard toolbar, click Save to save changes made to Short Film Project 06. Save the file without a baseline.

2   On the File menu, click Close to close the file.

If you are not continuing to other lessons:

●   On the File menu, click Exit.

Glossary

Accrual The method by which the project incurs the cost of a task or a resource. The three types of accrual are start, prorated, and end.

Base calendar A calendar that can serve as the project calendar or a task calendar. Microsoft Project includes three base calendars, named Standard, 24 Hours, and Night Shift. You can customize these, or you can use them as a basis for your own base calendar.

Calendar Settings that define the working time for a project, resources, and tasks.

Constraint A restriction, such as Must Start On or Finish No Later Than, that you can place upon a task's start or finish date.

Critical path A series of tasks that will push out the project's end date if they are delayed.

Deadline A date value you can enter for a task that indicates the latest date by which you want the task to be completed. The benefit of entering deadline dates is that they do not constrain tasks.

Fixed cost A set amount of money budgeted for a task. This amount is independent of resource costs and the task's duration.

Fixed duration A task type in which the duration value is fixed. If you change the amount of work you expect a task to require, Microsoft Project recalculates units for each resource. If you change duration or units, Microsoft Project recalculates work.

Fixed units A task type in which the units value is fixed. If you change the task's duration, Microsoft Project recalculates the amount of work scheduled for the task. If you change units or work, Microsoft Project recalculates duration.

Fixed work A task type in which the work value is fixed. If you change the task's duration, Microsoft Project recalculates units for each resource. If you change units or work, Microsoft Project recalculates duration.

Flexible constraint A constraint type that gives Microsoft Project the flexibility to change the start and finish dates (but not the duration) of a task. ASAP and ALAP are both flexible constraints.

Free slack The amount of time that a task can be delayed without delaying the start date of a successor task.

Hyperlink A link to another file, a specific location in a file, a page on the World Wide Web, or a page on an intranet.

Inflexible constraint A constraint type that forces a task to begin or end on a certain date. Must Start On and Must Finish On are both inflexible constraints.

Lag time A delay between tasks that have a task relationship. For example, lag time causes the successor task in a finish-to-start relationship to begin some time after its predecessor task concludes.

Lead time An overlap between tasks that have a task relationship. For example, lead time causes the successor task in a finish-to-start relationship to begin before its predecessor task concludes. In the Microsoft Project interface, you enter lead time as negative lag time.

Major scale In the timescale, the major scale appears above the minor scale and contains larger units of time, such as months or weeks.

Minor scale In the timescale, the minor scale appears below the major scale and contains smaller units of time, such as weeks or days.

Noncritical tasks Tasks that have slack. Noncritical tasks can finish later within the slack time without affecting the project completion date.

Note Any information (including linked or embedded files) that you wish to associate with a task, a resource, or an assignment.

Outline A hierarchy of summary tasks and subtasks within Microsoft Project, usually corresponding to major phases of work.

Predecessor A task that drives the start or finish of another task or tasks, called successor tasks.

Project calendar The base calendar that is used by the entire project. The project calendar defines normal working and nonworking time.

Recurring task A task that repeats at established intervals. You can create a recurring task that repeats for a fixed number of times, or ends by a specific date.

Relationship The type of dependency between two tasks, visually indicated by a link line. The types of relationships include finish-to-start, start-to-start, finish-to-finish, and start-to-finish. Also known as a link, a logical relationship, a task dependency, or a precedence relationship.

Risk Any event that decreases the likelihood of completing a task or a project on time, within budget, and to specification.

Fine-Tuning Task Details

142 Microsoft Project 2000 Step by Step

Scheduling formula A representation of how Microsoft Project calculates work, based on a task's duration and resource units. The scheduling formula is Duration × Units = Work.

Semi-flexible constraint A constraint type that gives Microsoft Project the flexibility to change the start and finish dates (but not the duration) of a task within one date boundary. Start No Earlier Than, Start No Later Than, Finish No Earlier Than, and Finish No Later Than are all semi-flexible constraints.

Slack The amount of time that a task can be delayed without delaying the start date of a successor task (free slack) or the project end date (total slack).

Split An interruption in a task, represented in the Gantt bar as a dotted line between two segments of a task. You can split a task multiple times.

Successor A task whose start or finish is driven by another task or tasks, called predecessor tasks.

Task calendar The base calendar that is used by a single task. A task calendar defines working and nonworking times for a task, regardless of settings in the project calendar.

Task type A setting applied to a task that determines how Microsoft Project schedules the task, based on which of the three scheduling formula values is fixed. The three task types are fixed units, fixed duration, and fixed work.

Timescale In the Gantt Chart and other views, the timescale appears in the upper portion of the view and contains major and minor time indicators, such as weeks and days.

Total slack The amount of time that a task can be delayed without delaying the project end date.

Quick Reference

To update the project calendar

1   On the Tools menu, click Change Working Time.
2   In the For box, select Standard (Project Calendar).
3   In the Selected Date(s) box, select the days of the week for which you want to change working or nonworking time.
4   In the From and To boxes, enter the working time you want.

To make holidays or other days nonworking time in the project calendar

1   On the Tools menu, click Change Working Time.

2   In the For box, select Standard (Project Calendar).

3   In the Selected Date(s) box, select the holiday date or other date you want to change to nonworking time.

4   Under Set Selected Date(s) To, click Nonworking Time.

To adjust the project's default start and end times

1   On the Tools menu, click Change Working Time.

2   Click Options.

3   In the Default Start Time and Default End Time boxes, type or select the start and end times you want.

To create a base calendar

1   On the Tools menu, click Change Working Time.

2   Click the New button.

3   In the Name box, type a name for the base calendar.

4   In the Make A Copy Of box, select the base calendar on which you want to base the new calendar.

5   Click OK.

6   In the Selected Date(s) box, select the days of the week for which you want to change working or nonworking time.

7   Under Set Selected Date(s) To, select Nonworking Time for those days you want to mark as nonworking.

8   For working days, in the From and To boxes, enter the working time you want.

To apply a task calendar to a task

1   In the Entry table, select a task.

2   On the Standard toolbar, click the Task Information button.

3   Click the Advanced tab.

4   In the Calendar box, select the task calendar you want to apply.

5   If you want the task calendar to override resource calendar settings, check the Scheduling Ignores Resource Calendars box.

To change a task relationship

1   In the Entry table, select a successor task.

2   On the Standard toolbar, click the Task Information button.

3   In the Type field for the predecessor task, select the relationship type you want.

To enter lead or lag time

1   In the Entry table, select a successor task.

2   On the Standard toolbar, click the Task Information button.

3   Click the Predecessors tab.

4   In the Lag field for the predecessor task, enter a positive time value or per-centage of the predecessor's duration for lag time, or enter a negative time value or percentage for lead time.

To change a task type in the Task Form

1   In the Gantt Chart view, select a task.

2   On the Window menu, click Split.

3   In the Task Type box in the Task Form, select the task type you want, and then click OK.

To change a task type in the Task Information dialog box

1   In the Entry table, select a task.

2   On the Standard toolbar, click the Task Information button.

3   Click the Advanced tab.

4   In the Task Type box, select the task type you want.

To interrupt work on a task

1   On the Standard toolbar, click the Split Task button.

2   Move the mouse pointer over the task's Gantt bar where you want to start the split, and then drag to the right.

To enter a fixed cost

1   On the View menu, point to Table: Entry, and then click Cost.

2   In the Fixed Cost field for the task you want, type or select an amount, and press Tab.

3   In the Fixed Cost Accrual field, select a method, and then press Enter.

To create a recurring task

1   In the Entry table, select the task above which you want to insert a recurring task.

2   On the Insert menu, click Recurring Task.

3   In the Recurring Task Information dialog box, select the options you want.

To apply a Start No Earlier Than constraint to a task

1   In the Entry table, select a task.

2   In the Start field, type or select the date you want.

To apply a Finish No Earlier Than constraint to a task

1   In the Entry table, select a task.

2   In the Finish field, type or select the date you want.

To apply other types of constraints to a task

1   In the Entry table, select a task.

2   On the Standard toolbar, click the Task Information button.

3   Click the Advanced tab.

4   In the Constraint Type box, select the type of constraint you want to apply.

5   If you choose a semi-flexible or an inflexible constraint type, type or select a date in the Constraint Date box.

To reorganize tasks

●   Drag the task ID for a task to a new location.

To enter a deadline date

1   In the Entry Table, select a task.

2   On the Standard toolbar, click the Task Information button.

3   Click the Advanced tab.

4   In the Deadline box, type or select the deadline date you want.

To view the project's critical path

1   On the View menu, select More Views.

2   In the More Views dialog box, select Detail Gantt, and then click Apply.

To filter for critical tasks

●   On the Project menu, point to Filtered for: All Tasks, and then click Critical.

To create a task note

1   In the Entry table, select a task.

2   On the Standard toolbar, click the Notes button.

3   In the Notes box, type the content of the note, and then click OK.

To create a hyperlink

1   In the Entry table, select a task.

2   On the Standard toolbar, click the Insert Hyperlink button.

3   In the Type The File Or Web Page Name box, type the address of the Web site to which you want to link.

4   If you want text to appear if you point to the Hyperlink indicator, type that text in the Text To Display box.

5   Click OK.

LESSON

7

Fine-Tuning Resource Details

**ESTIMATED TIME
40 min.**

After completing this lesson, you will be able to:

✔ *Update individual resource calendars.*

✔ *Set resource availability to change over time.*

✔ *Set up different pay rates for a resource.*

✔ *Set up different pay rates that will change over time for a resource.*

✔ *Look at resource costs.*

✔ *Look at how resources are scheduled to work over the duration of the project.*

✔ *Resolve resource overallocations.*

✔ *Create a resource note.*

This lesson continues the fine-tuning activities you started in Lesson 6, this time focusing on resources. Because people and equipment resources are often the most expensive part of a project, understanding how to make the best use of resources' time is an important project planning skill.

 Practice files for the lesson

To complete this lesson, you will use a file named Short Film Project 07. Open the Part 2 folder in the MS Project 2000 SBS Practice folder on your hard disk. Open the file 07A, and save it without a baseline as Short Film Project 07 in the Part 2 folder.

Adjusting Working Time for Individual Resources

PROJ2000-1-6

You might recall from Lesson 6 that Microsoft Project uses different types of calendars for different purposes. In this section we'll focus on the **resource calendar**. A resource calendar is an individual resource's working and nonworking times. Resource calendars apply only to work resources (people and equipment) and not to material resources.

When you initially create resources in a project, Microsoft Project creates a resource calendar for each resource. The initial working time settings for resource calendars exactly match those of the **Standard base calendar**. If all of your resources' working times match the working time of the Standard base calendar, then you don't need to edit any resource calendars. However, chances are that some of your resources will need exceptions to the Standard base calendar's working time—such as

- A flex-time work schedule.
- Vacation time.
- Other times when a resource is not available to work on the project, such as time spent training or attending a conference.

tip
If your team uses the Calendar module in Microsoft Outlook and Microsoft Project Central, resources can automatically report to you times they are not available to work on project activities. These times are based on calendar items marked as "busy" or "out of office" in Microsoft Outlook. Once the times are reported, you can easily update the resource's working time in the project plan without retyping anything. For more information, see "Import your nonworking time from Microsoft Outlook" in Appendix D.

There are two places you can edit a resource calendar: the Working Time tab of the Resource Information dialog box and the Change Working Time dialog box. Editing a resource calendar in either location has the same effect.

Any changes you make to the Standard base calendar are automatically reflected in all resource calendars that are based on the Standard calendar. Any specific changes you've made to a resource's working time are not changed, however.

tip

If you have a resource who is available to work on your project only part time, you might be tempted to set the resource's working time in your project to reflect a part-time schedule—for example, 9:00 A.M. to 1:00 P.M. daily. However, a better approach would be to adjust the resource's availability as recorded in their **Max. Units** field—for example, to 50%. Changing the resource's unit availability keeps the focus on the resource's capacity to work on the project, rather than on the specific times of the day when that work might occur. You set a resource's maximum units in the Resource Sheet view, which you display by selecting the Resource Sheet command from the View menu. For more information about resource units, see "Setting Up People Resources" in Lesson 4.

In this exercise, you specify the working and nonworking times for individual work resources.

1 On the Tools menu, click Change Working Time.

The Change Working Time dialog box appears.

2 In the For box, select Clair Hector.

Clair Hector's resource calendar appears in the Change Working Time dialog box. Notice the light shading in Clair's resource calendar during the work week. In the Legend box you can see that this shading represents edited working hours. In Lesson 6 you edited the Standard base calendar's default working time, and that change is reflected here in Clair's (as in every other resource's) resource calendar.

Clair Hector, the producer of the film, has told you she will not be available to work on Monday and Tuesday, May 21 and 22, 2001.

3 In the calendar below the Select Date(s) label, drag the vertical scroll bar or click the up or down arrow buttons until May 2001 appears.

To quickly select this date range, drag from 21 through 22.

4 Select the dates May 21 and 22.

5 Under Set Selected Date(s) To, click Nonworking Time.

When changing working time, make sure you have the right resource or base calendar selected in the For box.

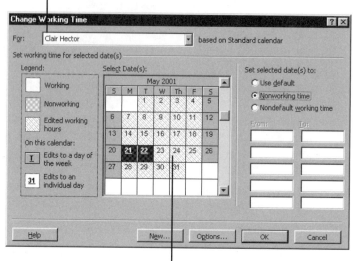

Clair Hector's normal working time is shaded to indicate that it's been edited (in this case, via changes made to the Standard base calendar).

Microsoft Project will not schedule work for Clair on these dates.

6 Next enter the following resource working time information. When asked to save each resource's information, click Yes.

Resource	Date	Working time issue
Kim Yoshida	June 4-5, 2001	Kim cannot work on these days; mark as nonworking time.
Jo Brown	July 12-13, 2001	Jo cannot work on these days; mark as nonworking time.

To conclude this exercise, you will set up a "4 by 10" work schedule (that is, 4 days per week, 10 hours per day) for a resource.

7 In the For box, select Florian Voss.

8 When prompted to save the resource calendar changes you made for Jo Brown, click Yes.

To quickly select the Monday through Thursday column headings, drag from the M through the Th.

9 Select the Monday through Thursday column headings.

Although you can only see one month at a time in the dialog box, selecting a day's column heading selects every occurrence of that day of the week—past, present, and future.

10 In the upper From box, type **8:00 AM**.

11 Select the Friday column heading.

12 Under Set Selected Date(s) To, click Nonworking Time.

Now Microsoft Project can schedule work for Florian beginning at 8:00 AM every Monday through Thursday, but will not schedule work for her on Fridays.

13 Click OK to close the Change Working Time dialog box.

tip

If you find that you must edit several resource calendars in a similar way (to handle a night shift, for example), it may be easier to assign a different base calendar to a resource or collection of resources. This is more efficient than editing each resource's individual resource calendar and allows you to make project-wide adjustments to a single base calendar if needed.

For example, if your project includes a day shift and a night shift, you can apply the **Night Shift** base calendar to those resources who work the night shift. You change a resource's base calendar in the Base Calendar box on the Working Time tab of the Resource Information dialog box. You can open this dialog box by selecting the Resource Information command on the Project menu when in a resource view. For collections of resources, you can do this directly in the Base Calendar column on the Entry table in the Resource Sheet view.

Setting Up Resource Availability to Apply at Different Times

PROJ2000E-1-7

In Lesson 4, you entered new resource information into Microsoft Project. Included in this was each resource's max. units value. This is the maximum capacity of a resource to accomplish tasks. A resource's working time settings (recorded in the individual resource calendars) determine when a resource is available to work. However, the resource's capacity to work (measured in **units**, and limited by their max. units value) determines the extent to which the resource can work within those hours.

You can specify different max. units values to be applied at different time periods for any resource. Setting a resource's availability over time allows you to control exactly what a resource's maximum units value is at any time. For example, two electricians may be available for the first eight weeks, three electricians available for the next six weeks, then two for the remainder of the project. You set resource availability over time in the Resource Availability grid on the General tab of the Resource Information dialog box. (You can open this dialog box by selecting the Resource Information command from the Project menu when in a resource view.)

In this exercise, you customize a resource's availability over time.

1   On the View bar, click Resource Sheet.

The Resource Sheet view replaces the Gantt Chart view.

2   In the Resource Name column, select the name of Resource 12, "Electrician."

3   On the Standard toolbar, click the Resource Information button.

4   Click the General tab.

You expect to have two electricians available to work on this project from the start of the project through July 6, three electricians from July 7 through July 20, and then just two for the remainder of the project.

5   Under Resource Availability, in the first row of the Available From column, leave "NA" (for Not Applicable).

6   In the Available To cell in the first row, type or select **7/6/01**.

7   In the Available From cell in the second row, type or select **7/7/01**.

8   In the Available To cell in the second row, type or select **7/20/01**.

9   In the Units cell in the second row, type or select **300%**.

10   In the Available From cell in the third row, type or select **7/21/01**.

11   Leave the Available To cell in the third row blank. (Microsoft Project will insert "NA" for you.)

12   In the Units cell in the third row, type or select **200%** and then press the Enter key.

When you enter dates in an abbreviated
format, such as 7/6/01, Microsoft Project
automatically converts them to this
expanded format.

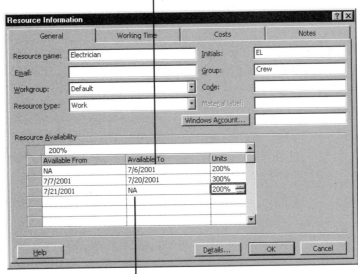

Microsoft Project automatically
inserts "NA," meaning not
applicable, here.

Now, for the period between July 7 and July 20, you can schedule up to
three electricians without overallocating them. Before and after this period,
you have just two electricians to schedule.

13   Click OK to close the Resource Information dialog box.

tip

The Max. Units field for the Electricians resource will display 300% only when
the current date (based on your computer's system clock) is within the July 7 to
July 20 range. At other times it will display 200%.

Entering Multiple Pay Rates for a Single Resource

PROJ2000E-1-2

Some resources may perform different tasks with different pay rates. For example, in our short film project, the director of photography could also serve as a camera operator. Because the pay rates for director of photography and camera operator are different, you can enter two **cost rate tables** for the resource. Then, after you assign the resource to tasks, you specify which rate table should apply. Each resource can have up to five cost rate tables.

In this exercise, you create a second cost rate table for a resource.

1   On the Resource Sheet, click Resource 17, "Jan Miksovsky."

2   On the Standard toolbar, click the Resource Information button.

The Resource Information dialog box appears.

You can also double-click the Resource Name field to display the Resource Information dialog box.

3   Click the Costs tab.

You see Jan's default pay rate of $18.75 per hour on rate table A.

4   Under Cost Rate Tables, click the B tab.

5   Select the default entry of $0.00/h in the field directly below the column heading Standard Rate, and then type **14/h**.

6   In the Overtime Rate field, type **21/h**, and then press the Enter key.

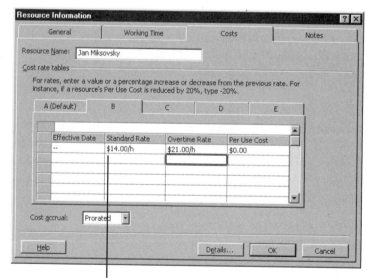

When you enter a pay rate Microsoft Project automatically supplies the currency symbol if you do not.

7   Click OK to close the Resource Information dialog box.

Notice that on the Resource Sheet, Jan's standard pay rate is still $18.75 per hour. This matches the value in her rate table A, the default rate table. This rate table will be used for all of Jan's task assignments unless you specify a different rate table. You will do this in a later lesson.

Setting Up Pay Rates to Apply at Different Times

In Lesson 4, you entered standard and overtime pay rates for resources. By default, Microsoft Project uses these rates for the duration of the project. However, you can change a resource's pay rates, effective as of the date you choose. For example, you could initially set up a resource on January 1 with a standard rate of $10 per hour, planning to raise the resource's standard rate to $13 per hour on July 1.

Microsoft Project uses these pay rates when calculating resource costs, based on when the resource's work is scheduled. You can assign up to 25 pay rates to be applied at different times to each of a resource's five cost rate tables.

In this exercise, you enter different pay rates for a resource to be applied later in the project.

Remember that double-clicking a resource name is a shortcut for displaying the Resource Information dialog box.

1   In the Resource Name column, double-click the name of Resource 10, "Doug Hampton."

The Resource Information dialog box appears.

2   Click the Costs tab.

You'll enter a second pay rate in cost rate table A.

3   In the Effective Date cell in the second row of cost rate table A, type or select **8/16/01**.

4   In the Standard Rate cell in the second row, type **30%**, and then press the Enter key.

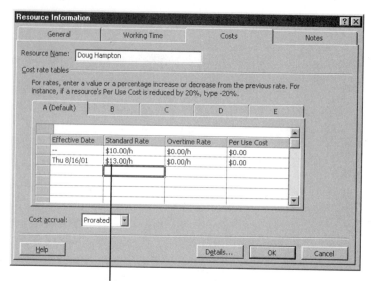

If you enter a positive or negative percentage value here, Microsoft Project automatically calculates the new rate value, based on the previous rate value.

Note that Microsoft Project calculates the 30% increase to produce a rate of $13 per hour. The previous rate of $10 per hour plus 30% equals $13 per hour. You can enter an exact value or a percentage increase or decrease from the previous rate.

5   Click OK to close the Resource Information dialog box.

Note that Doug Hampton's initial rate, $10.00/hr, appears in his Standard Rate field. This field will display $10 per hour until the current date changes to 8/16/01 or later. Then it will display his new standard rate of $13 per hour.

Examining Resource Costs

In many projects, resource costs are the primary factor that limits the overall scope of the project. If you have entered resource cost information into your plan, Microsoft Project provides several ways to view this data before and after you start tracking actual work.

You might recall from Lesson 4 that resources in the short film project are associated with one of five groups: Crew, Equipment, Film and Lab, Production, and Talent. These groups include all of the people, equipment, and material resources working on the project. For this type of project, focusing on cost information per group can be informative. In this exercise you view detailed cost data per resource, and then summary cost data per resource group.

1   On the View menu, click Table: Entry, and then select Summary.

    Microsoft Project displays the Summary table in the Resource Sheet view.

> ## tip
> You may have noticed the Cost table on the Table submenu. The Cost table is more useful after setting a baseline and tracking actual data. When initially planning, however, the Summary table is more helpful because it shows additional values such as pay rates and work values that affect cost.

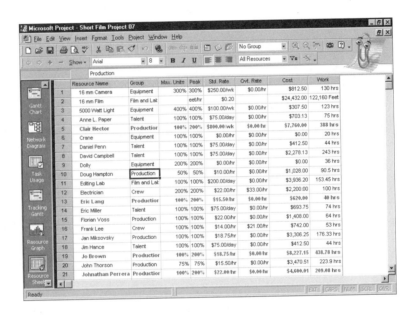

In this table you can see each resource's rate information and total costs, based on their current assignments. Next you look at summary costs per group.

2   On the Standard toolbar, locate the Group By button. Initially it contains "No Group." Click Resource Group.

    Microsoft Project organizes the resources according to the groups to which they are assigned and displays summary group-level units, cost, and work values. These summary rows are automatically formatted with a yellow background.

When information is grouped
in this way, you can collapse
all groups by using the buttons   ...or you can expand or collapse individual
on the Formatting toolbar...   groups by clicking here.

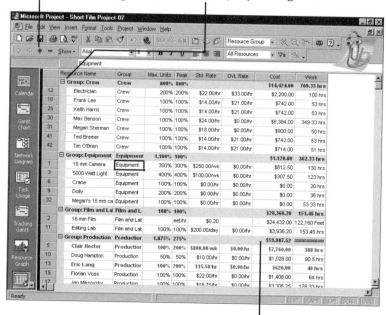

Since the summary values are calculated,
you cannot directly edit them.

This information is organized into an outline that you can expand or collapse.
Next you will collapse the outline in the table to see total costs per group.

3   Click the Resource Name column heading.

4   On the Formatting toolbar, click Hide Subtasks.

Microsoft Project collapses the Summary table to show just group names and
their summary information.

*If you see
pound signs
(###) in a col-
umn, you can
widen that
column. Move
the mouse
pointer to the
right edge of
the column,
and double-
click.*

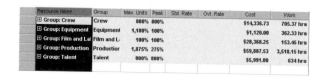

Resource Name	Group	Max. Units	Peak	Std. Rate	Ovt. Rate	Cost	Work
⊞ Group: Crew	Crew	800%	800%			$14,336.73	705.37 hrs
⊞ Group: Equipment	Equipment	1,100%	100%			$1,120.00	362.33 hrs
⊞ Group: Film and Lal	Film and L:	100%	100%			$28,368.25	153.45 hrs
⊞ Group: Production	Productior	1,875%	275%			$59,887.53	3,518.15 hrs
⊞ Group: Talent	Talent	800%	800%			$5,991.00	634 hrs

This view is a good way to see summarized cost projections per group. If you wish, you can expand individual groups by clicking the plus sign next to each group's name.

You cannot directly edit the values in the Cost column in this view. The cost values you see are calculated; they are the products of each resource's cost rate information multiplied by the work values of their task assignments. In the case of the group-level summary information, the resource costs per group are totaled. If you wish to change a resource's cost amount, you must change that resource's cost rates or assignments.

5   In the Group By box on the Standard toolbar, click No Group.

Examining Resource Allocations over Time

PROJ2000-2-5,
PROJ2000-5-10,
PROJ2000E-1-9

In this and the next exercise, you'll focus on resource allocation—how the task assignments you've made affect the workloads of the people and equipment resources of the project. How a resource's time is managed over time is called **allocation**, and specifically it's in one of three states:

- **Underallocated:** The resource's maximum capacity is not filled by the resource's assignments. For example, a full-time resource who has only 25 hours of work assigned in a 40-hour workweek is underallocated.

- **Fully allocated:** The resource's maximum capacity is just filled by assignments. For example, a full-time resource who has 40 hours of work assigned in a 40-hour workweek is fully allocated.

- **Overallocated:** The resource's maximum capacity is exceeded by assignments. For example, a full-time resource who has 65 hours of work assigned in a 40-hour workweek is overallocated.

You might recall from Lesson 4 that in Microsoft Project a resource's capacity to work is measured in units; a given resource's maximum capacity is called maximum units. Units are measured either as numbers (for example, 3 units) or as a percentage (for example, 300% units).

It is tempting to say that fully allocating all resources all the time is every project manager's goal—but that would be an oversimplification. Depending on the nature of your project and the resources working on it, some underallocations may be perfectly fine. Overallocation may not always be a problem either, depending on the scope of the overallocation. If one resource is overallocated for just a half hour, Microsoft Project will alert you, but such a minor overallocation might not be a problem you need to solve, depending on the resource involved and the nature of the assignment. Severe overallocation— for example, a resource being assigned twice the work he or she could possibly accomplish in one day—is always a problem, however, and you should know how to identify it and have strategies for addressing it.

In this exercise, you look at resource allocations and focus on two resources who are overallocated.

Resource Usage

For more in-formation about views and tables, see Lesson 2.

1   On the View bar, click Resource Usage.

The Resource Usage view appears.

On the left side of the Resource Usage view is a table (the Usage table by default), that shows assignments grouped per resource, the total work as-signed to each resource, and each assignment's work. This information is or-ganized into an outline that you can expand or collapse.

The right side of the view contains assignment details (work, by default) ar-ranged on a timescale. You can scroll the timescale horizontally to see differ-ent time periods. You can also change the major or minor timescale to display data in units of weeks, days, hours, and so on.

Next, you will collapse the outline in the table to see total work per resource over time.

2   In the Usage table, click the Resource Name column heading.

3   On the Formatting toolbar, click Hide Subtasks.

Microsoft Project collapses the Resource Usage view to show just resource names in the Usage Table, and their total work values over time in the timescaled grid on the right.

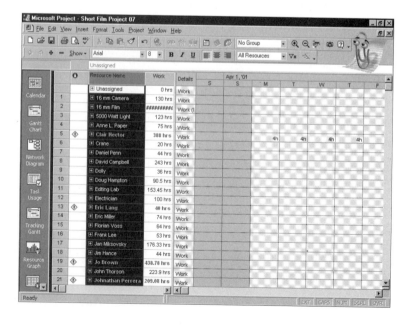

Notice the name of the first resource, "Unassigned." Who is this resource named "Unassigned," you might be wondering? Actually, it's nobody. "Unassigned" refers to all tasks to which no specific resources are assigned.

The other unusual resource here is named "16 mm Film." This is a material resource, and its value in the Work column contains the number of feet of film to be consumed based on the tasks to which this material resource is assigned. All other resources' work values are measured in hours.

Next you'll look at two people resources and their allocations.

4   In the Resource Name column, select the name of Resource 4, "Anne L. Paper."

5   On the Standard toolbar, click the Go To Selected Task button.

Microsoft Project scrolls the timescaled grid to show Anne L. Paper's earliest assignment: 8 hours on a Friday.

6   Point to the F column heading at the top of the timescaled grid.

In any timescaled view you can get details about dates by placing your mouse pointer on the timescale.

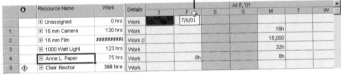

A ToolTip appears with the date of the assignment: 7/6/01. Such ToolTips are handy in any timescaled view such as the Resource Usage view and the Gantt Chart.

Currently the timescale is set to display weeks in the major scale and days in the minor scale. Now, change the timescale to see the work data summarized more broadly.

7   On the Format menu, click Timescale.

The Timescale dialog box appears.

8   In the Units box under Major Scale, select Years. In the Units box under Minor Scale, select Months. Be sure that 1 is the Count value for both scales.

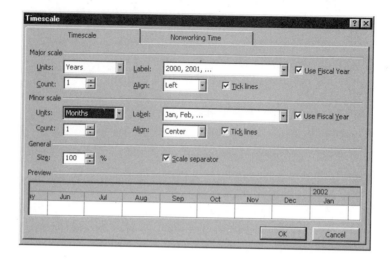

9 Click OK to close the Timescale dialog box.

Microsoft Project changes the timescaled grid to show work values per month.

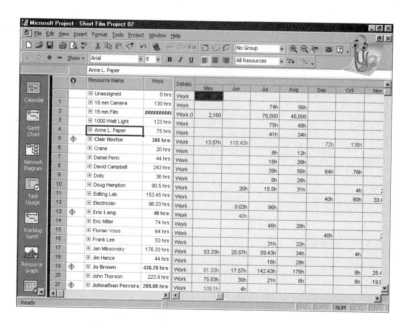

As you can see in the timescaled grid, Anne L. Paper is underallocated in each of the two months in which she has assignments in the project: July and August. Anne is one of the actors assigned to the scenes in which her character is needed, so this underallocation is really not a problem we need to address.

Notice the exclamation mark indicators next to the names of Clair Hector, Eric Lang, and other resources. Also note that their names are formatted in red. The indicators and the red formatting mean that these resources are overallocated: at one or more points in the schedule their assigned tasks exceed their capacity to work. We'll focus on Clair Hector, first by changing the timescale settings.

10 On the Format menu, click Timescale.

The timescale dialog box appears.

11 In the Units box under Major Scale, select Weeks. In the Units box under Minor Scale, select Days.

12 Click OK to close the Timescale dialog box.

13 In the Resource Name column, select the name of Resource 5, "Clair Hector."

14 On the Standard toolbar, click the Go To Selected Task button.

Microsoft Project scrolls the timescaled grid to show Clair Hector's earliest assignments. You can see that on Friday, April 6, Clair's 6 hours of work are formatted in red, indicating that she is overallocated on that day.

Given that Clair works full time, how could she be overallocated with just six hours of work? To determine this, you'll need to get a closer look at her assignments.

15 Click the plus sign next to Clair Hector's name in the Resource Name column.

Microsoft Project expands the Resource Usage view to show Clair Hector's individual assignments.

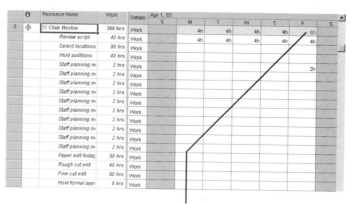

Even though this resource's assignments on this day don't exceed her capacity to work, they have been scheduled at times that overlap, resulting in an hour-by-hour overallocation.

There are only two assignments on April 6: the four-hour task "Review script" and the two-hour task "Staff planning meeting 1." It turns out that these two tasks have been scheduled at times that overlap between the hours of 5:00 P.M. and 7:00 P.M. (If you wish to see this, format the timescale to display days in the major scale and hours in the minor scale.) This is a real overallocation: Clair probably can't complete both tasks simultaneously. However, it's a relatively minor overallocation given the scope of the project, and we're not too concerned about resolving this level of overallocation.

There are more serious overallocations in the schedule, however. To conclude this exercise, you'll look at one of them.

16   In the Resource Name column, select the name of Resource 13, "Eric Lang."

17   On the Standard toolbar, click the Go To Selected Task button.

In the week of June 24, you can see that this resource is overallocated on four different days. On Tuesday and Wednesday, June 26 and 27, Eric Lang has 16 hours of work each day. Since this is twice his normal 8-hour workday, he is overallocated at 200% on these days. This is an example of a more serious overallocation, which we will attempt to address in the next section.

Here are a few more things to keep in mind when viewing resource allocation:

- By default, the Resource Usage view displays the Usage table. You can display different tables, however. On the View menu, click Table: Usage, and then select the table you want displayed.

- By default, the Resource Usage view displays work values in the timescaled grid. However, you can display additional assignment values such as cost and remaining availability. On the Format menu, click Details, and then select the value you want displayed.

 - Instead of using the Timescale command on the Format menu to change the major and minor scales of the timescale, you can click the Zoom In and Zoom Out buttons on the Standard toolbar. However, this method may not produce the exact level of detail you want. If it doesn't, use the Timescale command on the Format menu.

 - To see each resource's allocations graphed against a units scale, you can display the Resource Graph by selecting the Resource Graph command on the View menu or you can click the Resource Graph button on the View bar. Use the arrow keys or horizontal scroll bar to switch between resources in this view. You'll find examples of the Resource Graph view used in combination with another view in the next section.

Leveling Overallocated Resources

PROJ2000E-1-5

In the previous exercise you read about resource allocation and what causes overallocation. **Resource leveling** is the process of delaying a resource's work on a task to resolve an overallocation. Depending on the options you choose, this may involve delaying the start date of an assignment or the entire task or splitting up the work on the task.

For example, consider the following tasks, all of which have the same full-time resource assigned. (In this split view, the Resource Graph view appears below the Gantt Chart view.)

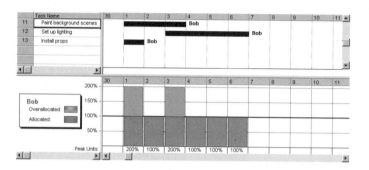

On day 1, the resource is overallocated at 200%. On day 2, the resource is fully allocated at 100%. On day 3, he's overallocated at 200% again. After day 3, the resource is fully allocated at 100%.

After leveling, Microsoft Project delays the start dates of the second and third tasks so that the resource is not overallocated.

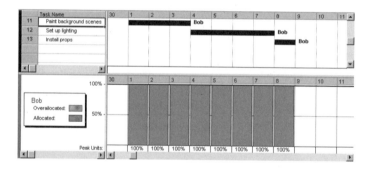

Note that the finish date of the latest task has moved from day 6 to day 8. This is common with resource leveling; resource leveling often pushes out the project finish date, unless you tell it not to. Before leveling, there was a total of eight days of work, but two of those days overlapped, causing the resource to be overallocated on those days. After leveling, all eight days of work are still there, but the resource is no longer overallocated.

Resource leveling is a powerful tool, but it basically does only a few things: it adds delay to tasks, splits tasks, and adjusts resource assignments. It does this following a fairly complex set of rules and options you specify in the Resource Leveling dialog box. (These options are explained below.) Resource leveling is a great fine-tuning tool, but it cannot replace your good judgment about task durations, relationships, and constraints or about resource availability. Resource leveling will work with all of this information as it's entered into your project plan, but it might not be possible to fully resolve all resource overallocations within the timeframe you want without changing more basic task and resource information.

In this exercise, you level resources and look at the effects on assignments and the project finish date.

1 On the View bar, click Resource Sheet.

The Resource Sheet view replaces the Resource Usage view.

2 On the View menu, click Table: Summary, and then select Entry.

Microsoft Project displays the Entry table, in which you can see the "Overallocated" indicators for those resources who are overallocated.

3 On the Tools menu, click Resource Leveling.

The Resource Leveling dialog box appears.

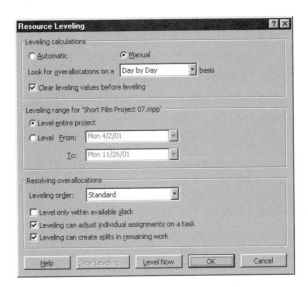

4 Under Leveling Calculations, click Manual.

These settings determine whether Microsoft Project levels constantly (Automatic) or only when you tell it to (Manual). Automatic leveling occurs as soon as a resource becomes overallocated.

5 In the Look For Overallocations On A box, click Day By Day.

This setting determines the timeframe in which Microsoft Project will look for overallocations. You might recall from the section "Examining Resource Allocations over Time" above that the resource Clair Hector was overallocated for two hours on one day, even though she worked only a total of six hours on that day. Choosing Hour By Hour here would cause Microsoft Project to attempt to resolve that overallocation. However, for most projects, leveling in detail finer than Day by Day can result in unrealistically precise adjustments to assignments.

6   Check the Clear Leveling Values Before Leveling box.

Sometimes you'll need to level resources repeatedly to get the results you want. For example, you might initially attempt to level week by week, then switch to day by day. If the Clear Leveling Values Before Leveling box is checked, Microsoft Project removes any existing delays from all tasks before leveling. Usually you clear this option only if you have delayed tasks manually and you want to keep those delays.

7   Under Leveling Range For "Short Film Project 07," check Level Entire Project.

Here you choose to level either the entire project or only those assignments that fall within a date range you specify. Leveling within a date range is most useful after you've started tracking actual work and you want to level only the remaining assignments in a project.

8   In the Leveling Order box, click Standard.

You control the priority Microsoft Project uses to determine which tasks it should delay to resolve a resource conflict. The ID Only option delays tasks only according to their ID numbers: higher numbers will be delayed before lower ID numbers. Use this option when your project plan has no task relationships or constraints. The Standard option delays tasks according to predecessor relationships, start dates, task constraints, slack, priority, and IDs. The Priority, Standard option looks at the task's priority value before the other standard criteria.

tip

In this project, we're not using task priorities. However, if you have specific tasks for which you want better control over the effects of resource leveling, you can change their priority values. When you level resources, Microsoft Project will delay a task with a lower priority before a task with a higher priority in order to resolve a resource overallocation. You set a task's priority on the General tab of the Task Information dialog box. The priority value range is zero to 1000. The default priority value for all tasks is 500; tasks with a priority of 1000 are never delayed by resource leveling. Use custom priorities sparingly, because many tasks with high priorities limit your scheduling flexibility with Microsoft Project.

9   Clear the Level Only Within Available Slack check box.

Checking this box prevents Microsoft Project from extending the project's finish date in order to resolve resource overallocations. Instead, Microsoft Project will use only the **free slack** of tasks, which, depending on the project, might not be adequate to fully resolve resource overallocations.

10   Check the Leveling Can Adjust Individual Assignments On A Task check box.

This allows Microsoft Project to adjust overallocated resources assigned to a task independent of any other resources assigned to the same task. This might cause resources to start and finish work on a task at different times.

11   Check the Leveling Can Create Splits In Remaining Work check box.

This allows Microsoft Project to split work on a task as a way of resolving an overallocation.

12   Click Level Now.

13   Microsoft Project asks whether you want to level the entire pool or only selected resources. Leave Entire Pool selected, and click OK.

Microsoft Project levels the overallocated resources.

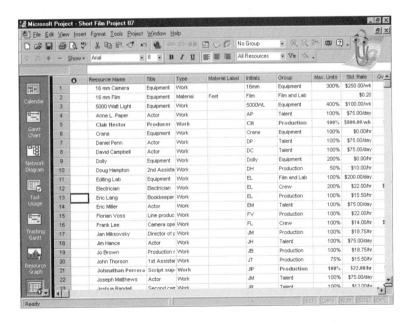

Notice that the "Overallocated" indicators are gone, although some resource names are still formatted in red. This means that some resources are still overallocated hour-by-hour (or minute-by-minute) but not day-by-day.

Next you'll look at the project plan before and after leveling using the Leveling Gantt view.

14 On the View menu, click More Views, select Leveling Gantt, and then click Apply.

Microsoft Project switches to the Leveling Gantt view.

15 Select the name of Task 6, "Select Locations."

16 On the Standard toolbar, click the Go To Selected Task button.

This gives you a better look at some of the tasks that were affected by leveling.

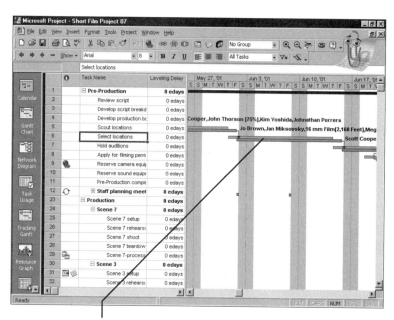

In the Leveling Gannt view, the green bar on top represent the preleveled schedule of the task. The blue bar below represents the schedule after leveling.

Notice that each task now has two bars. The green bar on top represents the preleveled task. You can see the preleveled start, finish, and duration pointing to a green bar. The blue bar on the bottom represents the leveled task.

Microsoft Project was able to resolve most resource overallocations by manually adjusting individual assignments on tasks. Microsoft Project had to apply a leveling delay to only one task (Task 76) .

Documenting Resource Details in Resource Notes

You might recall from Lesson 6 that you can record any additional information that you want about a task, resource, or assignment in a **note**. For example, if a resource is not available to work on a specific date range, it's a good idea to record why in a note. That way, the note resides in the Microsoft Project file and can be easily viewed or printed.

In this exercise, you enter resource notes to document why a resource is not available to work on certain dates.

Resource
Sheet

1   On the View bar, click Resource Sheet.

The Resource Sheet view appears.

2   In the Resource Name column, select the name of Resource 5, "Clair Hector."

3   On the Standard toolbar, click the Resource Notes button.

Microsoft Project displays the Resource Information dialog box with the Notes tab visible.

4   In the Notes box, type **Clair attending west coast film festival May 21 and 22, unavailable to work on project**, and click OK.

A note icon appears in the Indicators column.

5   Point to the note icon.

The note appears in a ToolTip. For notes that are too long to appear in a ToolTip, you can double-click the note icon to display the full text of the note.

Lesson Wrap-Up

This lesson covered how to apply a variety of important resource-related tools after creating your initial project plan but before tracking actual work.

If you are going on to other lessons:

1   On the Standard toolbar, click Save to save changes made to Short Film Project 07. Save without a baseline.

2   On the File menu, click Close to close the file.

If you aren't continuing to other lessons:

●   To quit Microsoft Project for now, on the File menu, click Exit.

Glossary

Allocation The portion of a resource's capacity to work devoted to a specific task. A full-time resource assigned to work full time on a task is fully allocated to that task. In Microsoft Project, a resource's work capacity is measured in units. One full-time resource has 100% units (recorded in the Max. Units field).

Cost rate table Resource pay rates that are stored on the Costs tab of the Resource Information dialog box. You can have up to five separate cost rate tables, named A through E, per resource.

Free slack The amount of time that a task can be delayed before it delays the start date of a successor task.

Fully allocated When a resource's assignments equal the resource's maximum capacity. For example, a full-time resource who has 40 hours of work assigned in a 40-hour workweek is fully allocated. In Microsoft Project, a resource's work capacity is measured in units. One full-time resource has 100% units (recorded in the Max. Units field).

Max. Units The maximum capacity of a resource to accomplish any task. A resource that is available to work full time has a maximum units value of 100% or 1.0.

Night Shift A base calendar included with Microsoft Project designed to accommodate an 11:00 P.M.–8:00 A.M. "graveyard" work shift.

Note Any information (including linked or embedded files) that you wish to associate with a task, resource, or assignment.

Overallocated When a resource is assigned to do more work on assigned tasks than can be done within the resource's normal work capacity. In Microsoft Project, a resource's work capacity is measured in units. One full-time resource has 100% units (recorded in the Max. Units field).

Resource calendar An individual work resource's working and nonworking times.

Resource leveling Resolving resource overallocation by delaying the start date of an assignment or an entire task or splitting up the work on a task. Microsoft Project can level resource automatically, or you can do it manually.

Standard base calendar A base calendar included with Microsoft Project designed to accommodate an 8:00 A.M.–5:00 P.M. work shift.

Underallocated When a resource's assignments are less than the resource's maximum capacity. For example, a full-time resource who has only 25 hours of work assigned in a 40-hour workweek is underallocated. In Microsoft Project, a resource's work capacity is measured in units. One full-time resource has 100% units (recorded in the Max. Units field).

Unit A standard way of measuring a resource's capacity to work when assigned to a task in Microsoft Project. Units is one variable in the scheduling formula: Duration × Units = Work.

Quick Reference

To change a resource's working time

1   On the Tools menu, click Change Working Time.

2   In the For box, select the name of the resource whose working time you want to change.

3   In the calendar below the Select Date(s) label, select the date range or day(s) of the week for which you want to adjust working time.

4   Under Set Selected Date(s) To, click the options you want.

To customize a resource's availability over time

1   Switch to a resource view such as the Resource Sheet view.

2   Select the name of the resource whose availability you want to change.

3   On the Project menu, click Resource Information.

4   Click the General tab.

5   In the Resource Availability grid, enter the date ranges and unit values you want.

To create multiple pay rates for a resource

1   Switch to a resource view such as the Resource Sheet view.

2   Select the name of the resource for whom you want to create an additional pay rate.

3   On the Project menu, click Resource Information.

4   Click the Costs tab.

5   Under Cost Rate Tables, the resource's initial pay rate information appears on tab A. Select one of the other tabs, then enter the rate information you want.

6   To apply different cost rate tables, pick the one you want in the Cost Rate Table field when you are in an assignment view.

To create multiple pay rates that apply at different times

1   Switch to a resource view such as the Resource Sheet view.

2   Select the name of the resource for whom you want to create an additional pay rate.

3   On the Project menu, click Resource Information.

4   Cick the Costs tab.

5   Click the tab of the rate table you want to edit.

6   In the second or later row of the Effective Date column, enter the date the new pay rate is to take effect.

7   In the Standard Rate column (and, if applicable, the Overtime Rate or Per Use Cost columns), enter either a dollar amount or a positive or negative percentage of the existing pay rate. If you enter a percentage value, Microsoft Project will calculate the new pay rate amount.

To view detailed and group-level summary resource costs

1   Switch to a resource view such as the Resource Sheet view.

2   On the View menu, click Table: Entry, and then select Summary.

3   On the Standard toolbar, click the down arrow for the Group By button, and click Resource Group.

4   To collapse the view to group-level summary data, click the Resource Name column heading. On the Formatting toolbar, click Hide Subtasks.

To view resource allocations over time

●   On the View bar, click Resource Usage.

To change the scale on the timescale

1   On the Format menu click Timescale.

2   In the Units boxes under Major Scale and under Minor Scale, select the options you want, and click OK.

To level overallocated resources

●   On the Tools menu, click Resource Leveling, and then choose the leveling options you want.

To create a resource note

1   Switch to a resource view such as the Resource Sheet view.

2   Select the name of the resource for which you want to create a note.

3   On the Standard toolbar, click the Resource Notes button.

4   In the Resource Information dialog box, type the note you want associated with this resource.

8

Fine-Tuning Assignment Details

ESTIMATED TIME
30 min.

After completing this lesson, you will be able to:

✔ *Replace one resource with another resource for an assignment.*

✔ *Apply different cost rates for a resource assigned to different types of tasks.*

✔ *Delay the start of a resource assignment.*

✔ *Control how a resource's work on a task is scheduled over time by using work contours.*

✔ *Set up variable consumption rates for material resources.*

✔ *Create an assignment note.*

This lesson concludes the fine-tuning activities you started in Lesson 6, this time focusing on assignments of resources to tasks.

Practice files for the lesson

To complete this lesson, you will use a file named Short Film Project 08. Open the Part 2 folder in the MS Project 2000 SBS Practice folder on your hard disk. Open the file 08A, and save it without a baseline as Short Film Project 08 in the Part 2 folder.

Replacing a Resource Assignment

At any point in the life cycle of a project, you might need to replace one resource assigned to a task with another. Here are some reasons why you might need to do this:

■ The resource who was initially assigned to a task is not available, and you don't want to delay the start of the task.

■ You want to replace an expensive resource with a less expensive one.

■ You want to replace a less qualified resource with a more qualified one.

■ You want to manually resolve a resource overallocation. For example, if a resource was overallocated because of multiple assignments on a single day, you could replace him on one of his assigned tasks with another resource.

Replacing a resource is simpler than unassigning the first resource from a task and then assigning a different resource. With the Replace button in the Assign Resources dialog box, you can perform both actions in one step. You can replace both work and material resources. You can also adjust the resource's units value (or for a material resource, the material amount or consumption rate). You cannot, however, replace a work resource with a material resource, or vice versa.

In the film project, you want the director of photography to replace one of the camera operators on what you expect to be a tricky film shoot. In this exercise, you replace one resource with another on a task assignment.

1   On the Edit menu, click Go To.

2   In the ID box, enter **63** and then click OK.

Microsoft Project scrolls to Task 63, "Scene 8 shoot."

3   On the Standard toolbar, click Assign Resources.

The Assign Resources dialog box appears.

4   In the Assign Resources dialog box, scroll through the resource list until you see the name "Frank Lee," and then select the name.

The check mark next to Frank Lee's name indicates that he is currently assigned to Task 63.

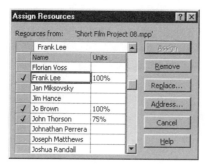

5   Click the Replace button.

The Replace Resource dialog box appears.

6   In the Replace Resource dialog box, select Jan Miksovsky, and then click OK.

Microsoft Project unassigns Frank Lee from this task and assigns Jan Miksovsky.

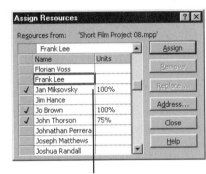

Here is the replacement resource assigned to the task.

Because you did not specify a different units value, Microsoft Project assigned the new resource at 100% units—the same units value at which the previous resource was assigned.

7   Click Close to close the Assign Resources dialog box.

tip
If you use either your e-mail program or Microsoft Project Central for project communication, you can quickly communicate assignment changes to the affected resources. For more information, see Appendix D, "Introducing the Workgroup Features ofMicrosoft Project."

Applying Different Cost Rates to Assignments

You might recall from Lesson 7 that you can set as many as five pay rates per resource. This allows you to apply different pay rates to different assignments for a resource, for example, depending on the skills required for each assignment. For each assignment, Microsoft Project initially uses Rate Table A by default, but you can specify when another rate table should be used.

In Lesson 7, you set up a second rate table for Jan Miksovsky to be applied for any assignments where she's functioning as a camera operator. In the previous section of this lesson, you assigned Jan to Task 63, "Scene 8 shoot," as a camera operator, but her assignment still reflects her default rate pay rate as director of photography. In this exercise, you change the pay rate table to be applied to Jan for her assignment to Task 63.

Resource Usage

Remember that Ctrl+G is a shortcut for displaying the Go To dialog box.

1   On the View bar, click Resource Usage.

The Resource Usage view appears.

2   On the Edit menu, click Go To, enter **17** in the ID box, and then click OK.

Microsoft Project scrolls the Resource Usage view to display Jan Miksovsky.

3   Click the plus sign next to Jan Miksovsky's name to display her individual assignments.

4   On the View menu, point to Table: Usage, and click Cost.

Microsoft Project displays the Cost Table.

In the Cost table you can see each assignment's total cost. To see other assignment cost values such as actual cost and variance, drag the vertical divider bar or scroll the table to the right.

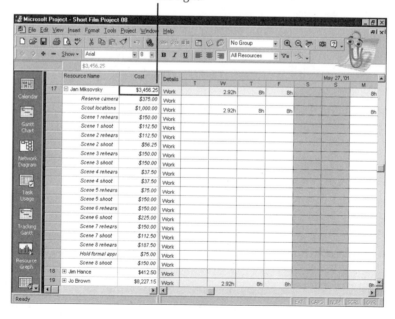

5 In the Resource Name column, select Jan Miksovsky's last assignment, "Scene 8 shoot."

Note the current cost of Jan's assignment to this task: $150.00.

6 On the Standard toolbar, click the Assignment Information button.

The Assignment Information dialog box appears.

7 If necessary, click the General tab.

8 In the Cost Rate Table box, type or select **B**, and then click OK to close the Assignment Information dialog box.

Microsoft Project applies Jan's Cost Rate Table B to the assignment. The new cost of the assignment, $112.00, appears in the Cost column.

Resource Name	Cost	Details	T	W	T	F	S	May 27, '01 S	M
17 ☐ Jan Miksovsky	$3,418.25	Work		2.92h	8h	8h			8h
Reserve camera	$375.00	Work							
Scout locations	$1,000.00	Work		2.92h	8h	8h			8h
Scene 1 rehears	$150.00	Work							
Scene 1 shoot	$112.50	Work							
Scene 2 rehears	$112.50	Work							
Scene 2 shoot	$56.25	Work							
Scene 3 rehears	$150.00	Work							
Scene 3 shoot	$150.00	Work							
Scene 4 rehears	$37.50	Work							
Scene 4 shoot	$37.50	Work							
Scene 5 rehears	$75.00	Work							
Scene 5 shoot	$150.00	Work							
Scene 6 rehears	$150.00	Work							
Scene 6 shoot	$225.00	Work							
Scene 7 rehears	$150.00	Work							
Scene 7 shoot	$112.50	Work							
Scene 8 rehears	$187.50	Work							
Hold formal appr	$75.00	Work							
Scene 8 shoot	$112.00	Work							
18 ☐ Jim Hance	$412.50	Work							

After you assign a different cost rate table to an assignment, Microsoft Project recalculates the total cost of the assignment.

tip

If you frequently change cost rate tables for assignments, you'll find it quicker to display the Cost Rate Table field directly in the Resource Usage or Task Usage view. Select a column heading and on the Insert menu, click Column. In the Field Name box, select Cost Rate Table from the drop-down list, and then click OK.

Fine-Tuning Assignment Details 8

Delaying the Start of Assignments

PROJ2000E-1-6

If more than one resource is assigned to a task, you might not want all of the resources to start working on the task at the same time. You can delay the start of work for one or more resources assigned to a task.

For example, let's say a task has four resources assigned. Three of the resources initially work on the task, and the fourth later inspects the quality of the work. The inspector should start work on the task later than the other resources.

> ## tip
> If you need to delay the start of all resources assigned to a task, rather than adjusting each resource's assignment, instead reschedule the start date of the task.

In this exercise, you delay the start of one resource's assignment on a task.

1   On the View bar, click Task Usage.

The Task Usage view appears. This view is similar to the Resource Usage view, except that assigned resources are listed under each task, rather than tasks being listed under resources.

2   On the Edit menu, click Go To, enter **84** in the ID box, and then click OK.

Microsoft Project displays the task, "Archive master film and audio tape."

	O	Task Name	Work	Details	T	F	S	S	M	T
84		⊟ Archive master film anc	20 hrs	Work		6.38h			13.62h	
		Doug Hampton	4 hrs	Work		1.28h			2.72h	
		Editing Lab	8 hrs	Work		2.55h			5.45h	
		Peter Kelly	8 hrs	Work		2.55h			5.45h	
85		⊟ Hand off masters to dis	8 hrs	Work					2.55h	5.45h
		Michael Patten	8 hrs	Work					2.55h	5.45h
				Work						

As you can see, this task currently has three resources (two people and the editing lab) assigned to it. You want to delay all of Doug Hampton's work on this task until Monday, December 10.

3   In the Task Name column, select the name of the resource Doug Hampton.

4   On the Standard toolbar, click the Assignment Information button.

The Assignment Information dialog box appears.

5   Click the General tab.

6 In the Start box, type or select **12/10/01**, and then click OK to close the Assignment Information dialog box.

	0	Task Name	Work	Details	T	F	S	Dec 9, '01 S	M	T	
84		⊟ Archive master film ar	20 hrs	Work		5.1h			14.9h		
		Doug Hampton	4 hrs	Work		0h			4h		
		Editing Lab	8 hrs	Work		2.55h			5.45h		
		Peter Kelly	8 hrs	Work		2.55h			5.45h		
85		⊟ Hand off masters to d	8 hrs	Work						8h	
		Michael Patter.	8 hrs	Work						8h	
				Work							

The start of this resource's work on this task is now delayed until Monday. The other assignments on the task are not affected.

Microsoft Project adjusts Doug Hampton's assignment on this task so that he works no hours on it Friday but four hours on it the following Monday. The other resources assigned to the task are not affected.

Applying Contours to Assignments

PROJ2000E-3-5

In the Resource Usage and Task Usage views, you can see exactly how long each resource is scheduled to work on each task. In addition to viewing assignment details, you can change the amount of time a resource works on a task in any given time period. There are two ways to do this:

■ Apply a predefined work **contour** to an assignment. Predefined contours generally describe how work is distributed over time in terms of graphical patterns. For example, the Bell predefined contour distributes less work to the beginning and end of the assignment, while distributing more work toward the middle. If you were to graph the work over time, the graph's shape would resemble a bell.

■ Directly edit the assignment details yourself. For example, in the Resource Usage or Task Usage view, you can change the assignment values directly in the timescaled grid.

How you contour or edit an assignment depends on what you need to accomplish. Predefined contours work best for assignments where you can predict a likely pattern of effort—a task that requires considerable ramp-up time might benefit from a back loaded contour, for example, to reflect the likelihood that the resource will be most productive toward the end of the assignment.

In this exercise, you apply a predefined contour to one task's assignments, and you manually edit another assignment.

1   On the Edit menu, click Go To, enter **79** in the ID box, and then click OK.

Microsoft Project scrolls to Task 79, "Record final narration." This task has four resources assigned to it.

	O	Task Name	Work	Details	T	W	T	F	S	Nov 4, '01 S
79		⊟ Record final narration	320 hrs	Work		32h	32h	32h		
		David Campbe	80 hrs	Work		8h	8h	8h		
		Michael Patten	80 hrs	Work		8h	8h	8h		
		Peter Kelly	80 hrs	Work		8h	8h	8h		
		Scott Cooper	80 hrs	Work		8h	8h	8h		

As you can see in the timescaled data at the right, all four resources are scheduled to work on this task at a regular rate of eight hours per day—that is, the assignments have a flat contour. This is the default work contour type Microsoft Project uses when scheduling work.

You want to change Michael Patten's assignment on this task so that, while the other assigned resources work full-time, he starts with a brief daily assignment and increases his work time as the task progresses. He should continue working on the task after the other resources have finished their assignments. To accomplish this, you will apply a back loaded contour to the assignment.

2   In the Task Name column, select Michael Patten, the second resource assigned to Task 79.

3   On the Standard toolbar, click the Assignment Information button.

Microsoft Project displays the Assignment Information dialog box.

4   Click the General tab.

5   In the Work Contour box, select Back Loaded, and then click OK to close the Assignment Information dialog box.

Microsoft Project applies the contour to this resource's assignment and reschedules his work on the task.

This indicator graphically represents the type of contour applied—in this case, a back loaded contour.

O	Task Name	Work	Details	T	W	T	F	S	Nov 4, '01 S	
79	⊟ Record final narration	320 hrs	Work		24.8h	24.93h	25.2h			
	David Campbe	80 hrs	Work		8h	8h	8h			
	Michael Patter	80 hrs	Work		0.8h	0.93h	1.2h			
	Peter Kelly	80 hrs	Work		8h	8h	8h			
	Scott Cooper	80 hrs	Work		8h	8h	8h			

A back loaded contour gives the resources a very short daily assignment initially, and gradually increases the daily time on the assignment.

If you scroll the timescaled data to the right, you see that, in each successive day of the task's duration, Michael Patten is assigned slightly more time to work on the assignment. You also see a contour indicator in the Indicators column, showing the type of contour that is applied to the assignment.

6 Point to the indicator.

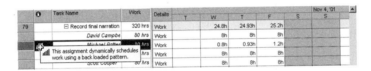

O	Task Name	Work	Details	T	W	T	F	S	Nov 4, '01 S	
79	⊟ Record final narration	320 hrs	Work		24.8h	24.93h	25.2h			
	David Campbe	80 hrs	Work		8h	8h	8h			
	Michael Patter		Work		0.8h	0.93h	1.2h			
	This assignment dynamically schedules work using a back loaded pattern.	hrs	Work		8h	8h	8h			
	Scott Cooper	80 hrs	Work		8h	8h	8h			

Microsoft Project displays a ToolTip describing the type of contour applied to this assignment.

tip

Applying a contour to this assignment caused the overall duration of the task to be extended. If you do not want a contour to extend a task's duration, change the task type to Fixed Duration before applying the contour. Applying a contour after changing the task type will cause Microsoft Project to recalculate the resource's work value so they work less in the same time period. For more information about task types, see "Changing Task Types" in Lesson 6.

Because Michael Patten's assignment to this task finishes later than the assignments of the other resources, Michael Patten determines the finish date of the task. One common way to phrase this is that Michael Patten is the driving resource of this task; his assignment determines, or drives, the finish date of the task.

Next you directly edit another task's assignment values.

7   On the Edit menu, click Go To, enter **2** in the ID box, type or select **4/9/01** in the Date box, and then click OK.

Microsoft Project scrolls vertically to Task 2, "Review script," and horizontally to display the last week of this task.

	❶	Task Name	Work	Details	Apr 8, '01 S	M	T	W	T	F
2		⊟ Review script	80 hrs	Work		8h	8h	8h	8h	8h
		Clair Hector	40 hrs	Work		4h	4h	4h	4h	4h
		Scott Cooper	40 hrs	Work		4h	4h	4h	4h	4h

You want to change the two resources' assignments on the last few days of this task so that they will work full time on it. To accomplish this, you will manually edit their assignment values.

8   Select Clair Hector's four-hour assignment for Tuesday, 4/10/01.

9   Type **8h** and then press the Enter key.

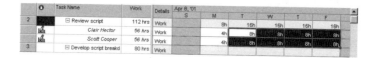

The fill handle is the small square in the lower right corner of the active cell.

10   Reselect the same assignment on Tuesday and drag the **fill handle** to the right through Friday's assignment.

This indicator means that this assignment has been manually edited.

	❶	Task Name	Work	Details	Apr 8, '01 S	M	T	W	T	F
2		⊟ Review script	96 hrs	Work		8h	12h	12h	12h	12h
		Clair Hector	56 hrs	Work		4h	8h	8h	8h	8h
		Scott Cooper	40 hrs	Work		4h	4h	4h	4h	4h

Use the fill handle to quickly copy a value from one cell to adjacent cells.

11   Drag the fill handle down one row, through Scott Cooper's assignments on Tuesday through Friday.

	❶	Task Name	Work	Details	Apr 8, '01 S	M	T	W	T	F
2		⊟ Review script	112 hrs	Work		8h	16h	16h	16h	16h
		Clair Hector	56 hrs	Work		4h	8h	8h	8h	8h
		Scott Cooper	56 hrs	Work		4h	8h	8h	8h	8h
3		⊟ Develop script breakd	80 hrs	Work						

Now both resources are assigned eight hours each on these days.

Entering Material Resource Consumption Rates

PROJ2000E-3-2

For a demonstration of fixed and variable material resource consumption rates, double-click Material Resource in the Multimedia folder on the Microsoft Project 2000 Step by Step CD-ROM.

In Lesson 4, you assigned one **material resource**—16 mm film—to a task. This assignment specified a fixed amount, or **fixed consumption rate**, of the material resource. Another way to use material resources is to assign them with a **variable consumption rate**. Here's the difference between the two rates:

- A fixed consumption rate means that, regardless of the duration of the task to which the material resource is assigned, an absolute quantity of the resource will be used. For example, pouring concrete for a house foundation requires a fixed amount of concrete, no matter how long it takes to pour it.

- A variable consumption rate means that the quantity of the material resource consumed depends upon the duration of the task. When shooting film, for example, you'll shoot more film in four hours than in two, and you can determine an hourly rate at which you shoot (or consume) film. After you enter a variable consumption rate for a material resource's assignment, Microsoft Project calculates the total quantity of the material resource consumed, based on the task's duration. The advantage of using a variable rate of consumption is that it's tied to the task's duration. If the duration changes, so too does the calculated quantity and cost of the material resource.

In either case, after you enter a standard pay rate for one unit of the material resource, Microsoft Project calculates the total cost of the assignment. For example, in Lesson 4, you specified that one foot of 16 mm film costs $.20 to purchase and process.

In this exercise, you enter an hourly variable consumption rate for each film shoot task. You've determined that the initial estimates of film consumption were too large. Now you'll use the following estimates: two cameras will consume, on the average, 1080 feet of film per hour, and three cameras will consume 1620 feet of film per hour.

1   On the View bar, click Resource Usage.

2   Click the plus sign next to the name of Resource 2, "16 mm Film," to display its assignments.

3   On the Window menu, click Split.

Microsoft Project displays the Resource Form below the Resource Usage view. Note that you can enter material resource consumption rates in the Assign Resources dialog box or in any view in which you can assign resources. You'll use the split view here because you'll change several assignments at once.

4   Click anywhere in the Resource Form. On the Format menu, point to Details, and then click Cost.

Microsoft Project now displays cost details in the Resource Form.

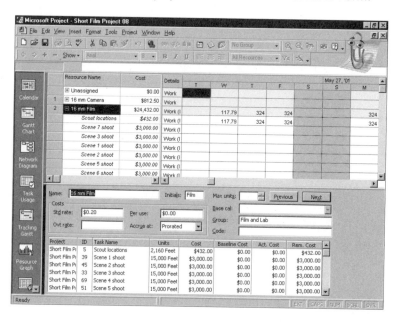

Here you can see the Units values for all of the 16 mm film's assignments.

5   In the Units column of the Resource Form, enter the following values.

Task Name	Units
Scene 1 Shoot	1620/h
Scene 2 Shoot	1080/h
Scene 3 Shoot	1080/h
Scene 4 Shoot	1080/h
Scene 5 Shoot	1080/h
Scene 6 Shoot	1620/h
Scene 7 Shoot	1620/h
Scene 8 Shoot	1080/h

6   Click OK in the Resource Form.

Microsoft Project recalculates the cost values of the material resource assignments based on the duration of each task to which it is assigned.

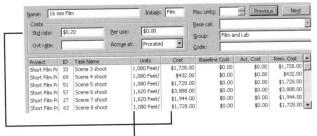

Microsoft Project calculates the cost per assignment for material resources as the standard cost rate (in dollars per unit, in this case feet) times the variable rate of consumption (in units per hour) times the duration of the task (in hours).

7   On the Window menu, click Remove Split.

8   In the Resource Usage view, click the minus sign next to Resource 2, "16 mm Film," to hide its assignments.

9   Scroll the timescaled data to the right through the month of July.

You can see the total calculated quantity of film (measured in feet) needed for each day's shooting starting in July. This is the product of the duration of each task to which the material resource is assigned multiplied by the variable consumption rate.

Comparing work and material resources

Following are some ways material resources are similar to and different from work resources.

For both material and work resources, you can edit and contour resource assignments, set up multiple pay rates, specify different pay rates to apply at different times, and share resources through a resource pool. (For more information on resource pools, see Lesson 13.) In addition, cost calculations for material resources work just about the same way as they do for work resources.

Unlike work resources, however, material resources do not use the following: overtime cost rates, resource calendars, or maximum units. Also, material resources are not affected by resource leveling, and they have no effect on a task's duration if effort-driven scheduling is enabled.

Fine-Tuning Assignment Details

Documenting Assignment Details in Assignment Notes

You might recall from Lessons 6 and 7 that you can record additional information that might be useful about a task, resource, or assignment in a **note**. For example, if you've edited resource assignments, it's a good idea to record why in a note. Notes reside in the Microsoft Project file, and they can be easily viewed or printed.

In this exercise, you enter resource notes to document why resource assignments have been edited.

1 On the View menu, point to Table: Cost, and then select Entry.

Microsoft Project displays the Entry Table, which includes the Indicators column.

2 On the Edit menu, click Go To, enter **17** in the ID box, and then click OK.

Microsoft Project displays Resource 17, "Jan Miksovsky."

3 Select her assignment, "Scene 8 shoot."

4 On the Standard toolbar, click the Assignment Notes button.

Microsoft Project displays the Assignment Information dialog box with the Notes tab visible.

5 In the Notes box, type **Scene 8's camera work will be especially tricky, so Jan will run the main camera**, and then click OK.

A note icon appears in the Indicators column.

6 Point to the note icon.

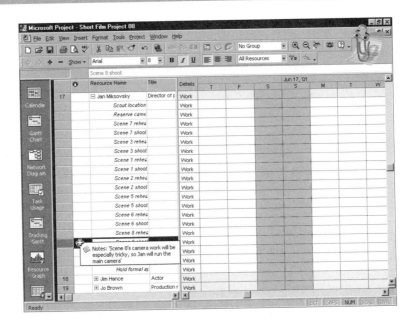

The note appears in a ToolTip. For notes that are too long to appear in a ToolTip, you can double-click the note icon to display the full text of the note.

This lesson concludes the "fine-tuning" portion of the project planning phase. Project planning—that is, all project management work up to the point when actual work on the project commences—might occupy the majority of a project manager's time. In fact, many project managers do nothing but project planning. In the next several lessons, we'll focus on viewing, formatting, and communicating the project plan.

Lesson Wrap-Up

This lesson covered how to apply a variety of important assignment-related tools after creating your initial project plan but before tracking actual work.

If you are going on to other lessons:

1 On the Standard toolbar, click Save to save changes made to Short Film Project 08. Save the file without a baseline.

2 On the File menu, click Close to close the file.

If you aren't continuing to other lessons:

● On the File menu, click Exit.

Glossary

Contour How a resource's work on a task is scheduled over time. Microsoft Project includes several predefined work contours that you can apply to an assignment. For example, a back loaded contour indicator schedules a small amount of work initially, then schedules increasing amounts of work as time progresses. You can also manually contour an assignment by editing work values in a usage view, such as the Resource Usage view. Applying a predefined contour or manually contouring an assignment causes Microsoft Project to display a work contour icon in the Indicators column.

Fill handle The small square in the lower right corner of the active cell in most table and usage views in Microsoft Project. Drag the fill handle in any direction to copy the value in the active cell to adjacent cells.

Fixed consumption rate A fixed quantity of a material resource to be consumed in the completion of an assignment. See also variable consumption rate.

Material resource Consumables that are used up as the project progresses. Like work resources, material resources are assigned to tasks, but they have no effect on the total amount of work scheduled to be performed on a task.

Note Any information (including linked or embedded files) that you wish to associate with a task, resource, or assignment.

Variable consumption rate A quantity of a material resource to be consumed that will change if the duration of the task to which it is assigned changes. See also fixed consumption rate.

Quick Reference

To replace a resource assignment

Gantt
Chart

1   On the View bar, click Gantt Chart.

2   In the Task Name column, select the task for which you want to replace a resource assignment.

3   On the Standard toolbar, click Assign Resources.

4   In the Name column of the Assign Resources dialog box, select the name of the resource you want to replace.

5   Click the Replace button.

6   In the Replace Resources dialog box, select the name of the replacement resource you want, and then click OK to close the Replace Resources dialog box.

7   Click Close to close the Assign Resources dialog box.

To apply a different cost rate to an assignment

1   On the View bar, click Resource Usage.

    -Or-

    On the View bar, click Task Usage.

2   Click the assignment for which you want to apply a different cost rate table.

3   On the Standard toolbar, click the Assignment Information button.

    The Assignment Information dialog box appears.

4   If the General tab is not visible, click the General tab.

5   In the Cost Rate Table box, type or select the rate table you want to apply to this assignment, and then click OK to close the Assignment Information dialog box.

To delay the start of an assignment

1   On the View bar, click Task Usage.

2   In the Task Name column, select the resource under the task for which you want to delay the start of an assignment.

3   On the Standard toolbar, click the Assignment Information button.

    The Assignment Information dialog box appears.

4   If the General tab is not visible, click the General tab.

5   In the Start box, type or select the date on which you want the selected resource to start work on this assignment, and then click OK to close the Assignment Information dialog box.

To apply a contour to an assignment

1   On the View bar, click Task Usage.

2   In the Task Name column, select the resource under the task for which you want to apply a contour to an assignment.

3   On the Standard toolbar, click the Assignment Information button.

    The Assignment Information dialog box appears.

4   If the General tab is not visible, click the General tab.

5   In the Work Contour box, select the contour you want, and then click OK to close the Assignment Information dialog box.

Gantt
Chart

To enter a fixed or variable material resource consumption rate

1   On the View bar, click Gantt Chart.

2   In the Task Name column, select the task to which you want to assign the material resource.

3   On the Standard toolbar, click Assign Resources.

4   In the Name column of the Assign Resources dialog box, select the name of the material resource you want to assign.

5   To assign a fixed consumption rate, in the Units field, type the quantity of the material resource to be consumed.

-Or-

To assign a variable consumption rate, in the Units field, type a quantity of the material resource to be consumed per time period. For example, if the task will consume 600 feet of film per hour, type **600/h**.

6   Click Assign.

To create an assignment note

1   On the View bar, click Resource Usage.

-Or-

On the View bar, click Task Usage.

2   Click the assignment for which you want to enter a note.

3   On the Standard toolbar, click the Assignment Notes button.

4   In the Assignment Information dialog box, type the note you want to associate with this assignment.

Review & Practice

You will review and practice how to:

✔ *Change working times for the entire project and for individual resources.*

✔ *Enter standard and overtime pay rates for resources.*

✔ *Enter or change task details such as deadline dates, lead time, duration, and task relationships.*

✔ *Identify and correct resource overallocations.*

ESTIMATED TIME
10 min.

Before you move on to Part 3, which covers various ways of sharing Microsoft Project information, you can practice the skills you learned in Part 2 by working through this Review & Practice section.

Scenario

Leonard Zuvela, manager of the band Fourth Coffee, liked the initial project plan for producing a music video. However, he's asked you to fine-tune some information to get a more accurate plan. He's also provided you with some time and cost constraints you'll have to meet for your film company, Industrial Smoke and Mirrors, to be awarded the project.

Practice files for the lesson

To complete this section, you will use a file named Music Video Project 2. Before you begin this section, open the Part 2 folder in the MS Project 2000 SBS Practice folder on your hard disk. Open the file Part2A, and save it without a baseline as Music Video Project 2 in the Part 2 folder.

For a demonstration of how to complete this step, double-click Part 2 Step 1 in the Multimedia folder on the Microsoft Project 2000 Step by Step CD-ROM.

You must complete the exercises in steps 1 through 4 sequentially.

Step 1: Change the Working Times

You know the approximate timeframe in which the music video must be produced, so you can enter some working time adjustments now. You can also fine-tune some of the individual resource assignments.

1   View the working time settings for the Standard project calendar.

2   Make May 10 and 11, 2001, nonworking time for the entire project.

3   Leonard Zuvela has informed you that the band members will not be available to work on this project during the week of May 6, 2001. Make these nonworking days for the resource named "Talent."

4   Locate Task 5, "Rehearsal" in the Task Usage view. View its timescaled work values.

5   Manually contour the Production Staff's assignment to the task "Rehearsal" so they are assigned to work 8 hours per day for each of the three days of the task's duration.

For more information about	See
Setting working time for the project	Lesson 6
Setting working time for a resource	Lesson 7
The Task Usage view	Lesson 8
Contouring resource assignments	Lesson 8

Step 2: Enter Resource Costs

For a demonstration, double-click Part 2 Step 2 in the Multimedia folder.

Although you don't plan to fill most of the resource positions on this project for some time, you can start putting together a project budget based on prevailing pay rates for various types of resources. Based on past projects and current advertised rates, you have good estimates of resource pay rates for all of the resources required for the music video. The Talent resource, members of the band Fourth Coffee, will not be paid out of your project budget, so for your purposes their cost to the project is zero.

1   Switch to the Resource Sheet view.

2   Enter the following resource cost information:

Resource Name	Standard Rate	Overtime Rate
Camera Operator	$22/hour	$33/hour
Choreographer	$300/day	(leave at zero)
Director	$1,400/week	(leave at zero)
Editor	$45/hour	$67.50/hour
Producer	$1,600/week	(leave at zero)
Production Staff	$20/hour	$30/hour
Sound Engineer	$800/week	(leave at zero)
Talent	(leave at zero)	(leave at zero)

3   In the Resource Sheet view, switch to a table that shows you total costs per resource.

For more information about	See
Setting resource pay rates	Lesson 7
Viewing resource costs	Lesson 7

Step 3: Fine-tune Task Details

For a demonstration, double-click Part 2 Step 3 in the Multimedia folder.

Leonard Zuvela, the manager of the band Fourth Coffee, has provided some constraints that you must meet to get the music video project. The first constraint is that final video must be available no later than Monday, July 2, 2001.

1   In the Gantt Chart view, enter a deadline for the milestone Task 11, "Hand off final video" of July 2, 2001.

2   Enter a three day lead between Task 9, "Add final music" and its predecessor Task 8, "Fine cut edit."

3   Change the duration of the task "Develop choreography" from 3 weeks to 12 days.

4   Change the task relationship between Task 9, "Add final music" and Task 10, "Clone dubbing master" to Finish-to-Finish.

For more information about	See
Entering deadline dates	Lesson 6
Setting lead time for tasks	Lesson 6
Changing a task's duration	Lesson 6
Changing task relationships	Lesson 6

Step 4: Improve Resource Usage

For a demonstration, double-click Part 2 Step 4 in the Multimedia folder.

The second constraint Leonard Zuvela gave you is that the total cost of the music video project (excluding equipment and supplies) cannot exceed $30,000. Also, as a good project manager, you want to ensure that none of your resources are assigned more work than they can handle.

1 Switch to the Resource Usage view. Locate the resources that are overallocated.

2 Level resources on a day-by-day basis.

3 Switch to the Leveling Gantt view.

4 View the effect on the project's finish date.

For more information about	See
The Resource Usage view	Lesson 7
The Leveling Gantt view	Lesson 7
Resolving resource overallocations by leveling	Lesson 7

Finish the Review & Practice

If you are going on to Part 3:

1 On the Standard toolbar, click Save to save changes made to Music Project Video 2. Save the file without a baseline.

2 On the File menu, click Close to close the file.

If you aren't continuing to Part 3:

● On the File menu, click Exit.

9

Getting Project Information to Look the Way You Want

ESTIMATED TIME
40 min.

After completing this lesson, you will be able to:

✔ *Sort task and resource data.*

✔ *Display task and resource data in groups.*

✔ *Filter or highlight task and resource data.*

✔ *Create a custom table and a custom view.*

✔ *Format the Gantt Chart, the Network Diagram, and the Calendar view.*

In this lesson, you use some of the many formatting tools in Microsoft Project to change the way your data appears. Microsoft Project includes powerful features that allow you to organize and analyze data that otherwise would require such separate tools as a spreadsheet application.

Practice files for the lesson

To complete this lesson, you use a file named Short Film Project 09. This is the completed project plan you developed in Parts 1 and 2. Before you begin this lesson, open the Part 3 folder in the MS Project 2000 SBS Practice folder on your hard disk. Open the file 09A, and save it without a baseline as Short Film Project 09 in the Part 3 folder.

Sorting Data in a View

Sorting is the simplest way to reorganize task or resource data in Microsoft Project. You can sort tasks or resources by predefined criteria, or you can create your own sort order with up to three levels of nesting. For example, you can sort resources by resource group and then sort by cost within each resource group.

PROJ2000-5-6

Like grouping and filtering, which you will work with in later sections, sorting does not (with one exception) change the underlying data of your project plan; it simply reorders the data you have. The one exception is the option it offers to renumber task or resource IDs after sorting. Once tasks or resources are renumbered, you cannot restore their original numbered sequence.

However, it's fine to permanently renumber tasks or resources if that's what you intend to do. For example, when building a resource list, you might enter resource names in the order in which the resources join your project. Later, when the list is complete, you might want to sort them alphabetically by name and permanently renumber them. Once this is done, the resource names will appear in alphabetical order in the Assign Resources dialog box and in resource views.

In planning your project's budget, you'd like to see all resources sorted by resource group. Further, within each group, resources should be sorted by cost from most to least expensive. In this exercise, you sort a resource view to see the data arranged this way.

tip

The Permanently Renumber Tasks (or when in a resource view, the Permanently Renumber Resources) check box in the Sort dialog box is a Microsoft Project–level setting; if checked, it permanently renumbers tasks or resources in any Microsoft Project file in which you sort. Because you might not want to permanently renumber tasks or resources every time you sort, it's a good idea to clear this check box.

1   On the View bar, click Resource Sheet.

The Resource Sheet view appears. By default, the Entry table appears in the Resource Sheet view; however, the Entry table does not display the cost field per resource. You will switch to the Summary instead.

2   On the View menu, point to Table: Entry, and then click Summary.

The Summary table appears. Your screen should look similar to the following illustration.

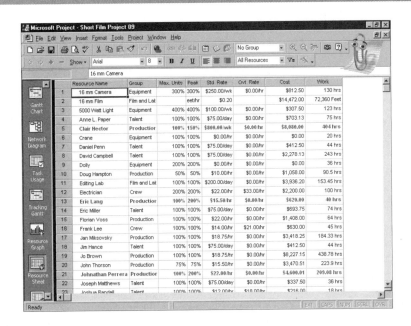

Now you are ready to sort the Resource Sheet view.

3 On the Project menu, point to Sort, and click Sort By.

The Sort dialog box appears

4 Under Sort By, select Cost from the drop-down list, and next to that click Descending.

5 Make sure that the Permanently Renumber Resources check box is cleared.

6 Make sure that the Sort Resources By Project check box is selected.

7 Check Sort.

The summary table in the Resource Sheet view is sorted by the Cost column, in descending order. Your screen should look similar to the following illustration.

The Resource Sheet view
is now sorted by cost, in
descending order.

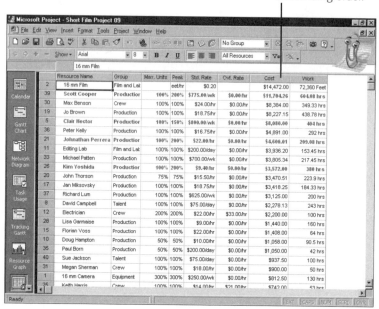

This arrangement is fine for looking at resource costs for the entire project, but you'd like to see this data organized by resource group. To see this, you'll apply a two-level sort order.

tip

When you sort data, the sort order applies to the active view, regardless of the specific table currently displayed in the view. For example, if you sort the Gantt Chart view by start date while displaying the Entry table and then switch to the Cost table, you'll see the tasks sorted by start date.

8   On the Project menu, point to Sort, and then click Sort By.

The Sort dialog box appears, in which you can apply up to three nested levels of sort criteria.

9   Under Sort By, select Group from the drop-down list, and next to that click Ascending.

10   Under Then By (in the center of the dialog box), select Cost from the drop-down list, and next to that click Descending.

11 Make sure that the Permanently Renumber Resources check box is cleared. The Sort Resources By Project check box should be selected.

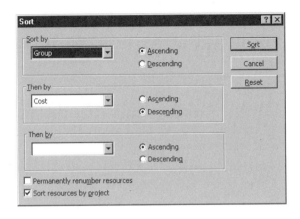

12 Click Sort.

Microsoft Project sorts the Resource Sheet view to display resources by group and then by cost within each group. Your screen should look similar to the following illustration.

Now the Resource Sheet view is sorted first by resource group, and within each group by cost.

This is an easy way to identify the most expensive resources in each functional group working on the short film project.

To conclude this exercise, re-sort the resource information to return it to its original order.

13 On the Project menu, point to Sort, and then click By ID.

Microsoft Project re-sorts the resource list by resource ID.

Note that there is no visual indicator that a task or resource view has been sorted other than the order in which the rows of data appear. Unlike grouping and filtering, you cannot save custom sort settings that you have specified. However, the sort order you most recently specified will remain in effect until you re-sort the view.

Grouping Data in a View

PROJ2000-5-3,
PROJ2000-5-4,
PROJ2000-5-11,
PROJ2000E-7-2

As you develop a project plan, the default views available in Microsoft Project give you several ways of viewing and analyzing your data. One important feature you can apply to task and resource views is **grouping**. Grouping allows you to organize task or resource information according to criteria you choose. For example, rather than viewing the task list in the Gantt Chart view sorted by task ID, you can view it sorted by task duration. Grouping goes a step beyond just sorting, however. Grouping adds summary values, or "roll-ups," at intervals that you can customize. For example, you can group resources by their cost with a $1000 interval between groups.

> **tip**
> In some respects, grouping in Microsoft Project is similar to the Subtotals feature in Microsoft Excel. In fact, grouping allows you to reorganize and analyze your Microsoft Project data in ways that previously would have required you to export your Microsoft Project data to a spreadsheet program.

Grouping can significantly change the way you view your task or resource data, allowing for a more refined level of data analysis and presentation. Grouping doesn't change the underlying structure of your project plan, however; it simply reorganizes and summarizes the data. As with sorting, when you group data in a view, the grouping applies to all tables you can display in the view.

Microsoft Project includes several predefined task and resource groups, such as grouping tasks by duration or resources by standard pay rate. You can also customize any of the built-in groups or create your own.

In this exercise, you group by Resource Group and show summary costs. This is similar to the sorting you did in the previous section but you're adding summary cost values.

1   On the Project menu, point to Group By: No Group, and then click Resource Group.

Microsoft Project reorganizes the resource data into resource groups, adds summary cost values per group, and presents the data in an expanded outline form. Your screen should look similar to the following illustration.

After grouping by the Resource Group field, Microsoft Project adds summary values per group. The summary values are formatted in yellow.

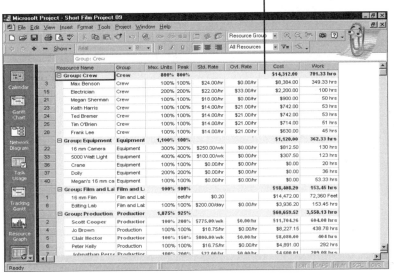

Microsoft Project applies colored formatting to the summary data rows, in this case, a yellow background. Because the summary data is derived from subordinate data, you cannot edit it directly. Displaying these summary values has no effect on the cost or schedule calculations of the project plan.

This arrangement of the resource cost information is similar to the sorting you did in the previous section. However, you'd like to have more control over how Microsoft Project organizes and presents the data. To accomplish this, you create a group.

2   On the Project menu, point to Group By: Resource Group, and then click More Groups.

The More Groups dialog box appears. In it, you can see all of the predefined groups for tasks and resources available to you. Your new group will be most similar to the Resource Group, so you'll start by copying it.

3   Ensure Resource Group is selected, and then click Copy.

The Group Definition dialog box appears.

4   In the Name box, type **Resource Groups by Cost**.

5   In the Field Name column, click the first empty cell below "Group."

6   Type or select **Cost**.

7   In the Order column, select Descending for the Cost field name.

The resources will be sorted within their groups by cost from highest to lowest values.

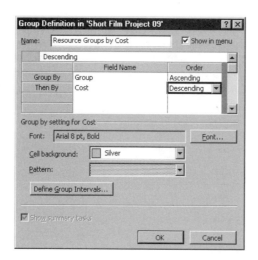

Next you'll fine-tune the cost intervals at which Microsoft Project will group the resources.

8   Click the Define Group Intervals button.

The Define Group Interval dialog box appears.

9   In the Group On box, select Interval.

10 In the Group Interval box, type **1000**, and then click OK.

11 Click OK again to close the Group Definition dialog box.

Resource Groups By Cost appears as a new group in the More Groups dialog box.

12 Click Apply.

Microsoft Project applies the new group to the Resource Sheet view. Your screen should look similar to the following illustration.

After applying a two-level group, information is grouped first by Resource Group and within each group by Cost.

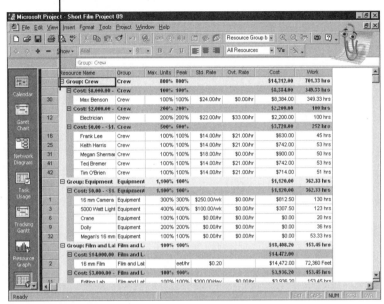

The resources are grouped by their group value (the yellow bands) and within each group by cost values at $1000 intervals (the gray bands).

To conclude this exercise, you remove the grouping.

13 On the Project menu, point to Group By: Resource Groups By Cost, and select No Group.

Microsoft Project removes the summary values and outline structure, leaving the original data. Displaying or removing a group has no effect on the subordinate data.

tip

All predefined groups and any groups you create are available to you through the Group By button on the Standard toolbar. The name of the active group appears on this button, which resembles a box with a drop-down list. Click the arrow in the Group By button to see other group names. If no group is applied to the current table, "No Group" appears on the button.

Use custom outline codes for more sophisticated needs

In complex projects, you might not find the work breakdown structure (WBS) or standard outline numbering schemes available in Microsoft Project adequate for your reporting or analysis needs. If this is the case, investigate Microsoft Project's capabilities to handle custom outline codes to identify a hierarchy within a project plan.

For example, you can define a custom outline code that associates different outline levels (or nested phases, subphases, and tasks) of a project plan with different levels of the organization's structure. The top level might be a division, the next lower level a business unit, and the third level a functional team. This results in the more informative outline code of "Promotionals-Commercial-Film Crew," for example. Alternatively, you could use custom outline codes to associate different outline levels of a project plan with different internal accounting or job tracking codes. If you can represent a hierarchy of any type as strings of numbers and letters, you can represent that hierarchy in your project plan through custom outline codes.

Once you've applied a custom outline code to your project plan, you can then group, sort, and filter tasks or resources by their outline codes. You can apply up to ten levels of a custom outline code for tasks and ten for resources in a single Microsoft Project file. To learn more about custom outline codes, ask the Office Assistant, "Tell me about custom outline codes."

Filtering Data in a View

PROJ2000-5-2,
PROJ2000-5-7,
PROJ2000-5-12

Another useful feature for changing the way you view Microsoft Project task and resource information is **filtering**. As the name suggests, filtering hides task or resource data that does not meet the criteria you specify, displaying only the data you're interested in. Like grouping, filtering does not change the data in your Microsoft Project file, only how it appears.

There are two ways to use filters: apply predefined filters to a view, or apply an **AutoFilter** to a view.

■ Apply a predefined or custom filter to see or highlight just the task or resource information that meets the criteria of the filter. For example, the Critical Task filter displays only the tasks that are critical. Some predefined filters, such as the Task Range filter, prompt you to enter specific criteria, for example, a range of task IDs.

▨ Use AutoFilters for more ad hoc filtering in any table in Microsoft Project. When the AutoFilter feature is turned on, small arrows appear next to the names of column headings. Clicking the arrow displays a list of criteria by which you can filter the data. The criteria you see depends on the type of data contained in the column—for example, AutoFilter criteria in a date column includes choices like "Today," "This month," as well as a "Custom" option with which you can specify your own criteria. You use AutoFilter in Microsoft Project in the same way you might use AutoFilter in Microsoft Excel.

Both types of filters hide rows in task or resource sheet views that do not meet the criteria you specify (or, if you prefer, highlight those that do). If a task or resource sheet view has a filter applied, the filter name appears in the Filter button on the Formatting toolbar. You might see gaps in the task or resource ID numbers. The "missing" data is only hidden and not deleted. As with sorting and grouping, when you filter data in a view, the filtering applies to all tables you can display in the view.

A commonly used format for communicating schedule information on a film project is called a shooting schedule. In this exercise, you create a filter that displays only the uncompleted film shoot tasks. In later sections, you'll combine this filter with a custom table and a custom view to create a complete shooting schedule that will inform everyone on the film project.

1   On the View bar, click Gantt Chart.

The Gantt Chart view appears. Before you create a filter, you can quickly see the tasks you're interested in by applying an AutoFilter.

2   On the Formatting toolbar, click the AutoFilter button.

Microsoft Project displays arrows to the right of the column headings. Your screen should look like the following illustration.

After turning on AutoFilters, these arrows appear next to column headings. Click them to choose the AutoFilter you want.

3   Click the down arrow in the Task Name column heading, and then select (Custom).

The Custom AutoFilter dialog box appears. You'd like to see just the tasks that contain the word "shoot."

4   Under Name, make sure "Contains" appears in the first box.

5   In the adjacent box, type **shoot**.

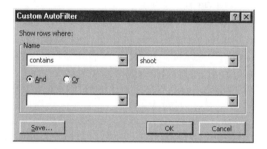

6   Click OK to close the Custom AutoFilter dialog box.

Microsoft Project filters the task list to show only the tasks that contain the word "shoot," and their summary tasks. Your screen should look similar to the following illustration.

After applying an AutoFilter, the filtered column name and its AutoFilter arrow are formatted in blue.

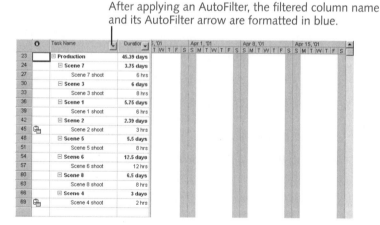

Note the blue formatting of the Task Name column heading and arrow. These are visual indicators that an AutoFilter has been applied to this view.

Next you turn off the AutoFilter and create a custom filter.

7   On the Formatting toolbar, click the AutoFilter button.

Microsoft Project toggles the AutoFilter off, redisplaying all tasks in the project. Now you are ready to create a custom filter.

8   On the Project menu, point to Filtered For: All Tasks and then click More Filters.

The More Filters dialog box appears. In it, you can see all of the predefined filters for tasks (when in a task view) and resources (when in a resource view) available to you.

9   Click the New button.

The Filter Definition dialog box appears.

10   In the Name box, type **Uncompleted Shoots**.

11   In the first row in the Field Name column, type or select **Name**.

12   In the first row in the Test column, type or select **contains**.

13   In the first row in the Value(s) column, type **shoot**.

That covers the first criterion for the filter; next you'll add the second criterion.

14   In the second row in the And/Or column, type or select **And**.

15   In the second row in the Field Name column, type or select **Actual Finish**.

16   In the second row in the Test column, type or select **equals**.

17   In the second row in the Value(s) column, type **NA**. This means "not applicable" and is the way Microsoft Project marks some fields that have no value yet. In other words, any shooting task that does not have an actual finish date must be uncompleted.

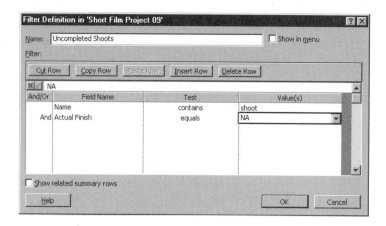

18   Click OK to close the Filter Definition dialog box.

The new filter appears in the More Filters dialog box.

19   Click Apply.

Microsoft Project applies the new filter to the Gantt Chart view. Your screen should look similar to the following illustration.

After applying a filter, Microsoft Project hides information that does not meet the filter's criteria. Note the gaps in the task IDs; this is one visual clue that a filter has been applied.

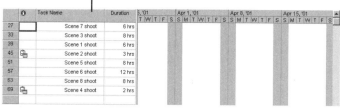

Now the tasks are filtered to show only the uncompleted shooting tasks. Because we haven't started tracking actual work yet, all of the shooting tasks are uncompleted at this time.

tip

Rather than hiding tasks that do not meet the filter criteria, you can highlight those that do in blue formatting without hiding the tasks that do not. Click the Highlight button instead of the Apply button in the More Filters dialog box.

To conclude this exercise, you will remove the filtering.

20   On the Project menu, point to Filtered For: Uncompleted Shoots, and then click All Tasks.

Microsoft Project removes the filter. As always, displaying or removing a filter has no effect on the original data.

tip

All filters are also available to you in the Filter button on the Formatting toolbar. The name of the active filter appears in this button; click the arrow next to the filter name to see other filters. If no filter is applied to the current view, "All Tasks" or "All Resources" appears on the button, depending on the type of view currently displayed.

Editing and Creating Tables

PROJ2000-5-8

As you might recall from Lesson 2, a table is a spreadsheet-like presentation of project data, organized into vertical columns and horizontal rows. Each column represents one of the many fields in Microsoft Project, and each row represents a single task or resource. The intersection of a column and a row can be called a cell (for those of you more oriented towards spreadsheets) or a field (for those of you who think in database terms).

Microsoft Project includes 15 predefined task tables and 10 resource tables that can be applied in views. You've already used several of these tables, such as the Entry table and the Summary table. Chances are that these tables will contain the fields you want most of the time. However, you can modify any predefined table, or you can create your own table with just the data you want.

In this exercise, you create a table to display the information found on a shooting schedule, a common format for presenting schedule information in film projects.

1   On the View menu, click More Views.

The More Views dialog box appears.

2   Select Task Sheet, and then click Apply.

Microsoft Project displays the Task Sheet view. This view does not include the chart portion of the Gantt Chart view, so it's easier to see more columns in the active table. Your screen should look similar to the following illustration.

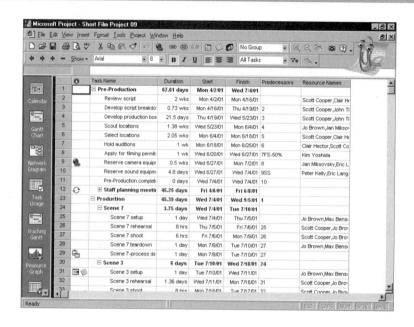

3 On the View menu, point to Table: Entry, and then click More Tables.

The More Tables dialog box appears. Based on the type of view (task or re-source) currently displayed, you can see all of the predefined tables for tasks or resources available to you.

4 Ensure that Task is the active option and that Entry is the selected table, and then click Copy.

The Table Definition dialog box appears.

5 In the Name box, type **Shooting Schedule Table**.

Next you will remove several fields, add others, and then put the remaining fields in the order you want.

6 In the Field Name column, select each of the following field names and then click Delete Row after selecting each field name:

Indicators

Duration

Finish

Predecessors

Resource Names

After you've deleted these fields, your screen should look similar to the fol-lowing illustration.

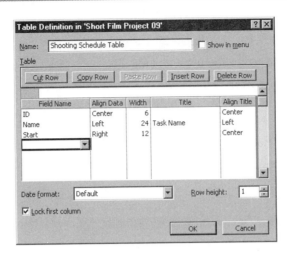

Next you will add some fields to this table definition.

7   In the Field Name column, click the down arrow in next empty cell below "Start," and then select Cast (Text9) from the drop-down list.

8   In the Align Data column in the same row, select Left.

As soon as Left is selected, Microsoft Project automatically completes row entries for the Cast field name by adding data to the Width column and to the Align Title column.

9   In the Width column, type or select **25**.

10   In the Field Name column in the next empty row below "Cast," select Location (Text10) from the drop-down list.

11   In the Align Data column, select Left.

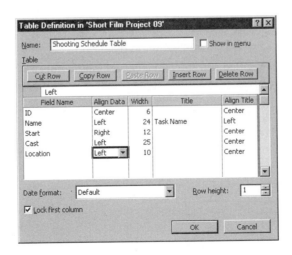

The two customized text fields Cast (Text9) and Location (Text10) contain the character names and film locations for the shooting tasks. These were previously added to the project plan.

The remaining work to complete this table definition is to reorder the fields to match the order commonly found on a shooting schedule.

12   In the Field Name column, select Start, and then click Cut Row.

13   In the Field Name column, select Name, and then click Paste Row.

After you've reordered these fields, your screen should look similar to the following illustration.

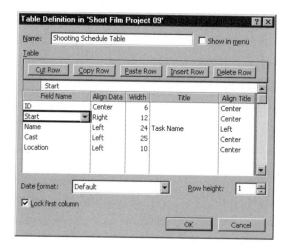

This matches the order in which information is commonly listed on a film shooting schedule.

14   In the Date Format box, select 1/31/00 12:33 PM.

15   Click OK to close the Table Definition dialog box.

The new table appears in the More Tables dialog box.

16   Click Apply.

Microsoft Project applies the new table to the Task Sheet view. If the Start column displays pound signs (###), double-click the column heading's right edge to widen it. Your screen should look similar to the following illustration.

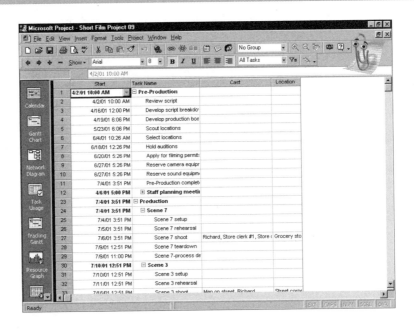

In the next section, you will combine the custom filter with this custom table to create a shooting schedule view for the film project.

Defining Custom Views

PROJ2000-5-9

In nearly all of the lessons in this book, you've switched between various pre-defined views in Microsoft Project. As you might recall from Lesson 2, a view might contain elements such as tables, groups, and filters. You can combine these with other elements (such as a timescaled grid in a usage view) or with graphic elements (such as the graphic representation of tasks in the chart portion of the Gantt Chart view).

Microsoft Project includes 23 views, which organize information for specific purposes. You might find that you need to see your project information in some way not available in the predefined views. Should this happen, you can edit an existing view or create your own view.

In this exercise, you create a film shooting schedule view that combines the custom filter and custom table you created in the previous sections. The view you create will more closely match the standard format used in the film industry.

1   On the View menu, click More Views.

 The More Views dialog box appears. In it, you can see all of the predefined views available to you.

2   Click the New button.

The Define New View dialog box appears. Most views occupy a single pane, but a view can consist of two separate panes.

3   Make sure Single View is selected, and then click OK.

The View Definition dialog box appears.

4   In the Name box, type **Shooting Schedule View**.

5   In the Screen box, select Task Sheet from the drop-down list.

6   In the Table box, select Shooting Schedule Table from the drop-down list.

7   In the Group box, select No Group from the drop-down list.

8   In the Filter box, select Uncompleted Shoots from the drop-down list.

9   Select the Show In Menu check box.

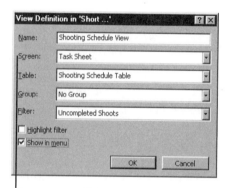

Here you see all the elements that can make up a view.

10   Click OK to close the View Definition dialog box.

The new view appears in the More Views dialog box.

11   Click Apply.

Microsoft Project applies the new view. Your screen should look similar to the following illustration.

The custom view is arranged like a shooting schedule, a standard format in the film industry.

	Start	Task Name	Cast	Location
27	7/6/01 3:51 PM	Scene 7 shoot	Richard, Store clerk #1, Store (	Grocery sto
33	7/16/01 12:51 PM	Scene 3 shoot	Man on street, Richard	Street corne
39	7/24/01 12:51 PM	Scene 1 shoot	Garth, Man on street, Store cle	Street corne
45	7/27/01 7:00 PM	Scene 2 shoot	Garth, Shelly	Shelly's livin
51	8/3/01 10:00 AM	Scene 5 shoot	Man on street, Garth, Old man,	Street corne
57	8/17/01 10:00 AM	Scene 6 shoot	Garth, Store Clerk #1, Shelly, C	Grocery sto
63	8/30/01 10:00 AM	Scene 8 shoot	Garth, Store clerk #1, Man on s	Street corne
69	9/4/01 7:00 PM	Scene 4 shoot	Shelly, Richard	Elevator

Now only uncompleted shoots are displayed, and the fields appear in an order consistent with a standard shooting schedule for a film project. Also, Microsoft Project added the Shooting Schedule view to the View bar. This view will be saved with this Microsoft Project data file, and you can use it whenever you wish.

To conclude this exercise, you will adjust row height and column width to display some information that is not currently visible.

12 While holding down the Ctrl key, select the task ID numbers for Tasks 27, 39, 51, 57, and 63.

In each of these selected rows, the names in the Cast column are truncated.

13 Drag the bottom edge of the task ID for Task 27 down approximately one row.

Microsoft Project resizes the selected rows. Your screen should look similar to the following illustration.

To resize a column's width, drag the right edge of the column label.

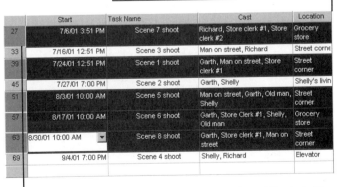

	Start	Task Name	Cast	Location
27	7/6/01 3:51 PM	Scene 7 shoot	Richard, Store clerk #1, Store clerk #2	Grocery store
33	7/16/01 12:51 PM	Scene 3 shoot	Man on street, Richard	Street corne
39	7/24/01 12:51 PM	Scene 1 shoot	Garth, Man on street, Store clerk #1	Street corner
45	7/27/01 7:00 PM	Scene 2 shoot	Garth, Shelly	Shelly's livin
51	8/3/01 10:00 AM	Scene 5 shoot	Man on street, Garth, Old man, Shelly	Street corner
57	8/17/01 10:00 AM	Scene 6 shoot	Garth, Store Clerk #1, Shelly, Old man	Grocery store
63	8/30/01 10:00 AM	Scene 8 shoot	Garth, Store clerk #1, Man on street	Street corner
69	9/4/01 7:00 PM	Scene 4 shoot	Shelly, Richard	Elevator

To resize a row's height, drag the bottom edge of the task ID. If you've previously selected multiple rows, all selected rows are also resized.

14 Double-click the right edge of the Location column heading.

Microsoft Project resizes the column width to accommodate the widest value in the column.

Formatting the Gantt Chart

PROJ2000-5-5,
PROJ2000E-4-2

For many people, a Gantt Chart is synonymous with a project plan. In Microsoft Project, the default view is the Gantt Chart. You are likely to spend a lot of your time in Microsoft Project in this view.

As you might recall from Lesson 2, the Gantt Chart view consists of two parts: a table on the left and a timescaled bar chart on the right. The bars on the chart graphically represent the tasks on the table in terms of start and finish dates, duration, and status (for example, if work on the task has started or not). Other elements on the chart, such as link lines, represent task relationships between tasks. In short, the Gantt Chart is a popular and widely understood representation of project information throughout the project management world.

The default formatting applied to the Gantt Chart view works well for onscreen viewing, sharing with other programs, or printing. However, you can change the formatting of just about any element on the Gantt Chart that you choose. In this exercise, you will focus on Gantt Chart bars. There are three distinct ways to format Gantt Chart bars:

- Format whole categories of items in the Bar Styles dialog box, which you can open by selecting the Bar Styles command on the Format menu. In this case, the formatting changes you make to a type of item (a milestone, for example) apply to all such items in the Gantt Chart.

- Format whole categories of items in the GanttChartWizard, which is available on the Format menu, though with fewer choices. This wizard contains a series of dialog boxes in which you select formatting options for the most-used items on the Gantt Chart.

- Format individual bars directly. The formatting changes you make have no effect on other elements in the Gantt Chart. You can double-click a bar on the Gantt Chart to see its formatting options.

In this exercise, you change a variety of items on the Gantt Chart through the Format Bar Styles dialog box.

Gantt
Chart

1 On the View bar, click Gantt Chart.

The Gantt Chart appears.

2   On the Format menu, click Bar Styles.

The Bar Styles dialog box appears.

The first item you'd like to change is the shape of the milestones on the Gantt Chart. Because many of the film project's resources are aspiring movie stars, a star shape seems appropriate.

3   In the Name column, select Milestone.

4   In the Shape box under the Start label, select the star shape, which is the last item in the drop-down list.

You can see the effect of your choice in the Appearance column of the dialog box. The star shape appears for the sample milestone.

The options you choose in the lower portion of the dialog box...

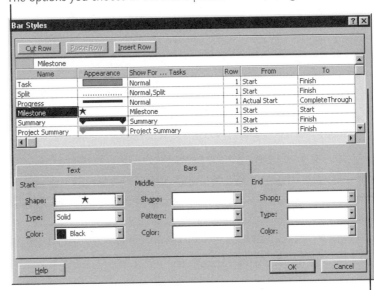

...are reflected in the upper portion of the dialog box.

The next change you'd like to make is to display resource initials instead of full names next to the task bars.

5   Click the Text tab.

6   In the Name column at the top of the dialog box, select Task.

7   In the Text tab, select Resource Names in the Right box, click the down arrow, and then select Resource Initials.

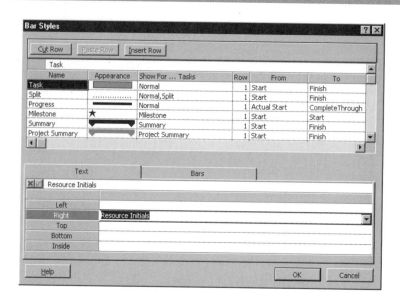

8   Click OK to close the Bar Styles dialog box.

Microsoft Project applies your formatting changes to the Gantt Chart. To get a better look at the formatting changes you made, you'll view a milestone.

Use flag fields to display unique graphical indicators on the Gantt Chart

As you saw in the Bar Styles dialog box, Microsoft Project has a lot of flexibility in how it displays items in the chart portion of the Gantt Chart view. However, you may have other issues you want to indicate on the Gantt Chart that don't fall within the list of items such as tasks or milestones in the Bar Styles dialog box. For example, some film projects employ child actors and in most cases special social workers are required by law to be present when child actors are employed. It would be useful to highlight, or flag, such shooting tasks in a film project's schedule by specially formatting the Gantt bars of such tasks. To accomplish this, you can use flag fields.

Microsoft Project supports up to 20 flag fields each for tasks, resources, and assignments. Flag fields accommodate simple yes/no values for task, resources and assignments. In the child actor example, you could use a task flag field to indicate if a task requires a child actor or not. Then, you could specify a unique indicator to appear in the Gantt Chart view for tasks that

(continued)

(continued)

have this flag set to yes. You can also sort, filter, and group tasks by this flag field or display different graphical indicators in a table depending on the value of the flag field.

Flag fields are handy whenever you need to mark tasks that meet criteria you cannot otherwise record in a specific Microsoft Project field. To set up a flag field, on the Tools menu point to Customize, and then click Fields. When the Customize Fields dialog box appears, click Flag in the Type box and then pick the options you want. For more information, ask the Office Assistant "How do I use flag fields" and then pick the specific type of flag field (task, resource, or assignment) that you're interested in.

9 Select the name of Task 11, "Pre-Production complete!" On the Standard toolbar, click the Go To Selected Task button.

The format changes you made to the Gantt Chart are visible here.

You can see the reformatted milestone and resource initials on the Gantt Chart.

PROJ2000E-7-1

Formatting the Network Diagram

In traditional project management, the Network Diagram (sometimes incorrectly called a PERT chart) is a standard way of representing project activities and their relationships. Tasks are represented as boxes, or nodes, and the relationships between tasks are drawn as lines connecting nodes. Unlike the Gantt Chart, which is a timescaled view, a network diagram allows you to see project activities in more of a flowchart format. This is useful if you'd like to focus more on the relationships between activities rather than on their durations.

Using the Network Diagram in Microsoft Project is a little bit like eating sushi in North America: people who like it *really* like it, and everybody else tends to stay away from it. So if the Network Diagram is to your taste, read on.

Microsoft Project 2000 provides substantially more formatting options for the Network Diagram. (Previous versions of Microsoft Project referred to this diagram as the PERT Chart.) In this section, you will use just a few of these formatting options. If you're a heavy-duty Network Diagram user, you'll want to explore the formatting options in greater detail on your own.

In this exercise, you format a few items on the Network Diagram view.

1 On the View bar, click Network Diagram.

The Network Diagram view appears. In this view, each task is represented by a box, or node, and each node contains several pieces of information about the task. Your screen should look similar to the following illustration.

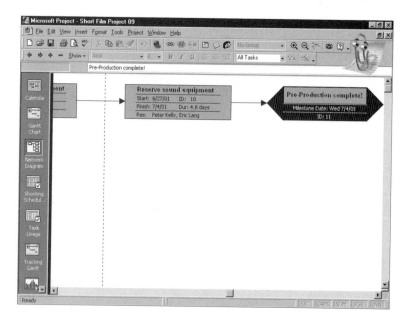

Although the Network Diagram is not a timescaled view, you can organize the nodes in a time sequence.

2 On the Format menu, click Layout.

The Layout dialog box appears.

3 In the Arrangement box, select Top Down By Month from the drop-down list.

4 Under Diagram Options, select Hide All Fields Except ID, and then click OK.

Microsoft Project rearranges the nodes into columns, each column representing a different month. The start date of the task determines the column into which each node is placed. Only the task ID appears in each node now.

tip

In this exercise you've hidden most details about the task in the Network Diagram. However, you can control the specific fields that appear in each box on the Network Diagram and how they appear. On the Format menu, click Box Styles, and then select the options you want. For more information, click the Help button in the Box Styles dialog box.

In this formatted Network Diagram view, task nodes are grouped by month, and task details are hidden.

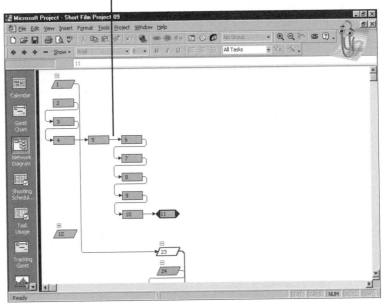

Project Information Look

9

5   To see detailed information about a specific node, point to the node. The task details appear in a ToolTip.

> ## tip
> To find out more about new formatting options for the network diagram, Gantt Chart, and other views, ask the Office Assistant, "Tell me all about formatting views."

Formatting the Calendar View

The Calendar view is probably the simplest view available in Microsoft Project; however, even the Calendar view offers several formatting options. This view is especially useful for sharing schedule information with resources or other stakeholders who prefer a traditional "month-at-a-glance" format rather than a more detailed view, such as the Gantt Chart.

In this exercise, you format the Calendar view to display just the assignments and working time of a single resource.

1   On the View bar, click Calendar.

The Calendar view appears. It displays four weeks at a time, and it draws task bars on the days on which tasks are scheduled.

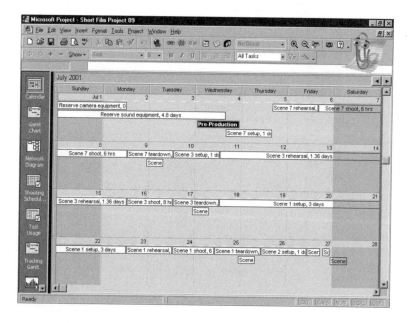

With a complex project, the Calendar view is not especially useful because it doesn't give you much information about the scheduled tasks or their relationships. However, it works well for viewing a single resource's tasks.

2   On the Project menu, point to Filtered For: All Tasks and then click Using Resource.

The Using Resource dialog box appears. You'd like to see assignments only for Jan Miksovsky in the Calendar view.

3   In the Show Tasks Using box, select Jan Miksovsky from the drop-down list, and then click OK.

Microsoft Project displays tasks for Jan Miksovsky in the Calendar view.

Your screen should look similar to the following illustration.

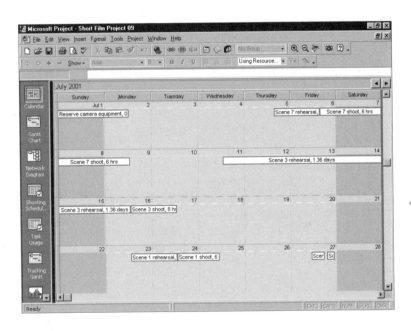

This is a good way of seeing an individual resource's tasks, but it would be even more useful if you could see that resource's working days represented on the calendar as well.

4   On the Format menu, click Timescale.

The Timescale dialog box appears.

5   Click the Date Shading tab.

6   In the Show Working Time For box, select Jan Miksovsky, and then click OK.

Microsoft Project reformats the Calendar view to show Jan Miksovsky's working time settings. For example, in a previous lesson, you specified that November 22 and 23 were nonworking days for Jan. In the Calendar view, these dates are formatted differently from her working days. If you wish to see these dates, scroll down until November 2001 is visible.

Lesson Wrap-Up

This lesson covered how to sort, filter, and group Microsoft Project data and how to build custom tables and views. It also covered how to format three common views in Microsoft Project: the Gantt Chart, Network Diagram, and Calendar views.

If you are going on to other lessons:

1   On the Standard toolbar, click Save to save changes made to Short Film Project 09. Save the file without a baseline.

2   On the File menu, click Close to close the file.

If you aren't continuing to other lessons:

●   On the File menu, click Exit.

Glossary

AutoFilter A quick way to view only the task or resource information in a table that meets the criteria you choose. To turn on AutoFilter, click the AutoFilter button on the Formatting toolbar. To AutoFilter a table, click the arrow next to a column heading, and choose the criteria you want.

Filter A way to see or highlight only the task or resource information in a table that meets the criteria you choose.

Group A way to reorder task or resource information in a table and to display summary values for each group. You can specify up to three nested levels of groups. (The term "group" is also used to refer to the Resource Group field, which is unrelated.)

Sort A way of ordering task or resource information in a view by the criteria you choose.

Quick Reference

To sort data in a view

1   Switch to the view and table you want to sort.

2   On the Project menu, click Sort, and then select the field by which you want to sort the view. To specify a custom sort, select Sort By, and then, in the Sort dialog box, choose the options you want.

To group data in a view

1   Switch to the view and table you want to group.

2   On the Project menu, click Group By: No Group, and then select the criteria by which you want to group the view. To specify different grouping options, select Customize Group By, and then choose the options you want in the Customize Group By dialog box.

To turn AutoFilter on or off

●   On the Formatting toolbar, click the AutoFilter button.

To filter data in a view

1   Switch to the view you want to filter.

2   On the Project menu, point to Filtered For, and select More Filters.

3   In the More Filters dialog box, choose the filter you want and then click Apply.

To create a custom table

1   On the View menu, point to Table: Entry, and then click More Tables.

2   In the More Tables dialog box, do one of the following:

   ●   To create a table, click New.

   ●   To redefine a table, select the table name, and then click Edit.

   ●   To create a table based on another table, select the table name, and then click Copy.

3   In the Table Definition dialog box, choose the options you want.

To create a custom view

1   On the View menu, click More Views.

2   In the More Views dialog box, do one of the following:

   ●   To create a view, click New. Select Single View or Combination View in the Define New View dialog box, and then click OK.

Project Information Look 9

- To redefine a view, select the view name, and then click Edit.
- To create a view based on another view, select the view name, and then click Copy.

3 In the View Definition dialog box, choose the options you want.

To format bar styles on the Gantt Chart

1 On the Format menu, click Bar Styles.

2 In the Bar Styles dialog box, select the options you want.

To start the Gantt Chart Wizard

1 On the Format menu, click GanttChartWizard.

2 Follow the instructions on your screen.

To format a bar on the Gantt Chart

1 Double-click the bar you want to format.

2 In the Format Bar dialog box, choose the options you want.

To format the Layout of the Network Diagram

Network Diagram

1 On the View bar, click Network Diagram.

2 On the Format menu, click Layout.

3 Choose the options you want.

To format the Calendar view

Calendar

1 On the View bar, click Calendar.

2 On the Format menu, click Layout.

3 In the Layout dialog box, choose the options you want.

LESSON

10

Printing Project Information

ESTIMATED TIME
20 min.

After completing this lesson, you will be able to:

✔ *Draw objects, such as text boxes or arrows, on a Gantt Chart.*

✔ *Change the page setup options for a view.*

✔ *Preview what you intend to print.*

✔ *View and edit reports designed for printing project data.*

In this lesson, you work with some of the many views and reports in Microsoft Project to print your project plan. One of the most important tasks of any project manager is communicating project information to **stakeholders,** and that often means printing on paper. You can use the predefined views and reports as is, or customize them to better suit your needs. You can also draw directly on a view using tools provided in Microsoft Project.

Practice files for the lesson

To complete this lesson, you use a file named Short Film Project 10. Open the Part 3 folder in the MS Project 2000 SBS Practice folder on your hard disk. Open the file10A, and save it without a baseline as Short Film Project 10 in the Part 3 folder.

Drawing on a Gantt Chart

PROJ2000-3-1

Microsoft Project includes a Drawing toolbar with which you can draw objects directly on a Gantt Chart. If you wish, you can link a drawn object to either end of a Gantt bar or to a specific date on the **timescale.** For example, if you'd like to note a particular event or graphically call out a specific item, you can draw text boxes, arrows, and other items directly on a Gantt Chart. If the

Drawing toolbar doesn't have the type of item you'd like to add, you can add bitmap images or documents as well.

In this exercise, you display the Drawing toolbar and add a text box to the Gantt Chart describing a film festival. Because you'll use the standard Gantt Chart view for other purposes later, you'll add text to the Detail Gantt view.

1   On the View menu, click More Views.

The More Views dialog box appears.

2   In the Views box, select Detail Gantt, and then click Apply.

The Detail Gantt view appears.

You can also click Drawing on the Insert menu to display the Drawing toolbar.

3   On the View menu, point to Toolbars and then click Drawing.

The Drawing toolbar appears.

tip
You can also right-click any toolbar to see the Toolbars shortcut menu and then display or hide a toolbar listed on that menu. For help using the mouse, see Appendix A.

4   On the Drawing toolbar, click the Text Box button, and then drag a small square anywhere on the chart portion of the Detail Gantt view.

5   Type **Film festival May 21 and 22**.

6   On the Format menu, point to Drawing and then click Properties.

tip
You can also double-click the text box's border to view its properties.

The Format Drawing dialog box appears.

7   Click the Line & Fill tab.

8   In the Color box under the Fill label, select Yellow.

9   Click the Size & Position tab.

You want to attach the text box to a specific date rather than to a specific Gantt bar.

10   Make sure that Attach To Timescale is selected, and in the Date box, select May 21, 2001.

11 In the Vertical box, type **1.25** and then click OK to close the Format Drawing dialog box.

Microsoft Project formats the text box with yellow fill and positions it below the timescale where you specified. Depending on the portion of the Detail Gantt view that is visible on screen, you might not see the text box. To see it, go to the date you specified.

12 On the Edit menu, click Go To.

The Go To dialog box appears.

13 In the Date box, select May 21, 2001 and then click OK.

Microsoft Project scrolls the Detail Gantt view to display the date you specified. Your screen should look similar to the following illustration.

The Drawing tool bar allows you to draw a variety of shapes and objects directly on a Gantt Chart view.

Double-click on the border of a drawn object to change its formatting or other properties.

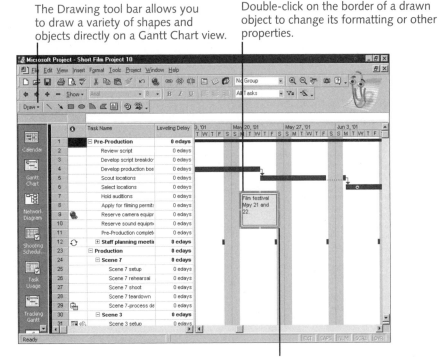

To resize a box, drag any of its corners.

Because you attached the text box to a specific date on the timescale, it will always appear near this date even if you zoom the timescale in or out. Had you attached the text box to a Gantt bar, it would move with the Gantt bar if the task were rescheduled.

To conclude this exercise, you'll hide the Drawing toolbar using the shortcut menu.

14 Right-click any of the visible toolbars, and in the shortcut menu that appears, click Drawing.

Microsoft Project hides the Drawing toolbar.

Customizing and Printing Views

PROJ2000-3-10

Printing a **view** allows you to get on paper just about whatever you see on your screen. Any customization you apply to a view, such as applying different **tables** or **groups,** will print as well. With a few exceptions, you can print any view you see in Microsoft Project. Here are the exceptions:

- You cannot print form views, such as the Task Form and the Relationship Diagram.

- If you have two views displayed in a combination view (one view in the top pane and the other view in the bottom pane), only the view in the active pane will print.

Keep in mind that the part of your project plan that you see on your screen at one time might be a relatively small portion of the full project, which might require a large number of pages to print. For example, the Gantt Chart of a six-month project with 85 tasks can require 14 or more letter-size pages to print in its entirety. Printing Gantt Chart or Network Diagram views can use quite a bit of paper; in fact, some heavy-duty Microsoft Project users print poster-size printouts of their project plans using plotters.

Whether you have a printer or a plotter, it's a good idea to preview any views you intend to print. By using the Page Setup dialog box in conjunction with the Print Preview window, you can control many aspects of the view to be printed. For example, you can control the number of pages on which the view will be printed, apply headers and footers, and determine content that appears in the legend of the Gantt Chart and some other views.

tip

Projects with several hundred tasks won't fit on a single letter-size or legal-size page in a legible form. If you have a project that large, you might get better results by printing summary or selected data. For example, a collapsed view showing only summary tasks and milestones might be more informative for people who just want an overall sense of the project plan. If you're interested in a specific time period, you can print just that portion of the timescale. Or you might apply a filter to display only the information that's of greatest interest to a particular audience: late or overbudget tasks, for example. For more information about changing what you see in a view, see Lesson 9.

In this exercise, you preview a Gantt Chart view and change options in the Page Setup dialog box.

Gantt
Chart

1　On the View bar, click Gantt Chart.

The Gantt Chart view appears.

2　On the File menu, click Print Preview.

Microsoft Project displays the Gantt Chart view in the Print Preview window. Your screen should look similar to the following illustration.

The Print Preview toolbar contains buttons for navigating between pages, zooming in or out, setting Page Setup options, printing, or exiting Print Preview.

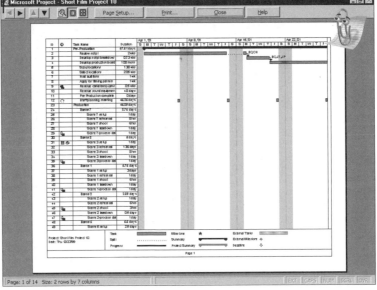

The Print Preview window has several options to explore. Let's start with the page navigation buttons.

3　On the Print Preview toolbar, click the Page Right button several times to display different pages.

4　Click the Page Down button once.

To get a broader view of the output, you'll switch to a multi-page view.

5   Click the Multiple Pages button.

The entire Gantt Chart appears in the Print Preview window. Your screen should look similar to the following illustration.

The multi-page Print Preview shows you the entire printed output laid out on separate sheets (the paper size is determined by your printer settings).

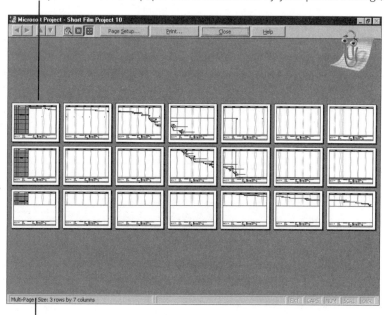

This status bar message refers to rows and columns of printed sheets, as they are laid out in the multi-page Print Preview.

If you have a plotter selected as your default printer or you have a different page size selected for your default printer, what you see in the Print Preview window will differ.

The status bar shows "3 rows by 7 columns." We refer to columns on the Gantt Chart and in other views; in the Print Preview window, however, these terms denote rows and columns of *pages*—in this case, three rows of pages by seven columns of pages, for a total of 21 pages. The status bar text can help you quickly determine the size (in pages) your printed view will be.

Next you'll change some options in the Page Setup dialog box.

6   On the Print Preview toolbar, click the One Page button.

Microsoft Project displays the first page of the Gantt Chart.

Page Setup...   **7**   Click the Page Setup button.

The Page Setup dialog box appears. This is the same dialog box you'd see if you selected the Page Setup command on the File menu. The first change we'll make to the printed Gantt Chart is to add the current date to the header that prints on every page.

8   Click the Header tab.

9   On the Header tab are Alignment tabs. Make sure that Center is selected, and then click the Insert Current Date button.

   Microsoft Project inserts the &[Date] code into the header and displays a preview in the Preview window of the Page Setup dialog box. Next you'll change the content of the Gantt Chart legend.

10   Click the Legend tab.

11   On the Legend tab are Alignment tabs. Click the Left tab.

   With the current settings, Microsoft Project will print the project title and the current date on the left side of the legend. Instead of the current date, you'd like to print the start date and the duration of the project.

12   In the Alignment window, select the "Date: &[Date]" code, and type **Start date:**.

13   In the General box, select Project Start Date from the drop-down list, and then click the Add button.

   Microsoft Project adds the label and code for the project start date to the legend.

14   Press the Enter key to add a third line to the legend and then type **Duration:**.

15   In the Project Fields box, select Duration from the drop-down list, and then click the Add button.

   Microsoft Project adds the label and code for project duration to the legend.

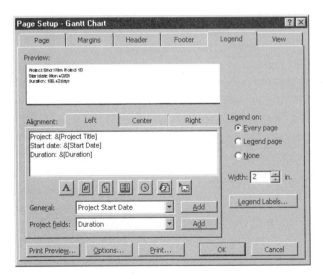

Printing Project Information 10

16   Click OK to close the Page Setup dialog box.

Microsoft Project applies the changes you specified to the legend. To get a closer look, you'll zoom in on the legend.

17   In the Print Preview window, click the lower left corner of the page with the magnifying-glass pointer.

Microsoft Project zooms in to show the page at a legible resolution. Your screen should look similar to the following illustration.

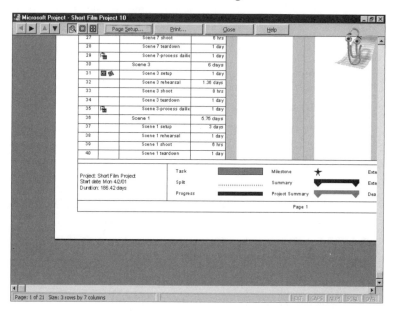

You can see the data you added to the legend, which will print on every page of the printed output.

18   On the Print Preview toolbar, click Close.

The Print Preview window closes, and the Gantt Chart view appears. Although you did not print, your changes to the header and the legend will be saved when you save the project file.

tip

You can print the project plan now if you wish; however, previewing the project plan is adequate for the purposes of the lesson. When printing in Microsoft Project, you have additional options in the Print dialog box, which you can open by choosing the Print command on the File menu. For example, you can choose to print a specific date range of a timescaled view, such as the Gantt Chart, or you can print a specific page range.

Customizing and Printing Reports

PROJ2000-3-6,
PROJ2000-3-11,
PROJ2000E-4-4

Reports are predefined formats intended for printing Microsoft Project data. Unlike views, which you can either print or work with online, reports are designed only for printing or for viewing in the Print Preview window. You don't enter data directly into a report. Microsoft Project includes several predefined task, resource, and assignment reports you can edit to get the information you want.

In this exercise, you view a report in the Print Preview window, and then you edit its format to include additional information.

1   On the View menu, click Reports.

The Reports dialog box appears, showing the six broad categories of reports available in Microsoft Project.

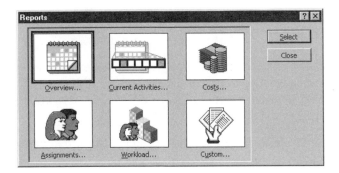

2   Click Custom, and then click the Select button.

The Custom Reports dialog box appears, listing all predefined reports in Microsoft Project and any custom reports that have been added.

3   In the Reports box, select Task, and then click the Preview button.

Microsoft Project displays the Task report in the Print Preview window. Your screen should look similar to the following illustration.

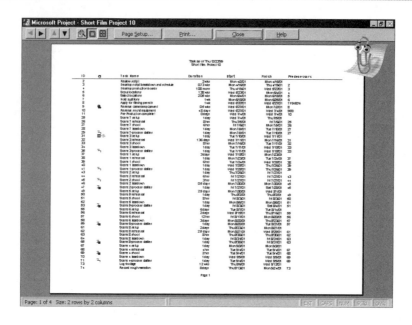

This report is a complete list of project tasks (except for summary tasks), similar to what you'd see in the Entry table of the Gantt Chart view. You'd like to see this data presented in a different way, so you'll edit this report.

4   On the Print Preview toolbar, click the Close button.

Close

The Print Preview window closes, and the Custom Reports dialog box reappears.

5   In the Reports box, ensure that Task is still selected, and then click the Copy button.

The Task Report dialog box appears.

6   In the Name box, select the displayed text, and then type **Custom Task Report**.

7   In the Period box, select Months from the drop-down list.

8   In the Table box, select Summary from the drop-down list.

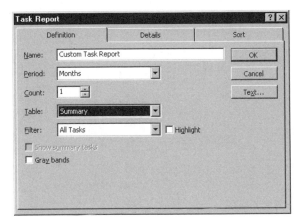

tip

The tables listed in the Task Report dialog box are the same as those you can apply to a view. In fact, the "Shooting Schedule Table" you created in Lesson 9 appears in the list here. When editing a report format, you can apply built-in or custom tables and filters, choose which categories of information to include in the report, and apply a sort order to the information—all in the dialog box for the report you're editing.

9   Click OK to close the Task Report dialog box.

10   In the Custom Reports dialog box, make sure that Custom Task Report is selected in the Reports box, and then click the Preview button.

Microsoft Project applies the custom report settings you chose to the report, and the report appears in the Print Preview window. Your screen should look similar to the following illustration.

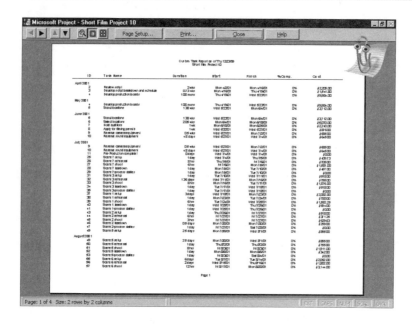

This custom report shows the fields displayed on the Summary Task table but divides the tasks by month.

11 On the Print Preview toolbar, click the Close button.

12 In the Custom Reports dialog box, click Close.

13 Click Close again to close the Reports dialog box.
    The Gantt Chart view reappears.

Lesson Wrap-Up

This lesson covered how to draw directly on a view and control printing options for views, as well as previewing and customizing a report before printing.

If you are going on to other lessons:

1 On the Standard toolbar, click Save to save changes made to Short Film Project 10.

    Save the file without a baseline.

2 On the File menu, click Close to close the file.

If you aren't continuing to other lessons:

● On the File menu, click Exit.

Glossary

Group To arrange task or resource information according to specific criteria and then to apply summary-level values, such as total costs or total hours. Microsoft Project includes several predefined groups, and you can define your own.

Report A format designed for printing. Microsoft Project includes several predefined reports, each focusing on specific aspects of your project data. You can also define your own reports.

Stakeholders All people or organizations that might be affected by project activities. This group includes those working on the project, as well as others (such as customers) external to the project work.

Table A spreadsheet-like presentation of project data, organized into vertical columns and horizontal rows. Each column represents one of the many fields in Microsoft Project, and each row represents a single task or resource.

Timescale In a Gantt Chart view, the timescale appears in the upper portion of the view, and it contains major and minor time indicators, such as weeks and days.

View The primary way you see data in Microsoft Project. The three categories of views are charts, sheets, and forms.

Quick Reference

To draw text boxes or other objects on the Gantt Chart

1   On the View menu, click Toolbars, and then select Drawing.

2   On the Drawing toolbar, click the object or shape you want to draw, and then draw it on the chart portion of a Gantt Chart view.

3   To set options for the drawn object (for example to link it to one end of a Gantt bar), double-click the object's border, and choose the options you want in the Format Drawing dialog box.

To work in the Print Preview window

1   On the File menu, click Print Preview.

2   Do one of the following:

- To navigate between pages of a multi-page print job, click a page navigation button.

- To zoom out to see all pages of the print job, click the Multiple Pages button.

- To change page setup options such as header or legend text, click the Page Setup button, and choose the options you want.

- To display the Print dialog box and set other options or to print what you see in the Print Preview window, click the Print button.

- To exit the Print Preview window, click Close.

To print a predefined report

1   On the View menu, click Reports.

2   In the Reports dialog box, select the category of report you want, and then click the Select button.

3   In the dialog box that appears next, select the specific report you want to print, and click the Select button.

4   In the Print Preview window, select the options you want.

To edit a predefined report

1   On the View menu, click Reports.

2   In the Reports dialog box, select the category of report you want, and then click the Select button.

3   In the dialog box that appears next, select the specific report you want to edit, and then click the Edit button.

4   In the dialog box that appears next, choose the options you want.

To create a custom report

1   On the View menu, click Reports.

2   In the Reports dialog box, click Custom, and then click the Select button.

3   In the Custom Reports dialog box, click the New button.

4   In the Define New Report dialog box, under the Report Type label, select the general category of report you want to create, and then click OK.

5   In the dialog box that appears next, choose the options you want.

LESSON

11

Publishing Project Information Online

ESTIMATED TIME

20 min.

After completing this lesson, you will be able to:

✔ Take a *"snapshot" of a Gantt Chart view.*

✔ *Publish Microsoft Project information in HTML format.*

✔ *Control how Microsoft Project information is saved in HTML format by customizing an export map.*

In this lesson, you work with the Web publishing features of Microsoft Project. These features include Copy Picture, which allows you to take a "snapshot" of the active view. You can either copy the snapshot to the Windows Clipboard or save it to an image file on your hard disk. You also export Microsoft Project information to HTML format and control how the exported information appears. In many organizations, publishing in HTML format on an intranet is the primary means by which project details are communicated to **stakeholders**.

To complete this lesson, you will use a file named Short Film Project 11. Open the Part 3 folder in the MS Project 2000 SBS Practice folder on your hard disk. Open the file11A, and save it without a baseline as Short Film Project 11 in the Part 3 folder.

Copying Project Information as a GIF Image

When communicating project details to resources, managers, and other stakeholders, chances are you'll need to copy information out of Microsoft Project and into other programs and formats. Microsoft Project supports the standard copy and paste functionality of most Windows programs, and it has an addi-

PROJ2000-3-4

tional feature, called **Copy Picture**, for taking "snapshots" of a view. You can take these "snapshots" by choosing the Copy Picture command on the Edit menu or clicking the Copy Picture button on the Standard toolbar.

 With Copy Picture, you have different options when taking snapshots of the active view:

- Copy the entire **view** visible on the screen or selected rows of a **table** in a view.

- Copy a range of time that you specify or show on the screen.

Either way, you can choose to copy onto the Windows Clipboard an image that is optimized for pasting into another program for onscreen viewing (Microsoft PowerPoint, for example), or for printing (Microsoft Word, for example). You can also save the snapshot to a Graphics Interchange Format (GIF) file in a location you specify. Once you save the image to a GIF file, you can use it in any of the many programs that support the GIF format. You can also combine it with HTML content on a Web page, as you'll do later in this lesson.

> ## tip
> If you want to copy text (to paste a task list into a spreadsheet, for example) rather than a graphic image, use the Copy command on the Edit menu. For more information, see Lesson 12, "Sharing Project Information with Other Programs."

In this exercise, you change what appears in the Gantt Chart view, and then you use Copy Picture to save a snapshot of this view as a GIF file. To begin, you filter the Gantt Chart to show only summary tasks.

1 On the Project menu, point to Filtered For: All Tasks, and then click Summary Tasks.

Microsoft Project filters the Gantt Chart to show only summary tasks. Next you'll zoom the **timescale** to see the entire project.

2 On the View menu, click Zoom.

The Zoom dialog box appears.

3 Click Entire Project, and then click OK.

Microsoft Project adjusts the timescale in the Gantt Chart to display the entire project's duration in the window. Your screen should look similar to the following illustration.

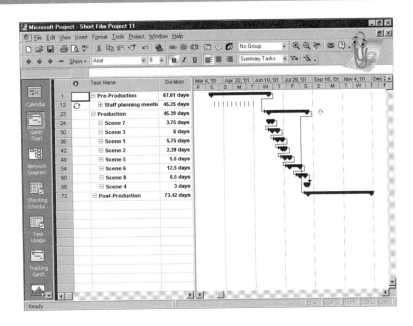

4   On the Standard toolbar, click the Copy Picture button.

The Copy Picture dialog box appears.

5   Under Render Image, click To GIF Image File.

Microsoft Project suggests that you save the file in the same location as the practice file and with the same name, except with a .gif extension.

6   Click OK to close the Copy Picture dialog box.

The GIF image is saved.

You could open your browser or a graphics program to view the GIF image you just saved, but you can also view it from within Microsoft Project.

7   On the View menu, point to Toolbars, and then click Web.

The Web toolbar appears.

8   On the Web toolbar, click Go, and then click Open.

The Open Internet Address dialog box appears.

9   Click Browse.

The Browse dialog box appears.

10   In the Files Of Type box, select GIF Files from the drop-down list.

11   Locate the GIF image named Short Film Project 11 in your Part 3 folder.

12   Select the GIF image, and then click Open.

13   In the Open Internet Address dialog box, click OK.

Microsoft Project opens the GIF image. If you have Microsoft Internet Explorer as your default program for viewing GIF files, your screen should look similar to the following illustration.

The Gantt Chart view snapshot is saved as a GIF format image, which you can view in a browser or graphics editing program.

ID	0	Task Name	Duration
1		Pre-Production	67.61 days
12	⟳	Staff planning meeting	45.25 days
23		Production	45.39 days
24		Scene 7	3.75 days
30		Scene 3	6 days
36		Scene 1	5.75 days
42		Scene 2	2.39 days
48		Scene 5	5.5 days
54		Scene 6	12.5 days
60		Scene 8	6.5 days
66		Scene 4	3 days
72		Post-Production	73.42 days

As noted above, what you see is a graphic image of the Gantt Chart view. The GIF image displays the view you displayed in Microsoft Project, almost exactly as you had it set up.

The Copy Picture feature is unavailable when a form view, such as the Task Form or the Relationship Diagram view, is displayed.

14 Close the program you used to view the GIF file, and then return to Microsoft Project.

Creating GIF images of views in Microsoft Project is useful on its own. However, you can also combine it with saving other Microsoft Project content as HTML for publishing to the Web or to an intranet site. You will do this in a later section.

Saving Project Information as a Web Page

PROJ2000-3-4

Another way to publish Microsoft Project information is to save it as a Web page. Unlike the Copy Picture feature, which produces a GIF image, saving as a Web page is better suited for publishing text. Microsoft Project uses **export maps** that specify the exact data to export and how to structure it. Export maps organize Microsoft Project data into HTML tables; the predefined maps resemble some of the predefined tables and reports in Microsoft Project. You can use export maps as they are or customize them to export only the Microsoft Project data you want.

In this exercise, you save Microsoft Project data as a Web page using an export map, and then you view the results in your browser.

1   On the File menu, click Save As Web Page.

The Save As dialog box appears. Microsoft Project suggests that you save the information as a Web page in the same location from which you opened the practice file. If you see a different location in the Save In box, navigate to the Part 3 folder on your hard disk.

2   Click Save.

The Export Mapping dialog box appears.

3   Under the Import/Export Map label, select Export To HTML Using Standard Template, and then click Save.

Microsoft Project saves the data to HTML format. This particular export map produces three tables that contain task, resource, and assignment informa-tion from the Short Film Project. All three tables will appear on the single Web page that you saved. Next you will view the Web page.

Go ▾

4   On the Web toolbar, click Go, and then click Open.

The Open Internet Address dialog box appears.

5   Click Browse.

The Browse dialog box appears.

6   In the Files Of Type box, select Web Pages from the drop-down list.

7   Locate the Web page named Short Film Project 11 in the Part 3 folder on your hard disk.

8   Select the Web page, and then click Open.

9   In the Open Internet Address dialog box, click OK.

Microsoft Project opens the Web page in your browser. If you have Microsoft Internet Explorer, your screen should look similar to the following illustration.

This is the result of saving Microsoft Project data as a Web page using Standard HTML template.

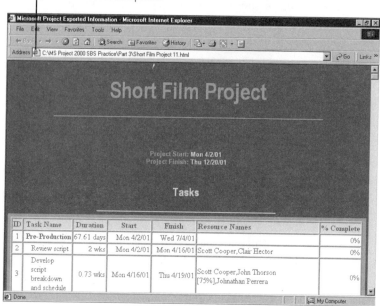

10   Scroll through the Web page to view the Tasks, Resources, and Assignments tables, which contains some of the same information as the Microsoft Project file.

11   Close your browser, and return to Microsoft Project.

The data you can export when saving to a Web page is not tied to the specific view you happen to be in at the time you save.

Saving information as a Web page allows you to publish large volumes of project information in HTML format.

You can do a few things to fine-tune the Web pages you can publish out of Microsoft Project.

- You can edit the export map. In the Export Mapping dialog box, click Edit. The Define Import/Export Map dialog box will appear, providing you a great deal of flexibility in choosing the exact task, resource, and assignment fields you want to export and how you want the exported data organized.

- You can apply a different HTML template to the Web page as you save it. This process is the subject of the next section.

- If you're HTML-savvy, you can edit the resulting Web page after saving it in Microsoft Project. For example, you can add several

Microsoft Project–specific tags to a Web page. For a list of those tags, ask the Office Assistant to "Tell me about HTML export templates and tags."

tip

Project managers, resources, and other stakeholders can use Microsoft Project Central to share project information via your origination's intranet or the Web. For more information, see Appendix D, "Introducing the Workgroup Features of Microsoft Project."

Changing the Look of a Project Web Page

Although export maps determine which Microsoft Project data you save as a Web page and how it's organized, **HTML templates** determine how that data is formatted. Microsoft Project includes several HTML templates that you can apply as you save a Web page.

In this exercise, you save project information as a Web page, apply a different template, and include in the Web page the GIF image you created earlier.

1   On the File menu, click Save As Web Page.

The Save As dialog box appears. Microsoft Project suggests that you save the information as a Web page in the same location from which you opened the practice file.

2   In the File Name box, type **Short Film Project 11 With Gantt Chart**, and click Save.

The Export Mapping dialog box appears. To keep the original export map intact, you'll create a copy of it and then customize the copy.

3   Under the Import/Export Map label, select Export To HTML Using Standard Template, and then click the Copy button.

The Define Import/Export Map dialog box appears. In the previous section, you saw that more information was exported to the Web page than you need, so you'll publish just task and resource information this time.

4   On the Options tab, under the Data To Import/Export label, clear the Assignments box.

Next you will pick a different HTML template to use. Under the HTML Options label, the Base Export On HTML Template box is selected, and the path to the current template appears.

5   Click the Browse button next to the path to the current template.

The Browse dialog box appears, showing all of the HTML templates that are included with Microsoft Project.

---

tip

If you installed Microsoft Project to the default location, the HTML templates it includes are in:

C:\Program Files\Microsoft Office\Templates\1033\Microsoft Project Web

---

6   In the list of templates, select Stripes Ivy, and then click OK.

There's just one more thing to do before creating the Web page. Earlier in this lesson, you created a GIF image of the Gantt Chart view named Short Film Project 11.gif. You'd like to include this image in the Web page.

7   Select the Include Image File In HTML Page check box.

If the GIF image file has the same name and is in the same folder as the Project file you're saving as a Web page, the path to that image file appears by default. Had you selected a different name or folder when creating the GIF image, you'd need to click the Browse button to locate it.

8   Click OK to close the Define Import/Export Map dialog box. In the Export Mapping dialog box, click Save.

Microsoft Project saves Microsoft Project data to HTML format. Next you will view the Web page you just created.

Go ▾   **9**   On the Web toolbar, click Go, and then click Open.

The Open Internet Address dialog box appears.

10   Click Browse.

The Browse dialog box appears.

11   In the Files Of Type box, select Web Pages. Locate the Web page named Short Film Project 11 With Gantt Chart in your Part 3 folder.

12   Select the Web page, and click Open.

13   In the Open Internet Address dialog box, click OK.

The Web page appears in your browser. If you have Microsoft Internet Explorer, your screen should look similar to the following illustration.

With a different template and the GIF image included, this is the result of saving Microsoft Project data as a Web page.

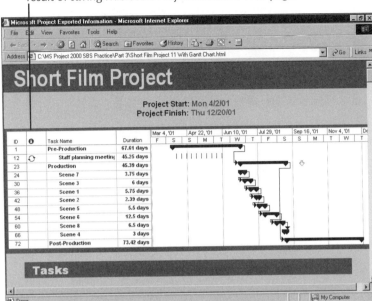

14 Scroll through the Web page to view the Gantt Chart image, the Tasks table, and the Resources table.

The new Web page doesn't have the Assignments table, and it shows different formatting from the page you created earlier.

15 Close your browser, and return to Microsoft Project.

16 Right-click any toolbar. In the shortcut menu that appears, click Web.

The Web toolbar disappears.

You've only scratched the surface of Microsoft Project's Web publishing capabilities. Depending on the communication needs you have as a project manager, you might use these features extensively. By modifying export tables, applying HTML templates, or editing the resulting Web pages, you can carefully tailor the information you provide over the Web.

Lesson Wrap-Up

This lesson covered how to use Microsoft Project's Web publishing features. You learned how to save GIF images of views, change the information you export to HTML, and format the Web pages you create.

If you are going on to other lessons:

1   On the Standard toolbar, click Save to save changes made to Short Film Project 11. Save the file without a baseline.

2   On the File menu, click Close to close the file.

If you aren't continuing to other lessons:

●   On the File menu, click Exit.

Glossary

Copy Picture The feature that allows you to copy images and create snapshots of a view.

Export map Specifications for exporting fields from Microsoft Project to other file formats, such as HTML. Microsoft Project includes several export maps, which you can use as they are or modify.

HTML template A set of HTML tags and codes that are applied to Microsoft Project data as it's exported via an export map. Microsoft Project includes several HTML templates, which you can use as they are or modify.

Stakeholders All people or organizations that might be affected by project activities. This group includes those working on the project, as well as others (such as customers) external to the project work.

Table A spreadsheet-like presentation of project data, organized in vertical columns and horizontal rows. Each column represents one of the many fields in Microsoft Project, and each row represents a single task or resource.

Timescale In the Gantt Chart and other views, the timescale appears in the upper portion of the view, and it contains major and minor time indicators, such as weeks and days.

View The primary way you see data in Microsoft Project. The three categories of views are charts, sheets, and forms.

Quick Reference

To copy a snapshot of a view to the Windows Clipboard

1   Set up the view with the specific details (such as table, filters, or groups) you want.

2 On the Standard toolbar, click the Copy Picture button.

3 In the Copy Picture dialog box, click For Screen to optimize the snapshot for online viewing or For Printer to optimize it for printing.

4 Select whatever other options you want, and click OK.

To save a snapshot of a view as a GIF image

1 Set up the view with the specific details (such as table, filters, or groups) you want.

2 On the Standard toolbar, click the Copy Picture button.

3 Under the Render Image label, click To GIF Image File, and then specify the file name and location you want.

4 Select whatever other options you want, and click OK.

To save Microsoft Project information as a Web page

1 On the File menu, click Save As Web Page.

2 Specify the filename and location you want, and then click Save.

3 In the Export Mapping dialog box, select Export To HTML Using Standard Template, and click Save.

To customize how Microsoft Project saves a Web page

1 On the File menu, click Save As Web Page.

2 Specify the filename and location you want, and click Save.

3 In the Export Mapping dialog box, select the specific import/export map you want to use, and do one of the following:

- To edit an existing export map, click the Edit button.

- To create a copy of the selected export map, click the Copy button.

4 In the Define Import/Export Map dialog box, select the options you want, and then click OK.

12

Sharing Project Information with Other Programs

**ESTIMATED
TIME
25 min.**

After completing this lesson, you will be able to:

✔ *Copy and paste data to and from Microsoft Project.*

✔ *Open a file produced in another program in Microsoft Project using import/export maps.*

✔ *Save Microsoft Project data to other file formats using import/ export maps.*

In this lesson, you focus on various ways of getting data into and out of Microsoft Project. In addition to the standard Windows copy and paste features with which you might be familiar, Microsoft Project offers a variety of options for importing and exporting data.

Throughout this lesson, you'll see the following terms:

▪ The **source program** is the program from which you copy or import information.

▪ The **destination program** is the program to which you paste or export information.

Practice files for the lesson ➡️ To complete this lesson, you will use a file named Short Film Project 12. Open the Part 3 folder in the MS Project 2000 SBS Practice folder on your hard disk. Open the file 12A, and save it without a baseline as Short Film Project 12 in the Part 3 folder.

Copying and Pasting with Microsoft Project

PROJ2000-3-7
PROJ2000-3-8

You can copy and paste data to and from Microsoft Project using the Copy, Copy Picture, Paste, and Paste Special commands on the Edit menu (or the corresponding buttons on the Standard toolbar). When copying data from Microsoft Project, you can choose one of two options, depending on the results you want.

- You can copy text (such as task names and dates) from a table, and paste it as text in a destination program.

- You can copy a graphic image of a view from Microsoft Project and paste it as a graphic image in the destination program. With the Copy Picture command on the Edit menu, you can create a graphic image of a view or a selected portion of a view. As you might recall from Lesson 11, the Copy Picture feature allows you to optimize the image for onscreen viewing (in Microsoft PowerPoint, for example) or for printing (in Microsoft Word, for example).

There is an important distinction between using Copy and Copy Picture. Using Copy allows you to edit the data in the destination program. However, using Copy Picture yields an image that you can edit only with a graphics editing program, such as Microsoft Paint.

tip
Many Windows programs, such as Microsoft Word and Microsoft Excel, have a Paste Special command on their Edit menus. This command gives you more options for pasting text from Microsoft Project into the destination program. For example, the Paste Special command in Word allows you to paste formatted or unformatted text, a picture, or a Microsoft Project Document Object (an **OLE** object). You can also choose to paste just the data or paste it with a link to the source data in Microsoft Project. For more information about using OLE with Microsoft Project, ask the Office Assistant "Tell me about linked and embedded objects."

You also have two options when pasting data into Microsoft Project from other programs.

- You can paste text (such as a list of task or resource names) into a table in Microsoft Project. For example, you can paste a range of cells from Excel or a sequence of paragraphs from Word to Microsoft Project. One example of this is pasting a series of task names that are organized in a vertical column from Excel or Word to the Task Name column in Microsoft Project.

tip
Pasting text as multiple columns requires some planning. First, make sure that the order of the information in the source program matches the order of the columns in the Microsoft Project table. You can either rearrange the data in the source program to match the column order in the Microsoft Project table, or vice-versa. Second, make sure that the columns in the source program support the same types of data—text, numbers, dates, and so on—as do the columns in Microsoft Project.

- You can paste a graphic image or an OLE object from another program into a graphical portion of a Gantt Chart view. You can also paste a graphic image or an OLE object to a task, resource, or assignment note; to a form view, such as the Task or Resource Form views; or to the header, footer, or legend of a view or report. For more information about printing views and reports, see Lesson 10.

For the short film project, you'd like to add a Gantt Chart image to a document you've prepared for a **stakeholder** of the project. In this exercise, you copy a snapshot of a Gantt Chart and paste it to WordPad (or to Word, if you prefer). You create the snapshot in the same way regardless of the destination program you have in mind. For example, you could paste the snapshot into a file from a word processor or an e-mail editor. To begin, you'll format the Gantt Chart view to show the information you want.

1   On the Project menu, point to Filtered For: All Tasks, and then click Summary Tasks.

   Microsoft Project displays only the summary tasks in the project.

2   On the View menu, click Zoom.

   The Zoom dialog box appears.

3   In the Zoom dialog box, click Entire Project, and then click OK.

Microsoft Project adjusts the timescale of the Gantt Chart to show the entire project. If the Duration column shows #####, double-click the right side of the column heading to adjust the column width. Your screen should look similar to the following illustration.

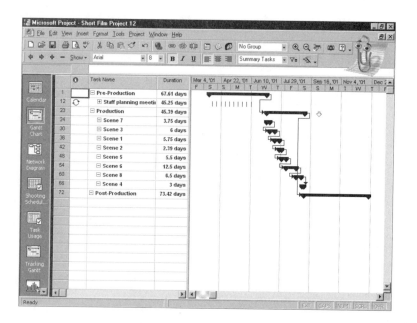

4   On the Standard toolbar, click the Copy Picture button.

The Copy Picture dialog box appears.

5   Under the Render Image label, select For Screen, and then click OK.

Microsoft Project copies a snapshot of the Gantt Chart view to the Windows Clipboard.

Next you'll open a proposal that's been created in a word processor. You can open this in WordPad or in Word if you have it.

6   Do one of the following:

●   If you do not have Word installed, click the Windows Start button, point to Programs, point to Accessories, and then click WordPad.

●   If you have Word installed, start it.

7   In WordPad or Word, on the File menu, click Open.

8   Locate and open the document named Letter To Client in your Part 3 folder.

9   Highlight the paragraph "(insert summary Gantt Chart)."

10 On the Edit menu, click Paste.

11 Microsoft Project pastes the snapshot of the Gantt Chart view from the Windows Clipboard to the document. If you are using WordPad, your screen should look similar to the following illustration.

This image of the Gantt Chart view has been pasted into a WordPad document. The Gantt Chart cannot be edited in this format, except as a graphic image.

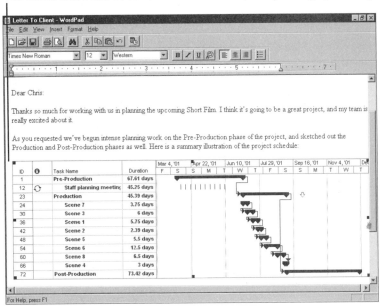

Again note that, rather than pasting into a word processor, you could paste this image into an e-mail message or another type of document.

12 On the WordPad or Word File menu, click Exit. When prompted to save the document, click No.

Opening Other File Formats in Microsoft Project

PROJ2000-1-1
PROJ2000-3-3

Information that you need to incorporate into a Microsoft Project document might come from many sources. A task list from a spreadsheet or resource costs from a database are two examples. You might want to use the unique features of Microsoft Project to analyze data from another program. For example, many people keep task lists and simple project schedules in Excel, but Excel has a very hard time with basic scheduling issues like working and nonworking time.

As you might recall from Lesson 11, Microsoft Project uses export maps when saving data to HTML and other formats. Microsoft Project uses import maps when opening data from another file format in Microsoft Project. In fact, the same maps are used for both opening and saving data, so they are referred to **import/export maps**. (You might also hear these referred to as "data maps.") Import/export maps allow you to specify how you want individual fields in the source program's file to be mapped to individual fields in the destination program. Once you set up an import/export map, it is available to use again.

A colleague has sent you an Excel workbook that contains her recommended tasks, durations, and sequence of activities for a television commercial Industrial Smoke and Mirrors will produce. In this exercise, you open the Excel workbook in Microsoft Project, and then you set up an import/export map to control how the Excel data is imported into Microsoft Project.

tip

If you have Excel installed on your computer, open the workbook named Sample Task List in the Part 3 folder. The important things to note about the workbook are the names and the order of the columns, the presence of a header row (the labels at the top of the columns), and that the data is in a worksheet named Tasks. When you're done viewing the workbook, close it without saving changes.

1   In Microsoft Project, on the File menu click Open.

   The Open dialog box appears.

2   Locate the Part 3 folder in the MS Project 2000 SBS Practice folder on your hard disk.

3   In the Files Of Type box, select Microsoft Excel Workbooks.

tip

While scrolling through the Files Of Type box, you can see the several file formats Microsoft Project can import. If you work with programs that can save in any of these file formats, you can import their data into Microsoft Project. For more information, ask the Office Assistant "Which file formats does Microsoft Project support?"

4   Open the file Sample Task List.

   The Import Mapping dialog box appears. You might recognize this from the work you did in "Changing the Look of a Project Web Page" in Lesson 11. This time, however, rather than exporting from Microsoft Project, you are importing into Microsoft Project.

5   Click the New Map button.

The Define Import/Export Map dialog box appears. In this dialog box, you will identify the source workbook, and you will specify how you want to map the data from the source workbook to Microsoft Project fields.

6   In the Import/Export Map Name box, type **Simple Task List**.

7   Under the Data To Import/Export label, select Tasks.

8   Click the Task Mapping tab.

9   In the Source Worksheet Name list, select Tasks.

Microsoft Project analyzes the header row names from the workbook, and it suggests the Microsoft Project field names that are probable matches.

In this dialog box you specify how Microsoft Project should import data from other file formats, in this case an Excel workbook.

Use the Preview area here to see how the data from another file format will be mapped to Microsoft Project fields, based on the settings you've made above.

10   Click OK to accept the field names it suggests and to close the Define Import/Export Map dialog box.

In the Import Mapping dialog box, note that the new data map appears in the Import/Export Map list.

11   Click Open.

Microsoft Project imports the Excel data into a new Microsoft Project file. Your screen should look similar to the following illustration. (The dates you see on the timescale will differ from those shown because Microsoft Project uses the current date as the project start date in the new file.)

Working with Microsoft Project file formats

To accommodate new capabilities and features, the Microsoft Project file format changes significantly with every major release of the product. Microsoft Project 2000 does a good job of opening and saving files in the Microsoft Project 98 format, but it can't directly open MPP files from versions of Microsoft Project prior to 98. These include Microsoft Project 3.0, Microsoft Project 4.0, and Microsoft Project 95.

On the other hand, Microsoft Project 2000 can open files in the MPX format, which is supported by a variety of project management programs. All previous versions of Microsoft Project can save in the MPX format, so you can convert old Microsoft Project files to the new format. However, it's a one-way trip. After you convert a project to the Microsoft Project 2000 format, you can't save it back to the MPX format or to formats of earlier versions prior to Microsoft Project 98.

When saving a Microsoft Project 2000 file in the Microsoft Project 98 format, you will lose data related to features that are new in the later version. These features include those that handle material resources, custom field formulas, and custom box styles in the Network Diagram view. You also lose timescale baseline data. Microsoft Project 2000 displays a warning when saving a project in the older format; from the warning, you can view additional details in Help.

Because of changes in the file format and in Microsoft Project itself, project schedules are calculated differently in Microsoft Project 2000 than in earlier versions. These differences mean that data that Microsoft Project generates—in some cases, start or finish dates—might change.

After importing the task names and durations, they appear
as an unlinked sequence of tasks, ready for editing.

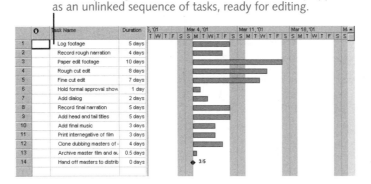

This task list will become a more fully developed schedule that you'll use in
a later lesson.

12 Close and save the new file as Wingtip Toys Commercial 12 in the Part 3
folder. When prompted, save the file without a baseline.

Saving to Other File Formats
from Microsoft Project

Pasting Microsoft Project data into other programs might be fine for one-time
or infrequent needs, but this technique might not work as well if you need to
export a large volume of data from Microsoft Project. Instead, you can save
Microsoft Project data in a variety of file formats. You can take one of two approaches to saving Microsoft Project data in other file formats.

- You can save the entire project as a database. The supported
  formats include Microsoft Project Database (.mpd) and Access
  Database (.mdb). These two formats are almost identical. One
  important difference is that the Microsoft Project Database format
  requires you to save the entire project, but the Access Database
  format allows you to save either the entire project or just the data
  you specify in an export map.

- You can save just the data you specify in a different format. The
  supported formats include Access database, Web page, Excel
  workbook, Excel PivotTable, or tab- or comma-delimited text. In
  Lesson 11, you worked with an export table when saving Microsoft
  Project data to a Web page. You use the same approach when
  specifying data you want to save in any format. You choose the

12

Sharing Project Information

format in which you want to save, you pick a built-in export map (or you create your own), and you export the data.

Although the short film project has not yet started, the project file already contains quite a bit of planned cost data. You'd like to give this data to the financial planner of Industrial Smoke and Mirrors so she can start work on detailed budgets. However, the financial planner uses a budget program that can't work with Microsoft Project files directly. You decide to provide her with cost data as tab-delimited text. This will allow her the greatest flexibility in importing the data into her budget program.

In this exercise, you save project cost data to a text file using a built-in export map. At this point, you should still have Short Film Project 12 open in Microsoft Project.

1 On the File menu, click Save As.

The Save As dialog box appears. Microsoft Project suggests saving the file in the same location from which you opened the practice file. If you see anything different in the Save As dialog box, locate the Part 3 folder.

2 In the File Name box, type **Short Film Project Costs**.

3 In the Save As Type box, click Text (Tab Delimited) from the list, and then click Save.

The Export Mapping dialog box appears. Remember that when using import/export maps, it makes no difference that the current view is in Microsoft Project..

4 Under the Import/Export Map label, select Cost Data By Task, and then click Save.

Microsoft Project saves the text file. To view it, you will open it in Notepad.

5 On the Windows Start menu, point to Programs, point to Accessories, and click Notepad.

Notepad starts.

6 In Notepad, make sure that Word Wrap is turned off.

7 On the File menu, click Open.

8 Open the document named Short Film Project Costs in your Part 3 folder. If you are running Notepad, your screen should look like the following illustration.

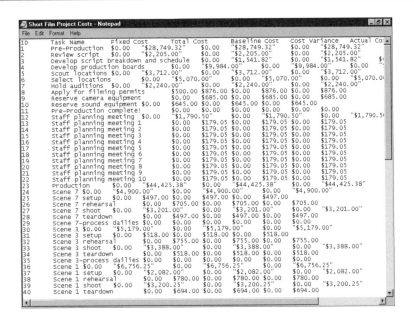

In this file, each field is separated by a tab. It might not be easy for you to read, but this format is easily imported into virtually any data-crunching program.

9   On the File menu, click Exit.

Notepad closes, and you return to Microsoft Project.

More about the database formats

As you might recall from Lesson 1, Microsoft Project is, in many respects, a database program that specializes in project management. So it's no surprise that Microsoft Project can save an entire project as a database. In fact, you can store multiple projects in a single database file for centralized administration or for other purposes. Saving a project in a database format might also help if you need to report or analyze data in ways that Microsoft Project doesn't support.

In addition to supporting the Microsoft Project Database and Access Database formats, Microsoft Project can also work with Microsoft SQL Server and Oracle Server databases through ODBC connectivity. The Microsoft Project Database format is thoroughly documented in the following file (assuming you installed Microsoft Project in the default location):

C:\Program Files\Microsoft Office\Office\1033\Projdb.htm

12

Sharing Project Information

Lesson Wrap-Up

This lesson covered how to exchange data between Microsoft Project and other programs. You learned how to use the Copy and Paste commands and how to import from and export Microsoft Project information to different file formats.

If you are going on to other lessons:

1   On the Standard toolbar, click Save to save changes made to Short Film Project 12. Save the file without a baseline.

2   On the File menu, click Close to close the file.

If you aren't continuing to other lessons:

●   On the File menu, click Exit.

Glossary

Destination program When exchanging data between Microsoft Project and another program, the program into which the data is placed.

Import/export map A set of specifications for importing or exporting specific data to or from Microsoft Project fields. Microsoft Project includes several built-in maps, which you can use as is or modify. Import and export maps are sometimes referred to as data maps.

OLE A protocol that allows you to transfer information, such as a chart or text (called an object), to documents in different programs.

Source program When exchanging data between Microsoft Project and another program, the program in which the data resides originally.

Stakeholders All people or organizations that may be affected by project activities. This group includes those working on the project, as well as others (such as customers) external to the project work.

Quick Reference

To copy text from a Microsoft Project table to the Windows Clipboard

1   Set up the table to display only the data you want to copy—for example, apply a filter or insert or hide columns.

2   Select the range of data you want to copy.

3   On the Edit menu, click Copy.

To copy a snapshot of a view to the Windows Clipboard

1   Set up the view with the specific details (such as tables, filters, or groups) you want.

2   On the Standard toolbar, click Copy Picture.

3   In the Copy Picture dialog box, click either For Screen, to optimize the snapshot for online viewing, or For Printer, to optimize it for printing.

4   Select whatever other options you want, and then click OK.

To open a file in a different format in Microsoft Project

1   On the File menu, click Open.

2   In the Files Of Type box, select the file format you want.

3   Locate and select the specific file you want to open, and then click Open.

4   If the file you selected is not in Microsoft Project format, the Import Mapping dialog box appears. You have the option to use an existing map or to create a map. Choose the options you want, and then click OK.

To save a Microsoft Project file in a different format

1   On the File menu, click Save As.

2   In the Save As dialog box, select the location, and enter the file name you want.

3   In the Save As Type box, select the format you want, and then click Save.

4   In the Export Mapping dialog box, select the export map you want to use, or click New to create a new export map, and then click Save.

13

Sharing Information Between Multiple Projects

ESTIMATED TIME
40 min.

After completing this lesson, you will be able to:

✔ *Create a resource pool.*

✔ *Look at resource allocation across multiple projects.*

✔ *Change resource assignments in a sharer file, and see the effects in the resource pool.*

✔ *Change a resource's working time in the resource pool, and see the effects in the sharer files.*

✔ *Make a specific date nonworking time in the resource pool, and see the effects in the sharer files.*

✔ *Create a project file and make it a sharer file for the resource pool.*

✔ *Manually update the resource pool from a sharer file.*

✔ *Insert project files to create a consolidated file.*

✔ *Link a task in one project to a task in another project.*

Most project managers must juggle more than one project at a time. These projects often share resources and are worked on simultaneously. They might also have dependency relationships between them or with other projects beyond the project manager's control.

Microsoft Project has several features to make it easier to work with multiple project files. In this lesson, you work with a resource pool, consolidate projects, and create cross-project links.

To complete this lesson, you start with two files. One is named Wingtip Toys Commercial 13 and the other is named Parnell Aerospace Promo 13. Close any open project files (including blank files), and open the Part 3 folder in the MS Project 2000 SBS Practice folder on your hard disk. Open the file 13A, and save it without a baseline as Wingtip Toys Commercial 13 in the Part 3 folder. Open the file 13B, and save it without a baseline as Parnell Aerospace Promo 13 in the Part 3 folder.

Creating a Resource Pool

PROJ2000E-1-4
PROJ2000E-1-10

When managing multiple projects, it's common for work resources (people and equipment) to be assigned to more than one project at a time. It might become difficult to coordinate the resources' time among the multiple projects, especially if those projects are managed by different people. For example, a sound engineer in a film studio might have task assignments for a TV commercial, a promotional program, and a documentary film—three projects proceeding simultaneously. In each project, the engineer might be **fully allocated** or even **underallocated**. However, if you add together all of her tasks from these projects, you might discover that she's been **overallocated**, or assigned to work on more tasks than she can handle at one time.

A **resource pool** can help you see how resources are utilized across multiple projects. The resource pool is a Microsoft Project file from which other project files draw their resource information. It contains information about all resources' task assignments from all the project files linked to the resource pool. You can change resource information—such as maximum units, cost rates, and nonworking time—in the resource pool, and all linked project files will use the updated information.

The project files that are linked to the resource pool are called **sharer files**. Here is one way of visualizing a resource pool and sharer files:

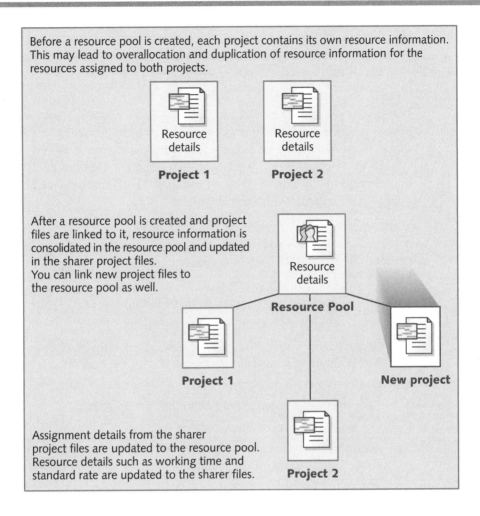

Before a resource pool is created, each project contains its own resource information. This may lead to overallocation and duplication of resource information for the resources assigned to both projects.

Resource details

Project 1

Resource details

Project 2

After a resource pool is created and project files are linked to it, resource information is consolidated in the resource pool and updated in the sharer project files.
You can link new project files to the resource pool as well.

Resource details

Resource Pool

Project 1

New project

Assignment details from the sharer project files are updated to the resource pool. Resource details such as working time and standard rate are updated to the sharer files.

Project 2

If you manage just one project with resources that are not used in other projects, using a resource pool provides you no benefit. However, in more complex project environments, setting up a resource pool allows you to do such things as:

■ View resources' assignment details from multiple projects in a single location.

■ View assignment costs per resource across multiple projects.

■ Find resources who are overallocated across multiple projects, even if those resources are underallocated in individual projects.

■ Enter resource information, such as nonworking time, in any of the sharer files or in the resource pool, so that it is instantly available in the other sharer files.

A resource pool is especially beneficial when working with other Microsoft Project users across a network. In those cases, the resource pool is stored in a central location, such as a network server, and the individual owners of the sharer files (which may be stored locally or on a network server) share the common resource pool. You can have up to 999 sharer files linked to a single resource pool. (You're more likely to exceed your computer's memory capacity than you are to reach this limit, however.)

In this exercise, you arrange the windows of two project files that will become sharer files; this helps you see the effects of creating a resource pool. You then create a file that will become a resource pool, and you link the two sharer files to it.

1   On the Standard toolbar, click the New button.

2   In the Project Information dialog box, click OK.

Because this resource pool will not contain any tasks of its own, you don't care what its start date is. Next you will save the new file.

3   On the File menu, click Save As.

You can name a resource pool anything you want, but it's a good idea to indicate that it is a resource pool in the filename.

4   Save the file as Resource Pool 13 in the Part 3 folder.

5   On the Window menu, click Arrange All.

Microsoft Project arranges the three project file windows within the Microsoft Project window. You don't need to arrange the project windows in this way to create a resource pool, but it's helpful, in this lesson, to see the results as they occur.

Next you switch the file Resource Pool 13 to the Resource Sheet view.

6   On the View bar, click Resource Sheet. Your screen should look similar to the following illustration.

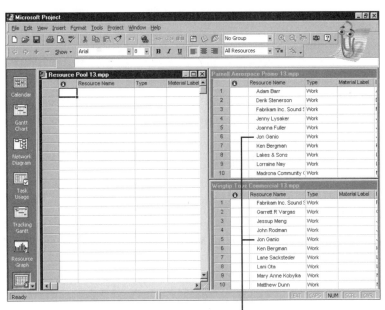

Prior to being linked to a resource pool, some resource names and other details are duplicated in these project files.

Looking at the resource names in the two project files (Parnell Aerospace Promo 13 and Wingtip Toys Commercial 13), you can see that several of the same resources appear in both project files. These include Fabrikam Inc. Sound Studio, Jon Ganio, Ken Bergman, and others. None of these resources are overallocated in either project.

7 Click the title bar of the Parnell Aerospace Promo 13 window.

8 On the Tools menu, point to Resources, and click Share Resources.

The Share Resources dialog box appears.

9 Under Resources For 'Parnell Aerospace Promo 13,' click Use Resources.

10 In the From list, click Resource Pool 13.

11 Click OK to close the Share Resources dialog box.

You see the resource information from the Parnell Aerospace Promo 13 project file appear in the Resource Pool 13 file. Next you will set up Wingtip Toys Commercial 13 project file as a sharer file with the same resource pool.

12 Click the title bar of the Wingtip Toys Commercial 13 window.

13 On the Tools menu, point to Resources, and then click Share Resources.

14 Under Resources For "Wingtip Toys Commercial 13," click Use Resources.

15 In the From list, click Resource Pool 13.

16 Under the On Conflict With Calendar Or Resource Information label, make sure that Pool Takes Precedence is checked.

Checking this option causes Microsoft Project to use resource information (such as cost rates) in the resource pool rather than in the sharer file should it find any differences between the two files.

17 Click OK to close the Share Resources dialog box.

You see the resource information from the Wingtip Toys Commercial 13 project file appear in the Resource Pool 13 file. Your screen should look similar to the following illustration.

Creating a dedicated resource pool

For more information about using Microsoft Project with others over a network or the Web, see Appendix D, "Introducing the Workgroup Features of Microsoft Project."

Any Microsoft Project file, with or without tasks, can serve as a resource pool. However, it's a good idea to designate a file that does not contain tasks as the resource pool. Why is this? Any project with tasks will almost certainly conclude at some point, and you might not want assignments for those tasks (with their associated costs and other details) to be included indefinitely in the resource pool.

Moreover, a dedicated resource pool file without tasks can allow people such as **line managers** or **resource managers** to maintain some information about their resources in the resource pool. These people might not have a role in project management, and they won't need to deal with task-specific details in the resource pool.

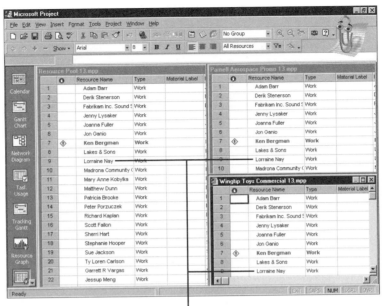

After these two sharer files have been linked to the resource pool, the combined resource information appears in all three files.

The resource pool contains the resource information from both sharer files. Microsoft Project will consolidate information from the sharer files based on the name of the resource. Jon Ganio, for example, is listed only once in the resource pool, no matter how many sharer files list him as a resource. However, Microsoft Project cannot match variations of a resource's name—for example, Jon Ganio from one sharer file and J. Ganio from another. It's a good idea to develop a convention for naming resources and stick with it. For more information about entering resource names, see Lesson 4.

Again, you don't have to arrange the project windows as you did in this exercise to link the sharer files to the resource pool. But it's helpful in this lesson to see the results as they occur.

tip
If you later decide you do not want to use a resource pool with a project file, you can break the link. On the Tools menu, point to Resources, and click Share Resources. Under Resources For "<Current Project Name>," click Use Own Resources.

Viewing Assignment Details in a Resource Pool

One of the most important benefits of using a resource pool is that it allows you to see how resources are allocated across projects. For example, you can identify resources that are overallocated across the multiple projects to which they're assigned.

Here's an example. As you might have noticed in the previous section, the resource Ken Bergman, who was not overallocated in either of the individual project files, did appear overallocated once Microsoft Project accounted for all of his assignments across the multiple projects. Why was this? When Ken's assignments from the two sharer files were combined, they exceeded his capacity to work on at least one day. Although Ken most likely was well aware of this problem, the project manager would not have been without setting up a resource pool (or hearing of the problem directly from Ken).

In this exercise, you look at the information in the resource pool.

Resource Usage

1   Double-click the title bar of the Resource Pool 13 window.

The resource pool window maximizes to fill the Microsoft Project window. In the resource pool, you can see all of the resources from the two sharer files. To get a better view of resource usage, you'll change views.

2   On the View bar, click Resource Usage.

The Resource Usage view appears.

If you cannot see the Resource Usage button on the View bar, click the down arrow button until the button appears.

3   In the Resource Name column, select Ken Bergman and then scroll the Resource Usage view up to display all of Ken's assignments below his name.

4   On the Standard toolbar, click the Go To Selected Task button.

The **timescaled** details on the right side of the Microsoft Project window scroll horizontally to show Ken Bergman's earliest task assignments.

5   Scroll the timescale details to the right to see more of Ken's assignments during the week of August 12.

The red numbers (for example, 16 hours on August 17) indicate days on which Ken is overallocated. For information about resolving problems with resource allocation, see Lesson 7, "Fine-Tuning Resource Details" and Lesson 16, "Identifying and Fixing Problems in Your Project."

Next you will display the Resource Form to get more detail about Ken's assignments.

6   On the Window menu, click Split.

Your screen should look similar to the following illustration.

In this combination view, you can see both the resource's assigned tasks and details about each assignment.

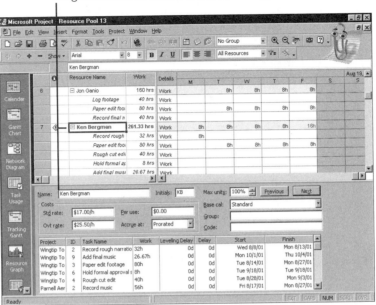

In this combination view, you can see all resources in the resource pool and their assignments (in the upper pane), as well as their additional details (in the lower pane) from all sharer files. Click different resource names in the Resource Usage View to see their assignment details in the Resource Form.

Updating Assignments in a Sharer File

You might recall from Lesson 5 that an assignment is the matching of a resource to a task. Because a resource's assignment details originate in sharer files, Microsoft Project updates the resource pool with assignment details as you make them in the sharer file.

In this exercise, you change resource assignments in a sharer file, and you see the change posted to the resource pool.

1   In the Resource Usage view, scroll up until you see Jenny Lysaker in the Resource Name column, and then click her name.

  You can see that Jenny Lysaker has no task assignments in either sharer file. Next you will assign Jenny to a task in one of the sharer files, and you will see the result in the resource pool.

2   On the Window menu, click Wingtip Toys Commercial 13.

3   On the View bar, click Gantt Chart.

4   On the Standard toolbar, click Assign Resources.

5   In the Task Name column, click Task 5, "Fine cut edit."

6   In the Name column in the Assign Resources dialog box, select Jenny Lysaker, and click Assign.

7   Click Close to close the Assign Resources dialog box.

8   On the Window menu, click Resource Pool 13 to switch back to the resource pool.

Jenny Lysaker's new task assignment appears in the resource pool. Your screen should look similar to the following illustration.

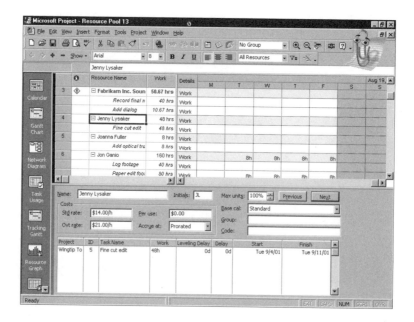

Updating a Resource's Working Time in a Resource Pool

PROJ2000E-1-8

Another important benefit of using a resource pool is that it gives you a central location in which to enter resource details, such as cost rates and working time. When a resource's information is updated in the resource pool, the new information is available in all of the sharer files. This can be especially useful in organizations with a large number of resources working on multiple projects. In larger organizations, people such as line managers, resource managers, or staff in a **program office** are often responsible for keeping general resource information up to date.

In this exercise, you update a resource's working time in the resource pool, and you see changes in the sharer files.

Ken Bergman has told you that he will be unavailable to work on August 30 and 31.

1   In the Resource Name column, select Ken Bergman and then scroll the Resource Usage view up to display all of Ken's assignments below his name.

2   On the Standard toolbar, click the Resource Information button

The Resource Information dialog box appears.

3   Click the Working Time tab.

4   In the calendar below the Select Date(s) label, drag the vertical scroll bar or click the up or down arrow buttons until August 2001 appears.

To select this date range with the mouse, drag from 30 to 31.

5   Select the dates August 30 and 31.

6   Under Set Selected Date(s) To, click Nonworking Time, and then click OK to close the Resource Information dialog box.

Scroll the timescale details to the right far enough to see that, on August 30 and 31, Ken has no work scheduled. (Previously, he had.) Your screen should look similar to the following illustration.

Since August 30 and 31 have been marked as nonworking days for this resource, no work is scheduled on these days.

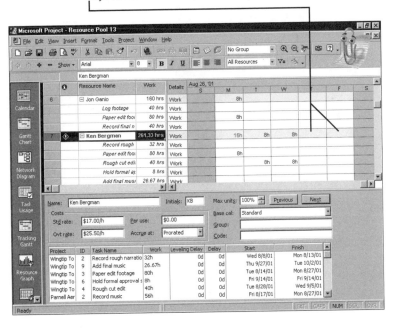

To verify that Ken's nonworking time setting was updated in the sharer files, you'll look at his working time in one of those files.

6   On the Window menu, click Wingtip Toys Commercial 13.

7   On the Standard toolbar, click Assign Resources.

8   In the Assign Resource dialog box, double-click Ken Bergman.

The Resource Information dialog box appears.

9   Click the Working Time tab.

10   In the calendar below the Select Date(s) label, drag the vertical scroll bar or click the up or down arrow buttons until August 2001 appears.

August 30 and 31 are flagged as nonworking days for Ken; the change to this resource's working time in the resource pool has been updated in the sharer files.

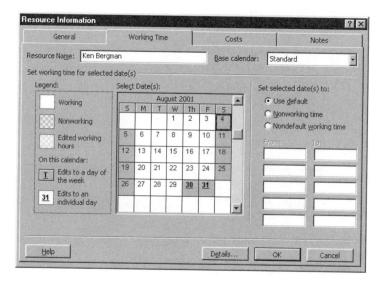

11   Click OK to close the Resource Information dialog box, and click Cancel to close the Assign Resources dialog box.

Updating All Projects' Working Times in a Resource Pool

In the previous exercise, you changed an individual resource's working time in the resource pool, and you saw the change posted to the sharer files. Another powerful capability of a resource pool is to allow you to change working times for a base calendar and to see the changes updated to all sharer files that use that calendar. For example, if you specify that certain days (such as holidays) are to be nonworking days in the resource pool, that change is posted to all sharer files.

tip

All sharer files share the same base calendars, and any changes you make to a base calendar in one sharer file are reflected in all other sharer files through the resource pool. If you have a specific sharer file for which you want to use different base calendar working times, change the base calendar that sharer file uses. For more information about working with base calendars, see Lesson 6, "Fine-Tuning Task Details."

In this exercise, you set nonworking time in the resource pool, and you see this change in all sharer files.

1   On the Window menu, click Resource Pool 13.

The entire company will be attending a local film festival on September 7, and you want this to be a nonworking day for all sharer projects.

2   On the Tools menu, click Change Working Time.

3   In the For box, click Standard (Project Calendar).

4   In the calendar below the Select Date(s) label, drag the vertical scroll bar or click the up or down arrow buttons until September 2001 appears, and then click September 7.

5   Under Set Selected Date(s) To, click Nonworking Time.

September 7 is marked as a nonworking
day in the resource pool.

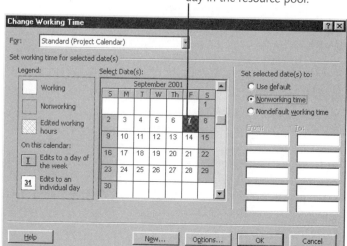

6   Click OK to close the Change Working Time dialog box.

To verify that the changes to the resource pool's Standard base calendar was updated in the sharer files, you'll look at working time in one of the sharer files.

7   On the Window menu, click Parnell Aerospace Promo 13.

8   On the Tools menu, click Change Working Time.

The Change Working Time dialog box appears.

9   In the For box, click Standard (Project Calendar).

10   In the calendar below the Select Date(s) label, drag the vertical scroll bar or click the up or down arrow buttons until September 2001 appears.

September 7 is flagged as a nonworking day.

In the sharer files linked to the resource pool, September 7 appears as a nonworking day in the Standard base calendar.

Change Working Time

For: Standard (Project Calendar)

Set working time for selected date(s)

Legend:
- Working
- Nonworking
- Edited working hours

On this calendar:
- **I** Edits to a day of the week
- **31** Edits to an individual day

Select Date(s):

September 2001

S	M	T	W	Th	F	S
						1
2	3	4	5	6	7	8
9	10	11	12	13	14	15
16	17	18	19	20	21	22
23	24	25	26	27	28	29
30						

Set selected date(s) to:
- ○ Use default
- ◉ Nonworking time
- ○ Nondefault working time

From: To:

Help   New...   Options...   OK   Cancel

11 Click OK to close the Change Working Time dialog box.

If you wish, you can switch to the Wingtip Toys Commercial 13 project file and verify that September 7 is also a nonworking day for that project.

12 Close all open files, and save them without baselines.

Linking New Project Files to a Resource Pool

You can make a project file a sharer file for a resource pool at any time: when initially entering the project file's tasks, after you've assigned resources to tasks, or even after work has begun. Once you've set up a resource pool, you might find it helpful to make sharer files of not only projects already underway but also all new projects. That way, you get used to relying on the resource pool for resource information.

In this exercise, you create a project file, and you make it a sharer file for the resource pool.

1 Open the Part 3 folder in the MS Project 2000 SBS Practice folder, select Resource Pool 13, and click Open. When prompted, click the second option to open the file read-write.

2 On the Standard toolbar, click the New button.

The Project Information dialog box appears.

3 In the Start Date box, type **8/6/01**, and then click OK.

4   On the File menu, click Save As.

5   Save the file as Hanson Brothers Project 13 in the Part 3 folder.

6   On the Standard toolbar, click Assign Resources.

The Assign Resources dialog box is initially empty because we have not yet entered any resource information in this file.

7   On the Tools menu, point to Resources, and then click Share Resources.

The Share Resources dialog box appears.

8   Under Resources For "Hanson Brothers Project 13," click Use Resources.

9   In the From list, click Resource Pool 13, and then click OK to close the Share Resources dialog box.

In the Assign Resources dialog box, you see all of the resources from the resource pool appear.

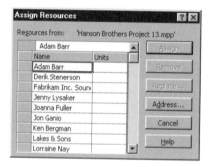

Now these resources are ready for assignments to tasks in this project.

10   Click Cancel to close the Assign Resources dialog box.

11   On the File menu, click Close. When prompted, click Yes to save your changes.

The Hansen Brothers Project 13 file closes, and the Resource Pool 13 file remains open.

12   On the File menu, click Close. When prompted, click Yes to save your changes.

Opening a Sharer File and Updating a Resource Pool

If you are sharing a resource pool with other Microsoft Project users across a network, whoever has the resource pool open as read/write prevents others from updating resource information such as standard cost rates. For this reason, it's a good idea to open the resource pool as read-only and to use the Update Resource Pool command only when you need to update the resource pool. You can select the Update Resource Pool command from the Resources submenu of the Tools menu. This command updates the resource pool file with new assignment information; once that's done, anyone else who opens the resource pool file will see the latest assignment information.

In this lesson, you're working with the resource pool and sharer files locally. If you are going to use a resource pool over a network, it's a good idea to understand the updating process. This exercise introduces you to that process.

In this exercise, you change assignments in a sharer file, and then you manually update the resource pool.

1   Open the Part 3 folder in the MS Project 2000 SBS Practice folder, select Wingtip Toys Commercial 13, and then click Open.

Because this file is a sharer file linked to a resource pool, Microsoft Project gives you the following options:

> ## tip
> If you do not have the Office Assistant displayed, you will see a similar message in a message box. For information about setting up your computer to more closely match the illustrations in this book, see Appendix B, "Matching the Exercises."

2   Choose the first option to open the resource pool as well as the sharer file.

Next you will change some assignments in the sharer file.

3   On the Standard toolbar, click Assign Resources.

4   In the Task Name column, click Task 12, "Archive master film and audio tape."

5   In the Name column in the Assign Resources dialog box, select Stephanie Hooper, and click Assign.

6   In the Task Name column, click Task 6, "Hold formal approval showing."

7   In the Name column in the Assign Resources dialog box, select Ray Zambroski, and then click Remove.

You've made two assignment changes in the sharer file. But, because the resource pool is opened as read-only, those changes have not been saved in the resource pool. Next you will update the resource pool.

This command is unavailable when the resource pool is open as read-write.

8   On the Tools menu, point to Resources, and then click Update Resource Pool.

Microsoft Project updates the assignment information in the resource pool file with the new details from the sharer file.

> ## tip
> Only assignment information is saved to the resource pool from the sharer file. Any changes you make to resource details, such as Max. Units, in the sharer file are not saved in the resource pool when you update. When you want to change the resource details, open the resource pool as read/write. Once it's open as read/write, you can change resource details in either the resource pool or the sharer file, and the other file will be updated automatically.

What to do when a sharer file changes locations

If the location of a sharer file changes (for example, if the file is moved from one network server to another), Microsoft Project cannot detect the move and will not find the sharer file in its new location. If this happens, you should first break the link to the old location in the resource pool by choosing options in the Share Resources dialog box. (You can open this dialog box from the Resources submenu of the Tools menu.) Then you should open the sharer file in its new location and relink the file to the resource pool by choosing options in the same dialog box.

Next you will change an assignment in the sharer file, close the file, and then update the resource pool.

9 In the Task Name column, click Task 3, "Paper edit footage."

10 In the Name column in the Assign Resources dialog box, select Lane Stacksteder, and then click Assign.

11 Click Close to close the Assign Resources dialog box.

12 On the File menu, click Close.

13 When prompted to save changes, click Yes.

14 When prompted, click OK to save the file without a baseline.

Microsoft Project determines that because the resource pool was open as read-only, the latest assignment changes from the sharer files have not been updated in the resource pool file. You are offered the choices shown in the following illustration.

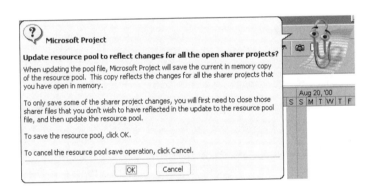

15 Click OK.

Microsoft Project updates the assignment information with the new details from the sharer file. The resource pool remains open as read-only.

Working with Consolidated Projects

PROJ2000-6-1
PROJ2000-6-2
PROJ2000-6-4
PROJ2000E-8-1
PROJ2000E-8-2

Complex projects often involve several people working on tasks at different times, in different locations, and frequently for different supervisors. Although a resource pool can help you manage resource details across projects, it might not give you the level of control that you want over tasks and relationships between projects.

A good way to pull together far-flung project information is to use a **consolidated project**. This is a Microsoft Project file that contains other Microsoft

Project files, called **inserted projects**. The inserted projects do not reside within the consolidated project, but they are linked to it in such a way that they can be viewed and edited from the consolidated project. If the inserted project is edited outside of the consolidated project, the updated information appears in the consolidated project the next time it is opened.

> ## tip
> Consolidated projects are also known as master projects, and inserted projects are also known as subprojects. In this lesson, we use the terms consolidated and inserted projects.

Using consolidated projects allows you to do such things as

- See all tasks from your organization's projects in a single view.
- "Roll up" project information to higher levels of management. For example, one team's project might be an inserted project for the department's consolidated project, which in turn may be an inserted project for the organization's consolidated project.
- Divide your project data to match the nature of your project, for example, by phase, component, or location.

Consolidated projects use the Microsoft Project outlining features. An inserted project appears as a summary task in the consolidated project, except its summary Gantt bar is gray and an inserted project icon appears in the Indicators column. When you save a consolidated project, any changes you've made to inserted projects are saved in the source files as well.

In this exercise, you insert a project into a new project.

1   On the Standard toolbar, click the New button.

     The Project Information dialog box appears.

2   In the Start Date box, type **8/6/01**, and then click OK.

3   On the File menu, click Save As.

4   Save the file as Consolidated Projects 13 in the Part 3 folder.

     Next you insert two projects into this new project.

5   On the Insert menu, click Project.

     The Insert Project dialog box appears.

6 In the Part 3 folder, click Parnell Aerospace Promo 13. Hold down the Ctrl key, click Wingtip Toys Commercial 13, and then click Insert.

Microsoft Project inserts the two projects into the consolidated project as collapsed summary tasks. Your screen should look similar to the following illustration.

Inserted projects initially appear as collapsed summary tasks in the consolidated project file. Note the Inserted Project icon in the Indicators column, and the gray task bars.

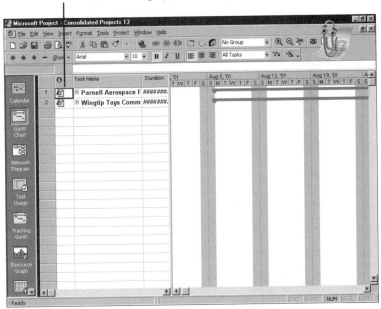

tip
If you point to the Inserted Project icon in the Indicators column, Microsoft Project displays the full path to the inserted project file.

7 Select the names of Tasks 1 and 2.

8 On the Formatting toolbar, click the Show button, and then click All Subtasks.

Microsoft Project expands the inserted projects' tasks.

9 On the View menu, click Zoom, click Entire Project, and then click OK.

Microsoft Project adjusts the timescale in the Gantt Chart so that all tasks in the two projects are visible. Your screen should look similar to the following illustration.

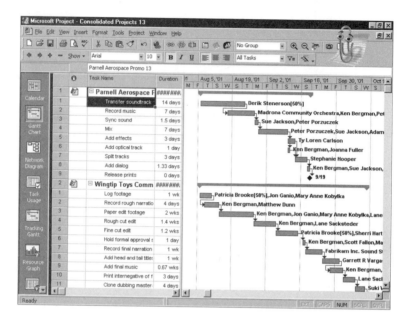

The two inserted projects are linked to the consolidated project file.

To remove an inserted project from a consolidated project, select the inserted project's summary task. On the Edit menu, click Delete Task.

Here are a few more things to keep in mind when working with consolidated project files:

- To remove an inserted project from a consolidated project, select the inserted project's summary task. On the Edit menu, click Delete Task.

- Rather than manually creating a consolidated project file and inserting projects into it, you can quickly consolidate all open project files. On the Window menu, click New Window. Select the names of the open project files you want to consolidate, and then click OK.

- If you frequently work on multiple projects that you don't want to consolidate, you can save them as a workspace. The workspace file consists of the names of the open project files, and it allows you to open several files with one action. On the File menu, click Save Workspace.

■ You can add tasks directly to a consolidated project file, independent of any inserted project files. You do this just as you would in a stand-alone project file; just make sure that the point at which you insert the new task is not within an inserted project's task list.

■ To save baseline values of tasks that reside directly within the consolidated project file, select the tasks, on the Tools menu point to Tracking, and then click Save Baseline. Tasks from inserted projects are not affected.

■ By default, Microsoft Project calculates all tasks from inserted projects and any tasks entered directly in the consolidated project as if they were all tasks in a single project file, and identifies a single critical path. However, you can display each inserted project's critical path within the consolidated project. To display this, clear the Inserted Projects Are Calculated Like Summary Tasks box on the Calculation tab of the Options dialog box (Tools menu).

Creating Dependencies Between Projects

PROJ2000-6-3

Other than the International Space Station, most projects do not exist in a vacuum. Tasks or phases in one project might depend on tasks in other projects. You can show such dependencies by linking tasks between projects.

Some of the reasons that you might need to create dependencies between projects include

■ The completion of one task in a project might enable the start of a task in another project. For example, another project manager might need to complete an environmental impact statement before you can start to construct a building. Even if these two tasks are managed in separate project files (perhaps because separate departments of a development company are completing them), one project has a logical dependency on the other.

■ A person or a piece of equipment might be assigned to a task in one project, and you need to delay the start of a task in another project until that resource completes the first task. The two tasks might have nothing in common other than that the same resource is required for both.

Task relationships between project files look similar to links between tasks within a project file, except that external predecessor and successor tasks have gray task names and Gantt bars. Such tasks are sometimes referred to as **ghost tasks,** because they are not linked to tasks within the project file, only to tasks in other project files.

In this exercise, you link tasks in two project files, and you see the results in the two project files, as well as in a consolidated project file.

1   Open the Part 3 folder in the MS Project 2000 SBS Practice folder on your hard disk, click Parnell Aerospace Promo 13, and then click Open.

2   On the View bar, click Gantt Chart.

3   In the Entry table, click the name of Task 8, "Add dialog."

4   On the Standard toolbar, click the Go To Selected Task button.

To the right of the task's Gantt bar, one of the resources assigned to this task is named Fabrikam Inc. Sound Studio. You want to use this sound studio for work on the Wingtips Toys project after this task is completed. Next you will link Task 8 to a task in the Wingtip Toys Commercial 13 project file.

5   Open the Part 3 folder in the MS Project 2000 SBS Practice folder, select Wingtip Toys Commercial 13, and then click Open.

6   Select the name of Task 7, "Record final narration."

7   On the Standard toolbar, click the Task Information button.

The Task Information dialog box appears. In it, you will enter the filename and task ID of the predecessor task in this format: File Name\Task ID.

8   Click the Predecessors tab.

9   In the ID column, click the next empty cell below Task 6, and type **Parnell Aerospace Promo 13\8**.

10   Press the Enter key, and then click OK to close the Task Information dialog box.

Microsoft Project inserts the ghost task named "Add dialog" to the project.

11   On the Standard toolbar, click the Go To Selected Task button.

The ghost task appears in the project to which it is linked with a gray task name.

The ghost task's Gantt bar is gray.

If you point to the ghost task's Gantt bar, Microsoft Project displays a ToolTip that contains details about the ghost task, including the full path to the external project file where the external predecessor task (the ghost task) resides.

Because the ghost task finishes on 9/19 and the tasks are linked with a finish-to-start relationship, the start date of Task 8, "Record final narration," moves out to 9/19. All subsequent successor tasks are also rescheduled. Next you'll look at the ghost task in the Parnell project.

12 On the Window menu, click Parnell Aerospace Promo 13.

Here you can see that ghost Task 9, "Record final narration," is a successor for Task 8, "Add dialog." Because Task 8 is a successor task with no other links to this project, it has no effect on other tasks here.

The link between these two project files will remain until you break it. Deleting a task in the source file or the ghost task in the destination file deletes the corresponding task or ghost task in the other file.

To conclude this exercise, you will display the link between these two projects in the consolidated project file.

13 On the Window menu, click Consolidated Projects 13.

You can see the link line between the task "Add dialog" in the first inserted project and the task "Record final narration" in the second inserted project.

tip
When viewing a consolidated project, you can quickly create cross-project links by clicking the Link Tasks button on the Standard toolbar. Dragging the mouse between two task bars will do the same thing.

Your screen should look similar to the following illustration.

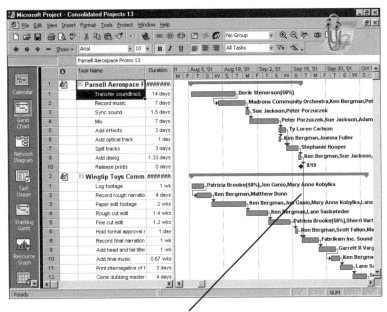

In the consolidated project file, the cross
project link appears as a normal task link.

Because you are looking at a consolidated project file, the cross-project link
does not appear as a ghost task.

tip

Each time you open a linked project file, Microsoft Project will prompt you to
update the cross-project links. You can suppress this prompt if you would rather
not be reminded, or you can tell Microsoft Project to automatically accept updated data from the linked project file. On the Tools menu, click Options, and
then click the View tab. Under Cross-Project Linking Options For <File Name>,
select the options you want.

Lesson Wrap-Up

This lesson covered how to create a resource pool and a consolidated project
file. You also learned how to link tasks between projects.

If you are going on to other lessons:

- Save and close all open files. When prompted, save without baselines and
  update the resource pool.

If you aren't continuing to other lessons:

●   On the File menu, click Exit.

Glossary

Consolidated project A Microsoft Project file that contains one or more inserted project files. The inserted projects are linked to the consolidated project so that any changes to the inserted projects are reflected in the consolidated file, and vice-versa. A consolidated project file is also known as a master project file.

Fully allocated The condition of a resource when the total work of its task assignments is exactly equal to that resource's work capacity. For example, a full-time resource assigned to work 40 hours per week is fully allocated. In Microsoft Project, a resource's work capacity is measured in units. One full-time resource has 100% units (recorded in the Max. Units field).

Ghost task A task that represents a link from one Microsoft Project file to another. Ghost tasks appear as gray bars.

Inserted project A Microsoft Project file that is inserted into another Microsoft Project file, called a consolidated file. An inserted project is also known as a subproject.

Line manager A manager of a group of resources; also called a functional manager. A line manager might also have project management skills and responsibilities, depending on the organization's structure.

Overallocated The condition of a resource when it is assigned to do more work than can be done within the resource's normal work capacity. In Microsoft Project, a resource's work capacity is measured in units. One full-time resource has 100% units (recorded in the Max. Units field).

Program office In project-driven organizations, a program office oversees a collection of projects (such as producing wings and producing engines), each of which contributes to a complete deliverable (such as an airplane) and the organization's strategic objectives.

Resource manager Someone who oversees resource usage in project activities specifically to manage the time and costs of resources. A resource manager might also have project management skills and responsibilities, depending on the organization's structure.

Resource pool A Microsoft Project file that other projects use for their resource information. Resource pools contain information about resources' task assignments from all project files (called sharer files) linked to the resource pool.

Sharer file Project files that are linked to a resource pool file. Sharer files share resource assignment details and other information, such as non-working time and project calendar settings, with the resource pool file.

Timescale In views such as the Gantt Chart view and the Resource Usage view, the timescale appears as a band across the top of the grid and denotes units of time. The timescale is divided into a major scale (such as weeks) and a minor scale (such as days). You can customize the timescale in the Timescale dialog box, which you can open from the Format menu.

Underallocated The condition of a resource when the total work of its task assignments is less than that resource's capacity to work. For example, a full-time resource working 25 hours per week is underallocated. In Microsoft Project, a resource's work capacity is measured in units. One full-time resource has 100% units (recorded in the Max. Units field).

Workspace A set of files and settings that you can save and reopen by opening a single workspace file. Workspace files have the .mpw extension.

Quick Reference

To create a resource pool

1   On the Standard toolbar, click the New button.
2   Save the new project file that will become a resource pool.
3   Open one of the Microsoft Project files you want to make a sharer file.
4   On the Tools menu, point to Resources, and click Share Resources.
5   Under Resources For <Sharer File Name>, click Use Resources.
6   In the From list, click the name of your resource pool file, and click OK to close the Share Resources dialog box.
7   If you have more than one sharer file, open another sharer file.
8   Repeat steps 4–6 for the other sharer files.

To view assignment details in the resource pool

1   On the View bar, click Resource Usage.
2   In the Resource Name column, select the name of a resource.

3   On the Standard toolbar, click the Go To Selected Task button.

4   Scroll the timescaled details to the right to see more of the resource's assignments.

5   On the Window menu, click Split to show the Resource Form.

6   On the Window menu, click Remove Split to hide the Resource Form.

To update assignments in a sharer file

1   On the View bar, click Gantt Chart.

2   On the Standard toolbar, click Assign Resources.

3   In the Task Name column, click the name of a task for which you'd like to assign or remove a resource.

4   In the Name column in the Assign Resources dialog box, select a resource name, and click Assign or Remove.

To update a resource's working time in the resource pool

1   On the View bar, click Resource Usage.

2   In the Resource Name column of the Resource Usage view, select the name of the resource whose working time you want to change, and click the Resource Information button.

3   In the Resource Information dialog box, click the Working Time tab.

4   In the calendar below the Select Date(s) label, drag the vertical scroll bar or click the up or down arrow buttons until the month you want appears.

5   Select the dates you want to designate as nonworking time.

6   Under Set Selected Date(s) To, click Nonworking Time, and click OK to close the Resource Information dialog box.

To update working time for all sharer files from the resource pool

1   Open the resource pool file as read/write.

2   On the Tools menu, click Change Working Time.

3   In the For box, click the base calendar you want to change, for example "Standard (Project Calendar)."

4   In the calendar below the Select Date(s) label, drag the vertical scroll bar or click the up or down arrow buttons until the month you want appears, and then select the specific days you want to make nonworking time.

5   Under Set Sselected Date(s) To, click Nonworking Time.

6   Click OK to close the Change Working Time dialog box.

To link new project files to the resource pool

1   Open the resource pool file as read/write.

2 On the Standard toolbar, click the New button.

3 In the Project Information dialog box, enter a project start date, and click OK.

4 On the Tools menu, point to Resources, and click Share Resources.

5 In the Share Resources dialog box, under Resources For <File Name>, click Use Resources.

6 In the From list, click the name of the resource pool, and click OK to close the Share Resources dialog box.

To edit a sharer file and update the resource pool

1 OpenIn a sharer file.

2 When prompted, open the resource pool as well as the sharer file.

3 In the sharer file, make changes to assignments.

4 On the Tools menu, point to Resources, and click Update Resource Pool.

To create a consolidated project file

1 On the Standard toolbar, click the New button.

2 Enter a project start date, and then save the new project file.

3 On the Insert menu, click Project.

4 In the Insert Projects dialog box, locate and select the Microsoft Project file you want to insert into the consolidated project file. To select multiple files, hold down the Ctrl key while you click the names of the files.

5 Click Insert.

To create task dependencies between projects

1 Open the two project files between which you want to create a task dependency.

2 Switch to the project file that contains the task you want to make the successor task.

3 On the View bar, click Gantt Chart.

4 In the Entry table, click the name of the task you want to make the successor task.

5 On the Standard toolbar, click the Task Information button.

6 Click the Predecessors tab.

7 In the ID column, click the next empty cell below any other predecessor tasks, and enter the name of the predecessor task from the other project file in this format: File Name\Task ID.

8 Press the Enter key, and click OK to close the Task Information dialog box.

Review & Practice

ESTIMATED
TIME
15 min.

You will review and practice how to:

✔ *Sort and filter data.*

✔ *View and customize a report, and save Microsoft Project data to another file format.*

✔ *Draw a text box on a Gantt Chart, and copy the Gantt Chart view to the Clipboard.*

✔ *Insert a Microsoft Project file into a consolidated file.*

Review & Practice

Before you move on to Part 4, which covers tracking actual work in a project, you can practice the skills you learned in Part 3 by working through this Review & Practice section.

Scenario

Before your film company, Industrial Smoke and Mirrors, can begin actual work on the music video for the band Fourth Coffee, you must provide more detailed information about the project plan to the band's management and the recording company. The people who want the additional information are mainly concerned with cost and schedule details. You'd also like to move the music video project plan into your organization's overall portfolio management file for organizational planning purposes.

Practice files
for the lesson ⇨ To complete this section, you will use files named Music Video Project 3 and Consolidated Projects 3. Before you begin this section, open the Part 3 folder in the MS Project 2000 SBS Practice folder on your hard disk. Open the file Part3A, and save it without a baseline as Music Video Project 3 in the Part 3 folder. Next, open the file Part3B, and save it without a baseline as Consolidated Projects 3.

Step 1: Display Only the Specific Information You Want

For a demonstration of how to complete this step, double-click Part 3 Step 1 in the Multimedia folder on the Microsoft Project 2000 Step by Step CD-ROM.

You must complete the exercises in steps 1 through 4 sequentially.

Leonard Zuvela, manager of the band Fourth Coffee, has asked you for some specific cost information. First, he'd like to see the resource costs listed from highest to lowest. Leonard has to secure management approval for any resources with a planned cost greater than $5,000, so he'd like to see who those resources are.

Next, you've identified a specific director for the project who has asked for a "plain-old month-at-a-glance" sort of schedule for her work on the project. You decide to give her a filtered Calendar view.

1   Switch to the Music Video Project 3 file, and then switch it to the Resource Sheet view.

2   Display the Cost table.

3   Sort the resources by cost.

4   Turn on AutoFilter and filter the Cost column to display only resources with a cost greater than $5,000.

5   Switch to Calendar view and filter to see only the tasks that use the resource "Director."

For more information about	See
Sorting resources or tasks	Lesson 9
Using AutoFilter	Lesson 9
Viewing and customizing the Calendar view	Lesson 9

Step 2: Print and Export Project Information

For a demonstration, double-click Part 3 Step 2 in the Multimedia folder.

On many projects, it's common for the work resources and others involved to have limited or no knowledge of traditional project management documents such as Gantt Charts or with project management programs such as Microsoft Project. To properly communicate project details to others involved with the music video project, you will need to print a report called "Who Does What" and export comparable data to Microsoft Excel format for others to import and work with.

1   View the available assignment reports.

2   View the "Who Does What" report in the Print Preview window.

3   Add the text "Industrial Smoke and Mirrors: Confidential" to the left side of the report's header.

4   Close the Print Preview window.

5   Save the project information as Video Project Who Does What in a Microsoft Excel Workbook format in the Part 3 folder and use the Who Does What Report export map.

6   If you have Excel, view the exported file.

For more information about	See
Viewing and customizing reports	Lesson 10
Customizing page elements such as headers and footers	Lesson 10
Exporting Microsoft Project data to other file formats	Lesson 12

Step 3: Draw On and Copy the Gantt Chart View

For a demonstration, double-click Part 3 Step 3 in the Multimedia folder.

You've probably noticed that people like to mark up project schedules such as Gantt Charts with related information. Even though you've recorded a deadline for the music video project, once it's printed the meaning of the deadline indicator on the Gantt Chart may be lost to some people who view it. To highlight the deadline, you'll find it effective to draw a text box on the Gantt Chart and attach it to the project's milestone task.

Leonard Zuvela has asked you for a graphic image of the Gantt Chart you showed him earlier so that he may include it in communications to his own organization. In this step you'll produce a snapshot of the Gantt Chart to send to him.

1   Switch to the Gantt Chart view.

2   Draw a text box on the Gantt Chart that says "Deadline 7/2/01." Change the box's fill to yellow and then attach the box to Task 11.

3   Take a snapshot of the Gantt Chart view rendered for the screen.

4   Paste the image into a WordPad document, or an e-mail message.

For more information about	See
Using the drawing tools in Microsoft Project	Lesson 10
Capturing a Gantt Chart view to the Clipboard	Lesson 11

Step 4: Consolidate Microsoft Project Files

For a demonstration, double-click Part 3 Step 4 in the Multimedia folder.

In addition to managing some of the individual projects Industrial Smoke and Mirrors is involved with, part of your job is to keep an eye on the aggregate or portfolio of active and planned projects. To conclude this Review & Practice, you insert Music Video Project 3 into a consolidated project file that contains links to other planned projects.

1   Switch to the Consolidated Projects 3 file .

2   Insert Music Video Project 3 into Consolidated Projects 3 above Promo Part 3.

3   In Consolidated Projects 3, expand all of the inserted projects to show all tasks.

4   Change the zoom settings to view all of the inserted projects in Consolidated Projects 3.

For more information about	See
Inserting projects into a consolidated project file	Lesson 13
Expanding and collapsing summary tasks in a consolidated project file	Lesson 13
Adjusting the zoom settings of the Gantt Chart view	Lesson 11

Finish the Review & Practice

If you are going on to Part 4:

1   On the Standard toolbar, click Save to save changes made to Consolidated Projects 3. Save the file without a baseline.

2   On the File menu, click Close to close the file.

3   Save and close Music Video 3 without a baseline.

If you aren't continuing to Part 4:

●   On the File menu, click Exit.

14

Tracking Progress Against the Project Plan

**ESTIMATED
TIME
40 min.**

After completing this lesson, you will be able to:

✔ *Save current values in the schedule as a baseline.*

✔ *Record actual work completed through a specific date.*

✔ *Record tasks as being a particular percent complete.*

✔ *Enter actual start, finish, and duration values for tasks.*

✔ *Enter daily actual work values for tasks and assignments.*

✔ *Change the remaining work or duration of tasks.*

✔ *Save an interim plan.*

PROJ2000-2-4

Up to now, these lessons have focused on project **planning**—developing and communicating the details of a project before actual work begins. After work begins, so does the next phase of project management: tracking progress. **Tracking** means recording project details such as who did what work, when the work was done, and at what cost. These details are often called **actuals**.

Tracking actuals is essential to properly managing, as opposed to just planning, a project. The project manager must know how well the project team is performing and when to take corrective action. Properly tracking project performance and comparing it against the original plan lets you answer such questions as:

- Are tasks starting and finishing as planned and, if not, what will be the impact on the project's finish date?

- Are resources spending more or less time than planned to complete tasks?

- Is it taking more or less money than planned to complete tasks?

Microsoft Project supports several ways to track progress, depending on the level of detail or control required by you, your project **sponsor**, and other **stakeholders**. Tracking progress to the lowest levels of detail requires more work from you and, possibly, from the resources working on the project. So before you begin tracking progress, you should determine the level of detail you need. The different levels of tracking described in this lesson include the following:

- Record project work as scheduled. This works best if everything in the project occurs exactly as planned. Hey, it could happen!

- Record each task's percentage of completion, either at precise values or at increments such as 25%, 50%, 75%, or 100%.

- Record each task's actual duration and start and finish dates when you need a finer level of detail than just the percentage complete.

- Track work by time period. This is the most detailed level of tracking. Here you record actual work values per day, per week, or by another interval.

You may find that you need to apply a combination of these approaches within a single project, because different portions of a project may have different tracking needs. For example, you might want to track high-risk tasks more closely than low-risk ones. Each of these approaches to tracking progress is described in this lesson.

To complete this lesson, you will use a file named Short Film Project 14. Before you begin this lesson, open the Part 4 folder in the MS Project 2000 SBS Practice folder on your hard disk. Open the file 14A, and save it without a baseline as Short Film Project 14 in the Part 4 folder.

Saving a Project Baseline

One of the most important activities of a project manager after developing a project plan is to record actuals and evaluate project performance. To judge project performance properly, you'll need to compare it against your original plan. This original plan is called the baseline plan, or just **baseline**. A baseline is a collection of important values in a project plan, such as the planned start and finish dates of the various tasks and assignments with their planned costs. When you save a baseline, Microsoft Project takes a "snapshot" of the existing values and saves it in the Microsoft Project file for future comparison.

The specific values saved in a baseline include the task, resource, and assignment **fields** and **timephased fields** listed in the following table.

Task	Resource	Assignment
Start field	Work and timephased work fields	Start field
Finish field	Cost and timephased cost fields	Finish field
Duration field		Work and timephased work fields
Work and timephased work fields		Cost and timephased cost fields
Cost and timephased cost fields		

tip

Timephased values are spread over time. For example, the value of a task's work field might be 40 hours, but its timephased values might be eight hours per day spread over five days. You can view timephased values in the timescale grid on the right side of views such as those for Task Usage or Resource Usage. Timephased values are always organized in a grid with the timescale at the top of the grid, which you can adjust.

You should save the baseline when:

- You have developed the project plan as fully as possible. (However, this doesn't mean you can't add additional tasks, resources, or assignments to the project after work has started; usually this is unavoidable.)

- You have not yet started entering actual values, such as for work completed.

The Short Film Project plan is now fully developed, and actual work is to begin on the project shortly. In this exercise, you save the baseline for the Short Film Project and then view various task, resource, and assignment baseline values.

1   On the Tools menu, point to Tracking and click Save Baseline.

The Save Baseline dialog box appears.

2   Click OK.

Microsoft Project saves the baseline, even though in the Gantt Chart view there's no indication that anything has changed. You'll now see some of the changes caused by saving the baseline.

3   On the View menu, click More Views.

The More Views dialog box appears.

4   In the Views box, select Task Sheet and click Apply.

In the Task Sheet view you have more room to see the fields in the table, because it doesn't include the Gantt Chart. Now switch to a different table in the Task Sheet view.

5   On the View menu, point to Table: Entry and click Work.

The Work table appears. This table includes both the Work and Baseline columns, shown side by side for easy comparison.

tip

If necessary, double-click the right edge of any column names that display pound signs (###) to see all of the field values.

Your screen should look similar to the following illustration.

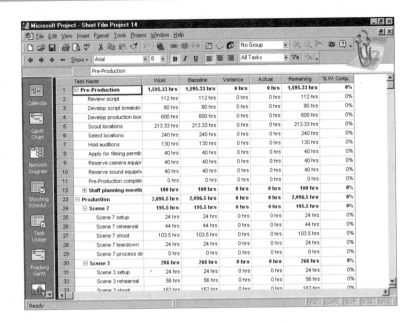

	Task Name	Work	Baseline	Variance	Actual	Remaining	% W. Comp.
1	⊟ Pre-Production	1,595.33 hrs	1,595.33 hrs	0 hrs	0 hrs	1,595.33 hrs	0%
2	Review script	112 hrs	112 hrs	0 hrs	0 hrs	112 hrs	0%
3	Develop script breakdo	80 hrs	80 hrs	0 hrs	0 hrs	80 hrs	0%
4	Develop production boa	600 hrs	600 hrs	0 hrs	0 hrs	600 hrs	0%
5	Scout locations	213.33 hrs	213.33 hrs	0 hrs	0 hrs	213.33 hrs	0%
6	Select locations	240 hrs	240 hrs	0 hrs	0 hrs	240 hrs	0%
7	Hold auditions	130 hrs	130 hrs	0 hrs	0 hrs	130 hrs	0%
8	Apply for filming permit:	40 hrs	40 hrs	0 hrs	0 hrs	40 hrs	0%
9	Reserve camera equipr	40 hrs	40 hrs	0 hrs	0 hrs	40 hrs	0%
10	Reserve sound equipm	40 hrs	40 hrs	0 hrs	0 hrs	40 hrs	0%
11	Pre-Production complet	0 hrs	0 hrs	0 hrs	0 hrs	0 hrs	0%
12	⊞ Staff planning meetii	100 hrs	100 hrs	0 hrs	0 hrs	100 hrs	0%
23	⊟ Production	2,096.5 hrs	2,096.5 hrs	0 hrs	0 hrs	2,096.5 hrs	0%
24	⊟ Scene 7	195.5 hrs	195.5 hrs	0 hrs	0 hrs	195.5 hrs	0%
25	Scene 7 setup	24 hrs	24 hrs	0 hrs	0 hrs	24 hrs	0%
26	Scene 7 rehearsal	44 hrs	44 hrs	0 hrs	0 hrs	44 hrs	0%
27	Scene 7 shoot	103.5 hrs	103.5 hrs	0 hrs	0 hrs	103.5 hrs	0%
28	Scene 7 teardown	24 hrs	24 hrs	0 hrs	0 hrs	24 hrs	0%
29	Scene 7-process de	0 hrs	0 hrs	0 hrs	0 hrs	0 hrs	0%
30	⊟ Scene 3	266 hrs	266 hrs	0 hrs	0 hrs	266 hrs	0%
31	Scene 3 setup	24 hrs	24 hrs	0 hrs	0 hrs	24 hrs	0%
32	Scene 3 rehearsal	56 hrs	56 hrs	0 hrs	0 hrs	56 hrs	0%
33	Scene 3 shoot	162 hrs	162 hrs	0 hrs	0 hrs	162 hrs	0%

At this point, because no actual work has occurred yet and no changes to the scheduled work have been made, the values in the Work and Baseline fields are identical. Once actual work has been recorded, the scheduled Work values might differ from the Baseline values, in which case you'd see the differences displayed in the Variance column.

What you see in the table are task-level values, which are closely related to, but not the same as, resource-level or assignment-level values. For example, in the table you see the total Work and Baseline values of each task, but you can't tell which resources will contribute work to each task.

Next you'll view resource-level and assignment-level baseline values.

6 On the View bar, click Resource Sheet.

The Resource Sheet view appears.

7 On the View menu, point to Table: Summary and click Work.

The Work table appears. Again you see the Work and Baseline fields for resources. Your screen should look similar to the following illustration.

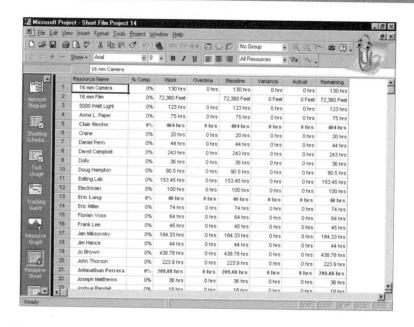

In the Work table you see resource-level values. You can identify the total Work and Baseline values for each resource, but you can't view the specific tasks to which each resource will contribute work. To conclude this exercise, you'll view assignment-level baseline values.

8   On the View bar, click Task Usage.

The Task Usage view appears.

9   On the Format menu, point to Details and click Baseline Work.

---

tip

You can also right-click anywhere in the Details column. In the submenu that appears, click Baseline Work.

Microsoft Project displays the baseline work timephased values below each scheduled work timephased value.

10   On the Standard toolbar, click the Go To Selected Task button.

Your screen should look similar to the following illustration.

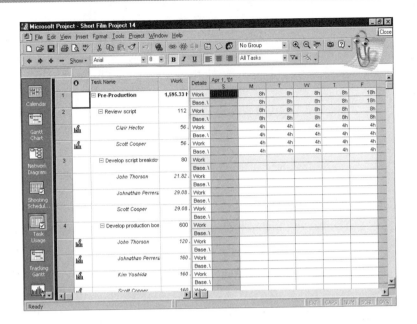

This time you see assignment-level values for Task 2, "Review script." As you might expect, because no actual work or changes to the schedule have been recorded, the schedule and baseline values are the same. These values are organized per resource in the timescaled grid. On the left side of the view you can see that resources are organized according to the task to which they are assigned.

Now that you've had a look at some task, resource, and assignment baseline fields and timephased values, it's time to enter some actuals!

Tracking a Project as Scheduled

The simplest approach to tracking progress is to report that the actual work is proceeding exactly as planned. For example, if the first month of a five-month project has elapsed and all of its tasks have started and finished as scheduled, you can quickly record this in the Update Project dialog box, which you can open by clicking the Tracking command on the Tools menu, and then selecting Update Project from the submenu.

In the short film project, some time has now passed since saving the baseline and so far so good. In this exercise, you record project actuals by updating work to the current date.

1   On the View bar, click Gantt Chart.

The Gantt Chart view appears.

2   On the Tools menu, point to Tracking and click Update Project.

The Update Project dialog box appears.

3   Make sure the Update Work As Complete Through option is selected. In the adjacent Date list, type or select **April 23, 2001**, and click OK.

Microsoft Project records the actual work for the tasks that were scheduled to start before April 23. Then it displays that progress by drawing **progress bars** in the Gantt bars for those tasks.

4   In the Task Name column, select the name of Task 4, "Develop production boards."

5   On the Standard toolbar, click the Go To Selected Task button.

Your screen should look similar to the following illustration.

Check marks appear in the
Indicators column for tasks
that have been completed.

This progress bar indicates the portion
of the task that has been completed.

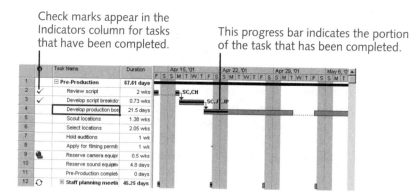

In the Gantt Chart view, the progress bar shows how much of each task has been completed. Because Tasks 2 and 3 have been completed, a check mark appears in the Indicators column for those tasks and the progress bar extends through the full length of the task's Gantt bars. By April 23, only a portion of Task 4 has been completed, however, so the progress bar for that task extends only to April 23.

Some of the recurring staff planning meetings have also been completed as scheduledby April 23, so progress bars appear in the summary Gantt bars before April 23.

Entering Percent Complete of Tasks

PROJ2000-2-2

Once work has begun on a task, you can quickly record progress on it as a percentage. There are different ways to do this, depending on your needs:

▪ Record that a task is 25%, 50%, 75%, or 100% complete by clicking a button on the Tracking toolbar.

▪ Enter an exact percent complete, for example, in the Task Information dialog box, which you can open by selecting the Task Information command on the Project menu.

In either case, when you enter a percentage other than 0% complete, Microsoft Project changes the task's actual start date to match its scheduled start date. It then calculates actual duration, remaining duration, actual costs, and other values, based on the percentage you enter. For example, if you specify that a four-day task is 50% complete, Microsoft Project calculates that it has used two days of actual duration and has two days of remaining duration.

In this exercise, you record percentages of tasks complete. You begin by displaying the Tracking toolbar.

1 On the View menu, point to Toolbars and click Tracking.

The Tracking toolbar appears. This toolbar contains several buttons relating to tracking activities, but the buttons that interest us now are the 0% through 100% complete buttons.

2 In the Task Name column, ensure that Task 4, "Develop production boards," is still selected.

3 On the Tracking toolbar, click the 100% Complete button.

Microsoft Project records the actual work for the task as scheduled, then it extends a progress line through the length of the Gantt bar.

4 Scroll the chart portion of the Gantt Chart view to the right until you see the end of Task 4.

Your screen should look similar to the following illustration.

Tracking Progress 14

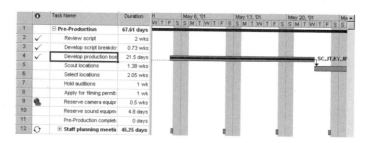

5   In the Task Name column, select the name of Task 5, "Scout Locations."

6   On the Standard toolbar, click the Task Information button.

The Task Information dialog box appears.

7   Click the General tab.

8   In the Percent Complete box, type or select **35** and click OK.

Microsoft Project records the actual work for the task as scheduled, then it drawsa progress line through 35% of the Gantt bar.

To finish this exercise, you'll record a few more tasks as complete.

9   In the Task Name column, select the names of Tasks 5 and 6.

10   On the Tracking toolbar, click the 100% Complete button.

Microsoft Project records the actual work for the task as scheduled.

You can use the percent complete buttons with an individual task or with a range of tasks.

So far you've recorded actual work that started and finished on schedule. While this may prove true for some tasks, usually you need to record tasks that start or finish early or late, or that last longer or shorter than planned. This is the subject of the next sections.

Entering Actual Start, Finish, and Duration Values of Tasks

Another way to keep your schedule up to date is to record what actually happens for each task in your project. You can record each task's actual start, finish, and duration values. With actual durations, you can enter the actual duration point when the task is completed or record it as a percent complete to the present time—even if the task is not yet complete.

When you enter actual start, finish, or duration values, Microsoft Project updates the schedule and calculates the task's percent complete. Microsoft Project uses the following rules:

■   When you enter a task's actual start date, Microsoft Project moves the scheduled start date to match the actual start date.

■ When you enter a task's actual finish date, Microsoft Project moves the scheduled finish date to match the actual finish date and sets the task to 100% complete.

■ When you enter a task's actual duration, if it's less than the scheduled duration, Microsoft Project subtracts the actual duration from the scheduled duration to determine the remaining duration.

■ When you enter a task's actual duration that is equal to the scheduled duration, Microsoft Project sets the task to 100% complete.

■ When you enter a task's actual duration that is longer than the scheduled duration, Microsoft Project adjusts the scheduled duration to match the actual duration and sets the task to 100% complete.

In this exercise, you record actual start and finish dates and durations for tasks.

1   On the Edit menu, click Go To.

     The Go To dialog box appears.

2   In the ID box, type **7** and click OK.

     Microsoft Project displays Task 7, "Hold auditions." This task started one day ahead of schedule (the Friday before its scheduled start date), so you'll record this.

3   On the Tools menu, click Tracking and then click Update Tasks.

> ## tip
> You can also click the Update Tasks button on the Tracking toolbar.

     The Update Tasks dialog box appears. Here you can see the scheduled start and finish values under Current.

4   Under the Actual label, in the Start box type or select **June 15, 2001**.

5   In the Actual Dur: box, type or select **1w**, and click OK to close the Update Tasks dialog box.

     Microsoft Project records the actual start date and work of the task. Your screen should look similar to the following illustration.

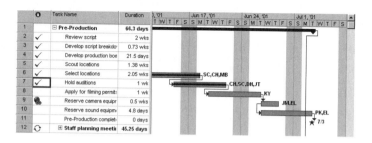

Next you'll record that Task 8 started on time, but took two days longer than planned to complete.

6   In the Task Name column, select the name of Task 8, "Apply for filming permits."

Is the project on track?

Properly evaluating a project's status can be tricky. Consider the following issues:

- For many tasks, it's very difficult to evaluate a percent complete. When is an engineer 50% complete in designing a new motor assembly, or a programmer 50% complete in coding a software module? Reporting work in progress is in many cases a "best guess" effort, and inherently risky.

- The portion of a task's duration that has elapsed does not always equate to a percentage accomplished. For example, a back-loaded task may require relatively little effort initially, so when 50% of its duration has elapsed far less than 50% of its total work will have been completed.

- The resources assigned to a task may have different criteria for what constitutes the task's completion than does the project manager—or the resources assigned to successor tasks.

Good project planning and communication can avoid or mitigate these and other problems that arise in project execution. For example, developing proper task durations and status reporting periods should identify tasks that have substantially varied from the baseline, early enough to make adjustments. Having well-documented and well-communicated task completion criteria should avoid "downstream" surprises. Nevertheless, in large, complex projects, variance from the baseline is almost certain to occur. For more information about identifying and analyzing variance, see Lesson 15.

7   Click the Update Tasks button on the Tracking toolbar.

The Update Tasks dialog box appears.

8   In the Actual Dur: box, type **7d** and click OK.

Microsoft Project records the actual duration of the task. Your screen should look similar to the following illustration.

Since the actual duration of Task 8 was longer than expected, Microsoft Project reschedules the start dates of successor tasks to start later.

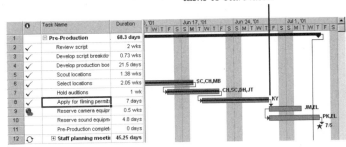

Because you didn't specify an actual start date, Microsoft Project assumes that the task started as scheduled, but the actual duration you entered causes Microsoft Project to calculate an actual finish date that is later than the originally scheduled finish date.

To conclude this exercise, you'll record that Task 9 was completed as scheduled but Task 10 took three days longer than scheduled to complete.

9   In the Task Name column, select the name of Task 9, "Reserve camera equipment."

10   On the Tracking toolbar, click the 100% Complete button.

11   In the Task Name column, select the name of Task 10, "Reserve sound equipment."

12   Click the Update Tasks button on the Tracking toolbar.

The Update Tasks dialog box appears.

13   In the Actual Dur: box, type or select **8d** and click OK.

Microsoft Project records the actual duration of the task.

14   On the Standard toolbar, click the Go To Selected Task button.

Your screen should look similar to the following illustration.

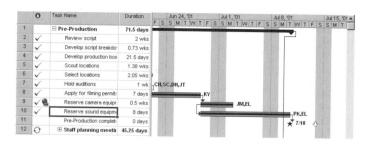

Now you can see that the Pre-Production phase of the Short Film Project has come in a few days ahead of its deadline.

Tracking Work by Time Period

PROJ2000-2-9

When you need to track actual work at the most detailed level possible, use the timescaled grid in the Task Usage or the Resource Usage view. In either view, you can enter actual work values for individual assignments daily, weekly, or as frequently as you wish. For example, if a task has three resources assigned to it and you know that two resources worked on the task for eight hours one day and the third for six hours, you enter these as three separate values on a timescaled grid.

Entering timephased values requires more work on the project manager's part and may require more work from resources to inform the project manager of their daily actuals. However, doing so gives you far more detail about the project's task and resource status than the other methods of entering actuals described in this lesson. Entering timephased values might be the best approach to take if you have a group of tasks or an entire project that have the following qualities:

- High-risk tasks.

- Relatively short-duration tasks where a variance of even a fraction of a day could put the overall project at risk.

- Tasks in which sponsors or other stakeholders have an especially strong interest.

- Tasks that require hourly billing for labor.

At this point in the Short Film Project, the Production phase has begun and the filming of scenes is under way. Because of the large number of resources involved, the high setup and teardown costs, and the limited availability of sites at which some scenes must be filmed, these tasks are the riskiest ones of the project. In this exercise, you enter daily actuals for Production tasks in the Task Usage view.

1 ·On the View bar, click Task Usage.

The Task Usage view appears. On the left is the Usage table, and on the right, the timescaled grid.

2 Click the minus sign next to Task 1, "Pre-Production," to collapse this phase of the project.

3 Select Task 23, "Production," and then on the Standard toolbar, click the Go To Selected Task button.

Collecting actuals from resources

The table you use in Step 8 of this section is similar to a time card. In fact, to enter assignment-level actual work values, you need some form of paper time card or its electronic equivalent. Several methods are used to collect such data from resources, assuming you need to track actuals at this level of detail. Some collection methods include the following:

- Collect actual values yourself. This method is feasible if you communicate with only a small group of resources on a frequent basis. It's also a good opportunity to talk directly to the resources about any surprises they may have encountered (either positive or negative) while performing the work.

- Collect actuals through a formal status reporting system. This technique may work through the already existing hierarchy of your organization and serve additional purposes besides project status reporting.

- Use Microsoft Project's e-mail-based collaboration features to collect assignment status data.

- Use Microsoft Project Central. This companion product for Microsoft Project enables intranet-based team communication, tracking, and status reporting.

For more information about Microsoft Project's e-mail-based team collaboration and the Microsoft Project Central companion product, see Appendix D.

Microsoft Project scrolls the timescaled grid to display the first scheduled work values of the Production phase.

4   On the Format menu, point to Details and click Actual Work.

Microsoft Project displays the Actual Work timephased fields for each assignment. Your screen should look similar to the following illustration.

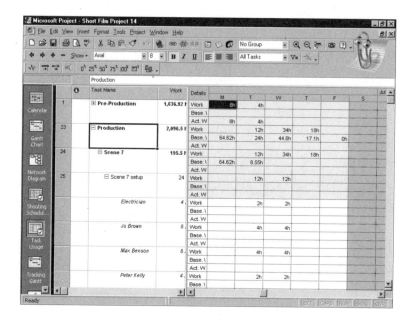

The first actual value to enter is for Task 25, "Scene 7 setup." This task was completed after 14 hours of work Tuesday and 10 hours Wednesday, although you don't know (or for this task, care) what the individual resource's actual work values were.

5   In the timescale grid, select the Act. Work field for "Scene 7 setup" on Tuesday, July 10, 2001.

tip

If you point to the name of a day on the timescale, Microsoft Project will display the full date of that day in a ToolTip.

6   Type **14h** and press the Right Arrow key.

Your screen should look similar to the following illustration.

When entering values in the Actual Work field in the
timescaled grid, you can see how Microsoft Project
distributes the actual work among assigned resources,
and rolls up the value to summary tasks.

O	Task Name	Work	Details	M	T	W	T	F	S	Jul
1	⊞ Pre-Production	1,636.92 h	Work	8h	4h					
			Base.\							
			Act. W	8h	4h					
23	⊟ Production	2,096.5 h	Work		14h	35.67h	15h			
			Base.\	64.62h	24h	44.6h	17.1h	0h		
			Act. W		14h					
24	⊟ Scene 7	195.5 h	Work		14h	35.67h	15h			
			Base.\	64.62h	.55h					
			Act. W		14h					
25	⊟ Scene 7 setup	24	Work		14h	10h				
			Base.\							
			Act. W		14h					
	Electrician	4	Work		2.33h	1.67h				
			Base.\							
			Act. W		2.33h					
	Jo Brown	8	Work		4.67h	3.33h				
			Base.\							
			Act. W		4.67h					
	Max Benson	8	Work		4.67h	3.33h				
			Base.\							
			Act. W		4.67h					
	Peter Kelly	4	Work		2.33h	1.67h				
			Base.\							

As soon as you enter this value, several things happen:

- The task's actual work value for Tuesday rolls up to the "Scene 7" summary task and then to the "Production" summary task.

- Because you entered the actual work value for the task and not for the individual resource assignments, Microsoft Project split up the actual work value among the assigned resources, in proportion to their scheduled work values.

7 In the Act. Work field for "Scene 7 setup" on Wednesday, July 11, 2001, type **10h** and press the Enter key.

Again Microsoft Project rolls up the actual work value to the summary tasks and splits up the actual work value among the assigned resources. Your screen should look similar to the following illustration.

Entering an actual work value at the task level
(Task 25 in this case) causes Microsoft Project
to distribute the actual work among the
assigned resources in the same proportion as
their scheduled work.

For Task 26, "Scene 7 rehearsal," you have individual resources' actual work
values for Wednesday and Thursday, July 11 and 12, 2001.

8   Enter the following actual work values into the timescale grid.

Resource Name	Wednesday's Actual Work	Thursday's Actual Work
Jan Miksovsky	3h	5h
Jo Brown	3h	5h
Joseph Matthews	2h	7h
Paul Born	1.5h	3h
Scott Cooper	2.5h	5.5h
Sue Jackson	4h	5h

When you are finished, your screen should look similar to the following illustration.

Entering an actual work value at the resource level causes Microsoft Project to add up the individual values and record it as the actual work value for the task (in this case, 30.5 hours for Task 26).

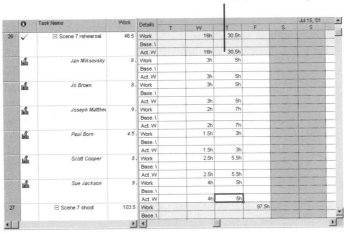

This time, the individual resources' actual work values were rolled up to the tasks' actual work values. Also, you may have noticed that as soon as you entered an actual work value for Wednesday, Microsoft Project recalculated the scheduled work for Thursday.

To finish this exercise, you can quickly record that the remaining tasks for Scene 7 were completed as scheduled.

9   In the Task Name column, hold down the Ctrl key and select Tasks 27, 28, and 29. You may have to scroll vertically to select these tasks.

10   On the Tracking toolbar, click the 100% Complete button.

Microsoft Project records the actual work values for all the assignments of these tasks.

Changing Remaining Work or Duration of Tasks

PROJ2000E-2-9
PROJ2000E-2-4

As you track actuals, not only can you adjust start and finish dates but also you can adjust remaining work or duration. You can do this only when reporting the partial completion of a task. Here are some examples:

■   A task that was scheduled for 32 hours of work is partially completed. According to the resources assigned to the task, they've performed 18 hours of work and expect to finish the entire task after working eight more hours. In Microsoft Project, you enter 18 hours of actual work and eight hours of remaining work. One way to enter actual and remaining work is in the Work table. On the View menu, point to Table, and click Work.

■ A task that was scheduled for three days of duration is partially complete. One day of duration has elapsed, and the resources working on the task now expect they'll need another four days to complete the task. In Microsoft Project, you enter one day of actual duration and four days of remaining duration. One way to enter actual and remaining duration is in the Update Tasks dialog box. On the Tools menu, point to the Tracking command and click Update Tasks.

In this exercise, you update actual and remaining work for a task.

Gantt
Chart

1   On the View bar, click Gantt Chart.

The Gantt Chart view appears.

2   On the Edit menu, click Go To.

The Go To dialog box appears.

3   In the ID box, type **31** and click OK.

Microsoft Project scrolls to Task 31.

4   On the Window menu, click Split.

The Task Form appears below the Gantt Chart.

Task
Usage

5   Click anywhere in the Task Form, and then on the View bar, click Task Usage.

Microsoft Project displays the Task Usage view in the lower pane and the Gantt Chart view in the upper pane. In a split view where both views include timescale data, selecting a task in the Gantt Chart view causes that task's details to appear in the Task Usage view. Likewise, when you horizontally scroll one view the other view scrolls with it.

6   Click anywhere in the Task Usage view in the lower pane, and then on the View menu click Table: Usage and select Work.

Microsoft Project displays the Work table in the Task Usage view.

7   In the Gantt Chart in the upper pane, click Task 31, "Scene 3 setup."

8   On the left side of the lower pane, scroll to the right to see the Actual column.

9   In the Actual column for Task 31, type **8h** and press the Right Arrow key.

Your screen should look similar to the following illustration.

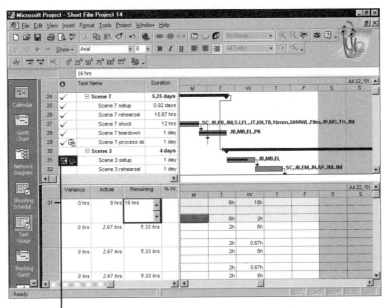

When working in a split view like this, entering data or navigating in one view affects what you see in the other view. In this window, the Gantt view appears above the Task Usage view. In both views you see different information about task 31.

Several things just happened. First, because you entered the actual work at the task level, it was distributed among the assigned resources. Second, the remaining work value was recalculated. Finally, Microsoft Project drew a progress bar through a portion of the task's Gantt bar in the Gantt Chart view in the upper pane.

10 In the Remaining column for Task 31, type **20h** and press the Right Arrow key.

Your screen should look similar to the following illustration.

Entering this remaining duration value in the Task Usage view...   ...causes Microsoft Project to recalculate the total duration of Task 31, and extend its Gantt bar.

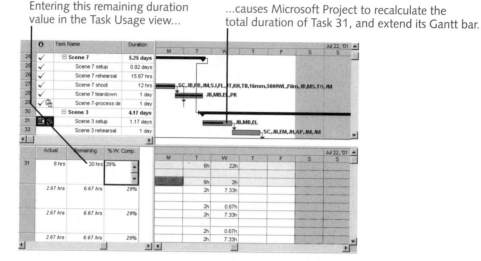

Again, several things happened. The new remaining work value was distributed among the assigned resources, and the Gantt bar grew in length to reflect the longer duration of the task.

11   On the Window menu, click Remove Split.

Manually entering actual costs

Whenever you've entered actual work values in this lesson, Microsoft Project has calculated actual cost values. By default, Microsoft Project calculates actual costs and you can't enter actual cost values directly. If you want to enter actual cost values yourself, on the Tools menu, click the Options command and click the Calculation tab in the Options dialog box that opens. Under the Calculation Options label, clear the Actual Costs Are Always Calculated By Microsoft Project check box.

Once automatic cost calculation is turned off, you can enter or import task- or assignment-level actual costs in the Actual field. This field is available in several locations, such as the Cost table. You can also enter actual cost values on a daily or other interval in any timescale view such as the Task Usage or the Resource Usage view. On the Format menu, point to the Details command and then click Actual Cost.

Saving an Interim Plan

PROJ2000E-2-5

At this point you've saved the baseline and entered a number of actual values into the project plan. In the next lesson you will compare actual performance against the baseline plan. However, after you've started tracking actual values, or any time you've adjusted your schedule, you might want to take another snapshot of the current values. You can do this with an **interim plan**. Like a baseline, an interim plan is a set of current values from the project plan that Microsoft Project saves with the file. Unlike the baseline, however, an interim plan saves only the start and finish dates of tasks, not resource or assignment values. You can save up to 10 different interim plans during a project.

Depending on the scope and duration of your projects, you may want to save an interim plan at any of the following junctures:

- At the conclusion of a major phase of work.

- At preset time intervals, such as weekly or monthly.

- Just before or after entering a large number of actual values.

In this exercise, you save an interim plan.

1   On the Tools menu, point to Tracking and click Save Baseline.
    The Save Baseline dialog box appears.

2   Click Save Interim Plan.

These boxes become active only
after you select Save Interim Plan.

As soon as you click Save Interim Plan, the Copy and Into boxes become active. Here you select start and finish values for tasks that you want to save into the specific interim start and finish fields that appear in the Copy and Into boxes. These fields are numbered Start1 through Start10 and Finish1 through Finish10. Because this is the first interim plan you've saved, use the default fields that appear in the Into box.

3   Click OK to save the interim plan and close the Save Baseline dialog box.

Microsoft Project saves each task's current start and finish values into the Start1 and Finish1 fields. In the next exercise you'll view these, along with the baseline values, against the current actual values.

Lesson Wrap-Up

This lesson covered how to save baseline and interim plans, and how to enter actual values.

If you are going on to other lessons:

1   On the Standard toolbar, click Save to save changes made to Short Film Project 14.

2   On the File menu, click Close to close the file.

tip
Now that you have saved a baseline for this file, Microsoft Project will no longer prompt you to save one when you save the file.

If you aren't continuing to other lessons:

●   On the File menu, click Exit.

Glossary

Actuals Project work completed and recorded in a Microsoft Project file. Prior to recording actuals, the project plan contains scheduled or planned information. Comparing planned versus actual project information helps the project manager better control project execution.

Baseline The original project plan saved for later comparison. The baseline includes the planned start and finish dates of the various tasks and assignments with their planned costs. Each Microsoft Project file can have only one baseline.

Field The lowest-level information about a task, resource, or assignment; also called a cell.

Interim plan Tasks' start and finish values saved for later comparison. Each Microsoft Project file can have, at most, 10 interim plans.

Planning The initial major phase of project management work. Planning includes all the work in developing a project schedule, up to the point where the tracking of actual work begins.

Progress bar A graphic representation in a Gantt Chart view that shows how much of a task has been completed.

Sponsor An individual or organization that provides financial support and champions the project team within the larger organization.

Stakeholder All the people or organizations that might be affected by a project's activities (those who "have a stake" in its success). This includes those working on the project as well as others such as customers outside the project.

Timephased field Task, resource, or assignment values that are distributed over time. The values of timephased fields appear in the timescale grid on the right side of views such as the Task Usage or Resource Usage views.

Tracking The second major phase of project management work. Tracking includes all the collecting, entering, and analyzing of actual project performance values such as work on tasks and actual durations.

Quick Reference

To save a project baseline

1   On the Tools menu, point to Tracking and click Save Baseline.

2   In the Save Baseline dialog box, select Save Baseline and click OK.

To track work on a project as scheduled through a specific date

1   On the Tools menu, point to Tracking and click Update Project.

2   In the Update Project dialog box, select Update Work As Complete Through.

3   In the Date list, select the date through which you want actual work to be recorded and click OK.

To enter a percent complete for a task with the Tracking toolbar

1   On the View menu, point to Toolbars and click Tracking.

2   In the Task Name column, select the task for which you want to record a percent complete.

3   On the Tracking toolbar, click the button for 0%, 25%, 50%, 75%, or 100% Complete.

To enter a percent complete for a task with the Task Information dialog box

1   In the Task Name column, select the task for which you want to record a percent complete.

2   On the Standard toolbar, click the Task Information button.

3   In the Task Information dialog box, click the General tab.

4   In the Percent Complete box, enter the value you want and click OK.

To enter an actual duration

1   In the Task Name column, select the task for which you want to record an actual duration.

2   On the Tracking toolbar, click the Update Tasks button.

3   In the Update Tasks dialog box, enter the value you want in the Actual Dur: box and click OK.

To enter daily actual work values per task or assignment

1   On the View bar, click Task Usage.

The Task Usage view appears.

2   Select the name of the task or assignment for which you want to enter actual values.

3   On the Standard toolbar, click the Go To Selected Task button.

4   On the Format menu, point to Details and click Actual Work.

5   In the timescale grid, enter the task or assignment value you want in the Act. Work field.

To split the Microsoft Project window to display the Gantt Chart and Task Usage views

1   On the View bar, click Gantt Chart.

2   On the Window menu, click Split.

3   Click anywhere in the lower pane, and then on the View bar, click Task Usage.

To save an interim plan

1   On the Tools menu, point to Tracking and click Save Baseline.

2   Click Save Interim Plan.

3   In the Copy and Into boxes, select the specific start and finish dates you want saved.

4   Click OK.

LESSON

15

Viewing and Reporting Project Status

**ESTIMATED TIME
50 min.**

After completing this lesson, you will be able to:

✔ *Determine which tasks were started or completed late.*

✔ *See the project's baseline, interim, and current schedules graphically in one view.*

✔ *Determine which tasks and resource assignments have cost more than originally planned.*

✔ *Create a "stoplight" report to quickly convey the project's budget status to stakeholders.*

✔ *Apply earned value analysis to the project to evaluate overall project performance and predict future performance trends.*

Once a project's baseline has been set and work has begun, the primary focus of the project manager shifts from planning to collecting, entering, and analyzing project performance details. For most projects, these performance details boil down to three primary questions or vital signs:

▪ How much work was required to complete a task?

▪ Did the task start and finish on time?

▪ What was the cost of completing the task?

Comparing the answers to these questions against the **baseline** gives the project manager and other **stakeholders** a good way to measure the project's progress, and to know when corrective action may be necessary. Where the scheduled or actual project details differ from the baseline details, you have **variance**. Variance is usually measured as time, such as days behind schedule, or as cost, such as dollars over budget. For many project managers, most of their time after initial project planning is complete is spent identifying, justifying, and, in many cases, responding to variance. Responding to variance is the subject of Lesson 16. However, before you can respond to variance, you must first identify, document, and report it. That is the subject of this lesson.

Practice files for the lesson ⇨   To complete this lesson, you will use a file named Short Film Project 15. Before you begin this lesson, open the Part 4 folder in the MS Project 2000 SBS Practice folder on your hard disk. Open the file 15A, and save it as Short Film Project 15 in the Part 4 folder.

At this point in the project, the first several scenes of the film have been shot and actuals for tasks associated with scenes 7, 3, and 1 have been entered into the project file.

Identifying Tasks that Have Slipped

One cause of variance is delays in starting or finishing tasks. You'd certainly want to know about tasks underway that started late or future tasks that may not start as scheduled. It's also helpful to identify completed tasks that did not start on time, and to try to determine why.

There are different ways to see delayed tasks, depending on the type of information you want:

▦   Filter for delayed or slipping tasks with the Slipped/Late Progress or Slipping Tasks filters. For information about applying filters, see "Filtering Data in a View" in Lesson 9.

▦   Apply the Variance table to a task view. For more information about tables, see "Editing and Creating Tables" in Lesson 9.

▦   Apply the Tracking Gantt view to compare tasks' baseline dates with their actual or scheduled dates.

In this exercise, you apply the Tracking Gantt view to display baseline and scheduled task information.

1   On the View menu, click Tracking Gantt.

Microsoft Project displays the Tracking Gantt view. This view is similar to the Gantt Chart view, except that different bars appear in the chart portion of the view.

*Remember
that Ctrl+G is
a keyboard
shortcut for
displaying the
Go To dialog
box.*

2 On the Edit menu, click Go To.

The Go To dialog box appears.

3 In the Date box, type or select **June 10, 2001**, and then click OK.

Microsoft Project scrolls the timescale portion of the Tracking Gantt view. Your screen should look similar to the following illustration.

The original baseline schedule appears
as gray bars in the Tracking Gantt view.

These blue bars represent the
tasks as they are currently scheduled.

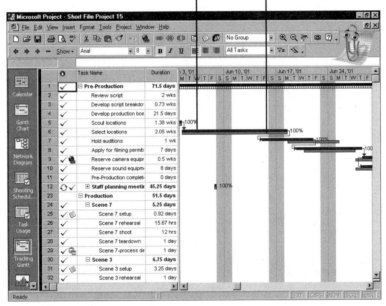

Here you can see where tasks began to vary from their baselines. Task 6 and prior tasks occurred as planned, Tasks 7 and 8 started earlier than planned, but Task 9 and later tasks started, or are now scheduled to start, later than planned.

4 On the Edit menu, click Go To.

The Go To dialog box appears.

5 In the ID box, type **36** and click OK.

Microsoft Project scrolls the Tracking Gantt view to display Task 36 and its adjacent tasks. Your screen should look similar to the following illustration.

Viewing and Reporting Status 15

These dark blue bars represent progress; in this case, this task is 100% complete.

These light blue bars represent tasks that have no progress.

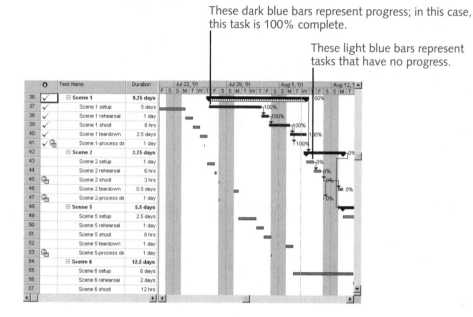

In this portion of the schedule, you can see baseline tasks (the patterned gray bars), completed tasks (the solid blue bars), and tasks scheduled but not yet not started (the patterned blue bars).

tip

To see details about any bar or other item in a Gantt Chart view, point to it with the mouse. After a moment a ToolTip appears with details. To see a legend of all Gantt bar color coding and symbols, on the Format menu click Bar Styles, and in the Bar Styles dialog box look at the Name and Appearance columns.

6   On the Edit menu, click Go To.

The Go To dialog box appears.

7   In the ID box, type **75** and click OK.

Microsoft Project scrolls the Tracking Gantt view to display Task 75 and its adjacent tasks. Your screen should look similar to the following illustration.

These red bars in the Tracking Gantt view represent tasks that are on the critical path; any delays in completing these tasks will delay the project finish date.

	ⓘ	Task Name	Duration
75		Paper edit footage	2 wks
76		Rough cut edit	1 wk
77		Fine cut edit	2 wks
78		Hold formal approval sr	1 day
79		Record final narration	3.33 wks
80		Add head and tail titles	0.64 wks
81		Add final music	1.64 wks
82		Print internegative of fil	3 days
83		Clone dubbing masters	4 days
84		Archive master film anc	1.32 days
85		Hand off masters to dis	1 day

At this point in the schedule, the scheduled start date of tasks has slipped quite a bit. These tasks' Gantt bars are formatted red to indicate that they are critical, meaning that any delay in completing these tasks will delay the project's finish date. For more information about the critical path, see "Viewing the Project's Critical Path" in Lesson 6.

tip

A useful report for describing tasks that are off schedule is the Slipping Tasks report. On the View menu, click Reports. In the Reports dialog box, double-click Current Activities and then double-click Slipping Tasks. For more information about using reports, see "Customizing and Printing Reports" in Lesson 10.

Comparing Baseline, Interim, and Current Plans

PROJ2000E-4-5

As you might recall from Lesson 14, you saved the first of up to ten **interim plans** for the Short Film Project. It's useful to compare baseline, interim, and actual plans in a single view. Doing so helps you evaluate how accurate your schedule adjustments to tasks (saved as interim plans) have been.

In this exercise, you display the current schedule along with the baseline and the interim plan you saved in Lesson 14. You begin by customizing a copy of the Tracking Gantt chart view.

1   On the View menu, click More Views.

The More Views dialog box appears.

Viewing and Reporting Status   15

2   In the Views list, make sure that Tracking Gantt is selected, and click Copy.

The View Definition dialog box appears.

3   In the Name box, type **Interim Tracking Gantt** and click OK.

The new view is listed in the More Views dialog box.

4   Click Apply.

Microsoft Project displays the new view, which at this point is identical to the Tracking Gantt view. Next, you'll add the interim plan bars to the view.

5   On the Format menu, click Bar Styles.

The Bar Styles dialog box appears.

6   Click the Insert Row button.

7   In the new cell directly below the Name column heading, type **Interim**.

8   In the same row, click the cell under the Show For...Tasks column heading and then select Normal from the drop-down list.

9   Click the cell under the From column heading and select Start1 from the drop-down list.

10   Click the cell under the To column heading and then select Finish1 from the drop-down list.

Your screen should look similar to the following illustration.

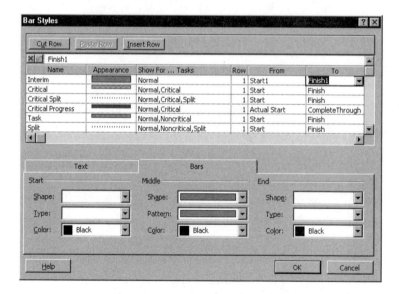

The Start1 and Finish1 items are the fields in which the first interim plan values were saved in Lesson 14. The current start date and finish date of each task in the project were saved to these fields when you saved the interim plan.

You've now instructed Microsoft Project to display the first interim plan start and finish dates as bars; next you'll specify what these bars should look like.

11 In the Pattern box under the Middle label, select the framed bar, the first option.

12 In the Color box, select Aqua.

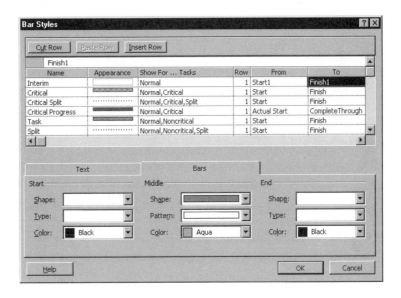

13 Click OK to close the Bar Styles dialog box.

Microsoft Project displays the interim bars on the Interim Tracking Gantt view. Next you'll get a better look at tasks where the interim plan matched the actual dates, and where, as currently scheduled, there will not be a match.

14 On the Edit menu, click Go To.

The Go To dialog box appears.

15 In the ID box, type **7** and click OK.

Microsoft Project scrolls the view to display Task 7 and its adjacent tasks. Your screen should look similar to the following illustration.

In this custom view, interim plans appear as aqua frame bars; this task was completed right on its interim schedule, but before its baseline schedule.

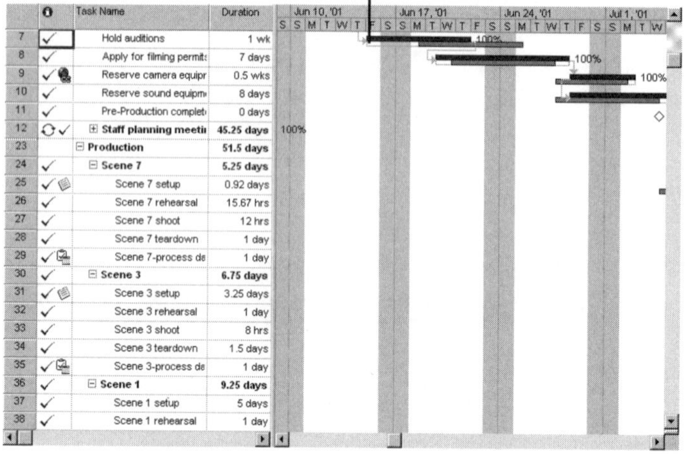

Here you can see that the completed Task 7 (shown as a solid blue bar) corresponds exactly to its interim plan bar (the aqua bar), and both were scheduled prior to the baseline. That's because after the baseline was saved, changes to the schedule were made that brought in the scheduled start date of the task. You then saved the interim plan, and later recorded the task as complete

16 On the Edit menu, click Go To.

The Go To dialog box appears.

17 In the ID box, type **31** and click OK.

Microsoft Project scrolls the view to display Task 31 and its adjacent tasks. Your screen should look similar to the following illustration.

At this point in the schedule, tasks
no longer match the interim plan.

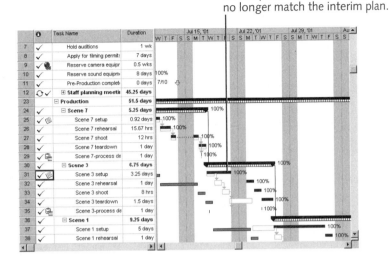

Here you can see that tasks executed before Task 31 were being completed
to match the interim plan (though not the baseline). However, Task 31's running over schedule has caused successor tasks to be rescheduled after their
interim start dates.

Identifying Tasks and Resources
That Are Over Budget

PROJ2000-2-8

The schedule ("Did tasks start and finish on time?"), while critical to nearly all
projects, is only one indicator of overall project health. For projects that include
cost information, another critical indicator is cost variance: Are tasks running
over or under budget? As you may recall from Lesson 6, task costs in Microsoft
Project consist either of fixed costs applied directly to tasks or of resource costs
derived from assignments, or both. Evaluating cost variance allows you to make
incremental budget adjustments for individual tasks to avoid exceeding your
project's overall budget.

In this exercise, you view cost variance first for tasks and then for resources. Although tasks and resources are directly related, it's informative to evaluate each
individually.

1   On the View menu, click More Views.

   The More Views dialog box appears.

2   In the Views list, select Task Sheet and click Apply.

Microsoft Project displays the Task Sheet view. Next, you'll switch to the Cost table.

3   On the View menu, point to Table: Entry, and click Cost.

tip

You also can right-click on the upper left corner of the active table, and in the shortcut menu that appears, click Cost.

The Cost table appears in the Task Sheet view. Your screen should look similar to the following illustration.

	Task Name	Fixed Cost	Fixed Cost Accrual	Total Cost	Baseline	Variance	Actual	Remair
1	⊟ Pre-Production	$0.00	Prorated	$29,296.13	$28,749.32	$546.81	$29,296.13	$
2	Review script	$0.00	Prorated	$2,205.00	$2,205.00	$0.00	$2,205.00	$
3	Develop script breakdo	$0.00	Prorated	$1,541.82	$1,541.82	$0.00	$1,541.82	$
4	Develop production boa	$0.00	Prorated	$9,984.00	$9,984.00	$0.00	$9,984.00	$
5	Scout locations	$0.00	Prorated	$3,712.00	$3,712.00	$0.00	$3,712.00	$
6	Select locations	$0.00	Prorated	$5,070.00	$5,070.00	$0.00	$5,070.00	$
7	Hold auditions	$0.00	Prorated	$2,240.00	$2,240.00	$0.00	$2,240.00	$
8	Apply for filming permit:	$500.00	Start	$1,026.40	$876.00	$150.40	$1,026.40	$
9	Reserve camera equipr	$0.00	Prorated	$685.00	$685.00	$0.00	$685.00	$
10	Reserve sound equipm	$0.00	Prorated	$1,041.41	$645.00	$396.41	$1,041.41	$
11	Pre-Production complet	$0.00	Prorated	$0.00	$0.00	$0.00	$0.00	$
12	⊞ Staff planning meetii	$0.00	Prorated	$1,790.50	$1,790.50	$0.00	$1,790.50	$
23	⊟ Production	$0.00	Prorated	$51,898.13	$44,425.38	$7,472.75	$21,204.00	$30,69
24	⊟ Scene 7	$0.00	Prorated	$5,415.25	$4,900.00	$515.25	$5,415.25	$
25	Scene 7 setup	$0.00	Prorated	$981.00	$497.00	$484.00	$981.00	$
26	Scene 7 rehearsal	$0.00	Prorated	$736.25	$705.00	$31.25	$736.25	$
27	Scene 7 shoot	$0.00	Prorated	$3,201.00	$3,201.00	$0.00	$3,201.00	$
28	Scene 7 teardown	$0.00	Prorated	$497.00	$497.00	$0.00	$497.00	$
29	Scene 7-process de	$0.00	Prorated	$0.00	$0.00	$0.00	$0.00	$
30	⊟ Scene 3	$0.00	Prorated	$6,603.50	$5,179.00	$1,424.50	$6,603.50	$
31	Scene 3 setup	$0.00	Prorated	$1,683.50	$518.00	$1,165.50	$1,683.50	$
32	Scene 3 rehearsal	$0.00	Prorated	$755.00	$755.00	$0.00	$755.00	$
33	Scene 3 shoot	$0.00	Prorated	$3,388.00	$3,388.00	$0.00	$3,388.00	$

In this table you can see each task's baseline cost, scheduled cost (in the Total Cost column), actual cost, and variance. The variance is the difference between baseline cost and the scheduled cost. (Of course, costs aren't scheduled in the same sense that work is scheduled; however because costs (other than fixed costs) are derived directly from the scheduled work, you can think of the costs as being scheduled.)

Next, you'll focus on summary level costs.

4   Click the Task Name column heading.

5   On the Formatting toolbar, click Hide Subtasks.

Microsoft Project displays only the top three summary tasks, which in this project correspond to the major phases of the project. Since we're currently working on tasks in the Production phase, we'll direct our attention there.

6   Click the plus sign next to Task 23, "Production."

Microsoft Project expands the Production summary task to show the summary tasks for the individual scenes. Your screen should look similar to the following illustration.

	Task Name	Fixed Cost	Fixed Cost Accrual	Total Cost	Baseline	Variance	Actual	Remair
1	⊞ Pre-Production	$0.00	Prorated	$29,296.13	$28,749.32	$546.81	$29,296.13	$
23	⊟ Production	$0.00	Prorated	$51,898.13	$44,425.38	$7,472.75	$21,204.00	$30,69
24	⊞ Scene 7	$0.00	Prorated	$5,415.25	$4,900.00	$515.25	$5,415.25	$
30	⊞ Scene 3	$0.00	Prorated	$6,603.50	$5,179.00	$1,424.50	$6,603.50	$
36	⊞ Scene 1	$0.00	Prorated	$9,185.25	$6,756.25	$2,429.00	$9,185.25	$
42	⊞ Scene 2	$0.00	Prorated	$2,209.88	$2,209.88	$0.00	$0.00	$2,20
48	⊞ Scene 5	$0.00	Prorated	$6,003.00	$5,375.00	$628.00	$0.00	$6,00
54	⊞ Scene 6	$0.00	Prorated	$13,184.00	$11,588.00	$1,596.00	$0.00	$13,18
60	⊞ Scene 8	$0.00	Prorated	$7,063.50	$6,535.50	$528.00	$0.00	$7,06
66	⊞ Scene 4	$0.00	Prorated	$2,233.75	$1,881.75	$352.00	$0.00	$2,23
72	⊞ Post-Production	$0.00	Prorated	$27,816.02	$27,816.02	$0.00	$0.00	$27,81

Looking at the Variance column, you can see that Scene 7 had some variance, Scene 3 had more, and Scene 1 significantly more. Next you'll focus on Scene 1 details.

7   Click the plus sign next to summary Task 36, "Scene 1."

Microsoft Project expands the Scene 1 summary task to show the individual tasks. Your screen should look similar to the following illustration.

But what about all those other costs?

In many projects, cost budgets don't fully reflect all the costs of completing the project. For example, in the Short Film Project we're not accounting for such overhead costs as renting or acquiring studio space, electricity, or replacement parts for equipment. Depending on your organization's needs and practices, you may or may not need to track such overhead costs in your project plan. If you do need to track overhead costs, then you may be able to use a **burdened labor rate**—resource rates that factor in such overhead costs. Using burdened labor rates has the additional benefit of hiding each resource's exact pay rate—often considered highly confidential information—in the project plan. Here's one caveat, though: if you plan to use cost information from your project plan for accounting purposes, especially for capitalizing specific task types, check with an accounting expert about how salary, benefit, and overhead cost rates should be handled.

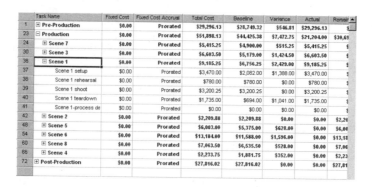

	Task Name	Fixed Cost	Fixed Cost Accrual	Total Cost	Baseline	Variance	Actual	Remain
1	⊞ Pre-Production	$0.00	Prorated	$29,296.13	$28,749.32	$546.81	$29,296.13	$
23	⊟ Production	$0.00	Prorated	$51,898.13	$44,425.38	$7,472.75	$21,204.00	$30,69
24	⊞ Scene 7	$0.00	Prorated	$5,415.25	$4,900.00	$515.25	$5,415.25	$
30	⊞ Scene 3	$0.00	Prorated	$6,603.50	$5,179.00	$1,424.50	$6,603.50	$
36	⊟ Scene 1	$0.00	Prorated	$9,185.25	$6,756.25	$2,429.00	$9,185.25	$
37	Scene 1 setup	$0.00	Prorated	$3,470.00	$2,082.00	$1,388.00	$3,470.00	$
38	Scene 1 rehearsal	$0.00	Prorated	$780.00	$780.00	$0.00	$780.00	$
39	Scene 1 shoot	$0.00	Prorated	$3,200.25	$3,200.25	$0.00	$3,200.25	$
40	Scene 1 teardown	$0.00	Prorated	$1,735.00	$694.00	$1,041.00	$1,735.00	$
41	Scene 1-process de	$0.00	Prorated	$0.00	$0.00	$0.00	$0.00	$
42	⊞ Scene 2	$0.00	Prorated	$2,209.88	$2,209.88	$0.00	$0.00	$2,20
48	⊞ Scene 5	$0.00	Prorated	$6,003.00	$5,375.00	$628.00	$0.00	$6,00
54	⊞ Scene 6	$0.00	Prorated	$13,184.00	$11,588.00	$1,596.00	$0.00	$13,18
60	⊞ Scene 8	$0.00	Prorated	$7,063.50	$6,535.50	$528.00	$0.00	$7,06
66	⊞ Scene 4	$0.00	Prorated	$2,233.75	$1,881.75	$352.00	$0.00	$2,23
72	⊞ Post-Production	$0.00	Prorated	$27,816.02	$27,816.02	$0.00	$0.00	$27,81

Looking at the Variance column, you can see that the Scene 1 setup and teardown tasks account for all of the variance for the Scene 1 summary task. In the next lesson, you'll investigate this issue further and determine whether changes to the remaining setup and teardown tasks are required.

Since cost values in the Short Film Project are almost entirely derived from the costs of resource assignments, you'll next look at resource cost variance.

Resource
Sheet

8   On the View bar, click Resource Sheet.

The Resource Sheet view appears.

9   On the View menu, point to Table: Summary and click Cost.

The Cost table appears.

Remember that you also can right click on the Select All button in the upper left corner of the active table to switch to a different table.

10   On the Project menu, point to Sort and click Sort By.

The Sort dialog box appears.

11   In the Sort By box, select Cost Variance, and click Descending.

12 . Make sure the Permanently Renumber Resources box is cleared, and then click Sort.

Microsoft Project sorts the Cost table by cost variance per resource, from highest to lowest amount. Your screen should look similar to the following illustration.

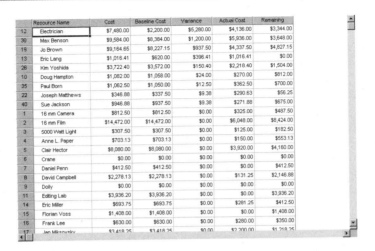

	Resource Name	Cost	Baseline Cost	Variance	Actual Cost	Remaining
12	Electrician	$7,480.00	$2,200.00	$5,280.00	$4,136.00	$3,344.00
30	Max Benson	$9,584.00	$8,384.00	$1,200.00	$5,936.00	$3,648.00
19	Jo Brown	$9,164.65	$8,227.15	$937.50	$4,337.50	$4,827.15
13	Eric Lang	$1,016.41	$620.00	$396.41	$1,016.41	$0.00
26	Kim Yoshida	$3,722.40	$3,572.00	$150.40	$2,218.40	$1,504.00
10	Doug Hampton	$1,082.00	$1,058.00	$24.00	$270.00	$812.00
35	Paul Born	$1,062.50	$1,050.00	$12.50	$362.50	$700.00
22	Joseph Matthews	$346.88	$337.50	$9.38	$290.63	$56.25
40	Sue Jackson	$946.88	$937.50	$9.38	$271.88	$675.00
1	16 mm Camera	$812.50	$812.50	$0.00	$325.00	$487.50
2	16 mm Film	$14,472.00	$14,472.00	$0.00	$6,048.00	$8,424.00
3	5000 Watt Light	$307.50	$307.50	$0.00	$125.00	$182.50
4	Anne L. Paper	$703.13	$703.13	$0.00	$150.00	$553.13
5	Clair Hector	$8,080.00	$8,080.00	$0.00	$3,920.00	$4,160.00
6	Crane	$0.00	$0.00	$0.00	$0.00	$0.00
7	Daniel Penn	$412.50	$412.50	$0.00	$0.00	$412.50
8	David Campbell	$2,278.13	$2,278.13	$0.00	$131.25	$2,146.88
9	Dolly	$0.00	$0.00	$0.00	$0.00	$0.00
11	Editing Lab	$3,936.20	$3,936.20	$0.00	$0.00	$3,936.20
14	Eric Miller	$693.75	$693.75	$0.00	$281.25	$412.50
15	Florian Voss	$1,408.00	$1,408.00	$0.00	$0.00	$1,408.00
16	Frank Lee	$630.00	$630.00	$0.00	$280.00	$350.00
17	Jan Miksovsky	$3,418.25	$3,418.25	$0.00	$2,200.00	$1,218.25

With the data arranged this way, you can see that several resources have cost variances, and that the Electrician has the highest variances. In Lesson 16, you will further analyze the Electrician's cost variances and take corrective actions.

tip

Two useful reports for describing tasks and resources that are over budget are the Overbudget Tasks and Overbudget Resources reports. On the View menu, click Reports. In the Reports dialog box, double-click Costs, and then double-click the report category you want. For more information about using reports, see "Customizing and Printing Reports" in Lesson 10.

Reporting Project Status

PROJ2000E-7-4

Communicating project status to key stakeholders such as customers and sponsors is arguably the most important function of a project manager, and one that may occupy much of your working time. While even a perfect communications flow can't guarantee a project's success, a project with poor communications flow is almost guaranteed to fail.

A key to properly communicating project status is knowing:

■ Who needs to know project status and why?

■ What format or level of detail do these people need?

The time to answer these questions is in the initial planning phase of the project. Once work on the project is underway, your main communications task will be reporting project status. This can take several forms:

- Status reports that describe where the project is in terms of cost, scope, and schedule (these are the three sides of the project triangle introduced in Lesson 1).

- Progress reports that document the specific accomplishments of the project team.

- Forecasts that predict future project performance.

If you work in an organization that is highly focused on projects and project management, chances are that standard formats already exist within your organization for these and many other types of project reporting documents. If your organization does not already have standardized formats for such information, you may be able to introduce project status formats that are based on clear communication and project management principles.

Some of the techniques you can use in Microsoft Project to help you report project status include the following:

- Print the Project Summary report. For more information about using reports, see "Customizing and Printing Reports" in Lesson 10.

- Copy Microsoft Project data to other applications—for example, copy the Gantt Chart view to Microsoft Word or to Microsoft PowerPoint. For more information about using Microsoft Project data in other applications, see Lesson 12.

- Save Microsoft Project data in other formats, such as in HTML, using the Compare To Baseline export map. For more information, see Lesson 12.

- Share project status through Microsoft Project Central, allowing the stakeholders you choose to view project details through their Web browsers. For more information, see Appendix D.

In this exercise, you focus on creating what is often called a "stoplight" report. This is a status report that represents key indicators such as schedule or budget status for tasks as a simple red, yellow, or green light, much as you'd find on a traffic signal.

1   On the View menu, click More Views.

The More Views dialog box appears.

2   Select Task Sheet, and click Apply.

Microsoft Project displays the Task Sheet view. It currently contains the Cost table.

To save time, a field in this project file has been customized to contain a formula that evaluates each task's cost variance. Next, you will view the formula to understand what it does, and then view the graphical indicators assigned to the field.

3   On the Tools menu, point to Customize, and then click Fields.

The Customize Fields dialog box appears.

4   In the Type box, select Number from the drop-down list.

5   In the list box, select Overbudget (Number3).

2000
New!

6   Under the Custom Attributes label, click the Formula button.

The Formula dialog box appears. Your screen should look similar to the following illustration.

The Number3 field has been renamed "Overbudget"
and customized with a formula.

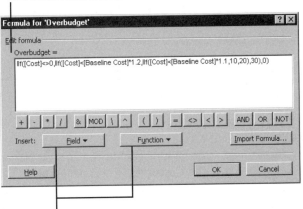

When writing a formula, use these buttons to insert
Microsoft Project fields or functions into your formula.

This formula evaluates each task's cost variance. If the task's cost fell within 30 percent above baseline, the formula assigns the number 30 to the task, if within 20 percent, a 20, and if within 10 percent, a 10.

7   Click Cancel to close the Formula dialog box.

8   In the Customize Fields dialog box, under the Values To Display label, click Graphical Indicators.

The Graphical Indicators dialog box appears. Here you specify a unique graphical indicator to display, depending on the value of the field for each task. To save you time, indicators already have been selected.

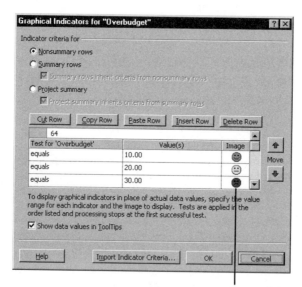

Depending on the value returned by the formula, Microsoft Project will display one of these three graphical indicators in the Overbudget column.

9   In the first cell under the Image column heading, click the drop-down arrow.

Here you can see the many graphical indicators you can associate with the values of fields.

10   Click Cancel to close the Graphical Indicators dialog box, and then click Cancel again to close the Customize Fields dialog box.

To conclude this exercise, you will display the Overbudget (Number3) column in the Cost table.

11   Select the Fixed Cost column heading.

12   On the Insert menu, click Column.

The Column Definition dialog box appears.

13   In the Field Name box, select Overbudget (Number3) from the drop-down list and then click OK.

Microsoft Project displays the Overbudget column in the Cost table. Your screen should look similar to the following illustration.

The custom field Overbudget (Number3) displays a graphical indicator that represents one of three different levels of cost variance. Now anyone can quickly scan the column to locate tasks that need further investigation.

	Task Name	Overbudget	Fixed Cost	Fixed Cost Accrual	Total Cost	Baseline	Variance	Actual
1	⊞ Pre-Production	☺	$0.00	Prorated	$29,296.13	$28,749.32	$546.81	$29,296
23	⊟ Production	☺	$0.00	Prorated	$51,898.13	$44,425.38	$7,472.75	$21,204
24	⊞ Scene 7	☺	$0.00	Prorated	$5,415.25	$4,900.00	$515.25	$5,415
30	⊞ Scene 3	●	$0.00	Prorated	$6,603.50	$5,179.00	$1,424.50	$6,603
36	⊟ Scene 1	●	$0.00	Prorated	$9,185.25	$6,756.25	$2,429.00	$9,185
37	Scene 1 setup	●	$0.00	Prorated	$3,470.00	$2,082.00	$1,388.00	$3,470
38	Scene 1 rehearsal	☺	$0.00	Prorated	$780.00	$780.00	$0.00	$780
39	Scene 1 shoot	☺	$0.00	Prorated	$3,200.25	$3,200.25	$0.00	$3,200
40	Scene 1 teardown	●	$0.00	Prorated	$1,735.00	$694.00	$1,041.00	$1,735
41	Scene 1-process de		$0.00	Prorated	$0.00	$0.00	$0.00	$0
42	⊞ Scene 2	☺	$0.00	Prorated	$2,209.88	$2,209.88	$0.00	$0
48	⊞ Scene 5	☺	$0.00	Prorated	$6,003.00	$5,375.00	$628.00	$0
54	⊞ Scene 6	☺	$0.00	Prorated	$13,184.00	$11,588.00	$1,596.00	$0
60	⊞ Scene 8	☺	$0.00	Prorated	$7,063.50	$6,535.50	$528.00	$0
66	⊞ Scene 4	☺	$0.00	Prorated	$2,233.75	$1,881.75	$352.00	$0
72	⊞ Post-Production	☺	$0.00	Prorated	$27,816.02	$27,816.02	$0.00	$0

Since this task has no cost, the graphical indicator settings do not display any indicator for this task.

As each task's cost variance changes, so too do the graphical indicators according to the ranges specified in the formula. This is a handy format for identifying tasks whose cost variance is higher than you'd like, as indicated by the yellow and red lights.

tip

To see a value behind a graphical indicator, point at the indicator. A ToolTip appears with a value.

Up to now you've identified schedule and budget variance in a task view and budget variance in a resource view—each an important measure of project status. This is a good time to remind ourselves that the final qualifier of project status is not the exact formatting of the data in Microsoft Project, but the needs of your project's stakeholders. Determining what these needs are requires your good judgment and communication skills.

15

Viewing and Reporting Status

Measuring Performance with Earned Value Analysis

PROJ2000E-2-6
PROJ2000E-5-2
PROJ2000E-6-2

Looking at task and resource variance throughout the project's duration is an essential project management activity, but it doesn't give you a complete picture of the project's long-term health. For example, a task may be over budget and ahead of schedule (possibly not good), or over budget and behind schedule (definitely not good). Viewing schedule or budget variance in isolation doesn't tell you much about performance trends that may continue for the duration of the project.

To get a more complete picture of overall project performance in terms of both time and cost, you can use **earned value analysis**. The purpose of earned value analysis is to measure the project's progress and help predict its outcome. Earned value analysis has its origins in large projects carried out for the U.S. government, and remains one of the essential project status reporting tools for major government projects. However, because of earned value analysis' usefulness in predicting future project performance, it is gaining popularity in the private sector and on smaller projects as well.

The main thing that distinguishes earned value analysis from the simpler schedule and budget variance analysis you did in the previous exercises can be summed up like this:

- Simple variance analysis answers the question, "What current performance results are we getting?"

- Earned value analysis addresses the question, "For the current performance results we're getting, are we getting our money's worth?"

The difference is subtle but important. Here's an example. The short film project has a baseline duration of about 186 days and a budget of about $101,000. After barely half of the baseline duration has elapsed, the actual costs incurred total about $50,500. What is the project's status? It turns out that you can't tell based on only this information. A simple distribution of cost over time would suggest that $50,500 spent by the midpoint of a $101,000 project is just about right. But perhaps the project is running ahead of schedule—more work has been completed by midpoint than planned. That would be good news; the project might finish ahead of schedule. On the other hand, the project may be running behind schedule—less work has been accomplished than was planned. This would be bad news; the project will likely miss its planned finish date, exceed its budget, or both.

Earned value analysis allows you to look at project performance in a more sophisticated way. It allows you to determine two important things: the true cost of project results to date, and the performance trend that is likely to continue for the remainder of the project.

Let's get back to the short film project. Midway through the project, the value of the work planned is about $53,000, slightly more than half of the amount budgeted. Or, to use earned value terms, this is the budgeted cost of work scheduled, or **BCWS** for short. So far, however, only about $49,000 was actually spent; this is the actual cost of work performed, or **ACWP**. To calculate earned value, Microsoft Project determines, per task, if you've spent more than you planned for the actual work that has been completed to date. Earned value also is called budgeted cost of work performed, or **BCWP**. Microsoft Project calculates earned values per task, per summary task, and for the entire project. For the Short Film Project at the midpoint of its duration, BCWP is around $45,000. With these numbers we can calculate (or let Microsoft Project do it for us) some important indicators of project performance:

■ The project's cost variance, or **CV**, is the difference between the budgeted and actual cost of work performed. In our project, this turns out to be around $4000. Put another way, so far in the project we've spent about $4000 more than planned for the actual work performed (or the value earned). This is not good.

■ The project's schedule variance, or **SV**, is the difference between the budgeted cost of work performed and the budgeted cost of work scheduled. In our project, this turns out to be around $8000. We are behind schedule by about $8000 worth of work. This, too, is not good.

Although it may seem odd, and even confusing, to think of being ahead of or behind schedule in terms of dollars, remember that dollars buy work, and work drives the completion of tasks. You'll soon find that viewing both cost and schedule variance in the same unit of measure makes it easier to compare the two, and other earned value numbers as well, most of them also measured in dollars.

The final earned value numbers we'll consider here are two very helpful indicators called cost performance index (**CPI**) and schedule performance index (**SPI**). These values are derived from other earned value numbers. They allow you to compare the performance of multiple projects in a consistent way. And it turns out that once a project gets underway, CPI and SPI can be used to calculate—with uncanny accuracy—the project's best-case and worst-case final actual budget. In this exercise, you view earned value numbers for the Short Film Project, and then display custom fields that calculate CPI and SPI values for the project. You begin by setting the project's **status date**. This is the date you want Microsoft Project to use when calculating earned value numbers; it need not match the current date.

1 On the Project menu, click Project Information.

The Project Information dialog box appears.

2 In the Status Date box, type or select **August 6, 2001** and click OK.

3 On the View menu, point to Table: Cost and click More Tables.

The More Tables dialog box appears.

4 In the Tables list, select Earned Value and click Apply.

Microsoft Project displays the Earned Value table in the Task Sheet view. Next you will display the **project summary task** to see project-level earned value numbers.

5 On the Tools menu, click Options.

6 In the Options dialog box, click the View tab.

7 Under the Outline Options label, select the Project Summary Task box and then click OK.

Microsoft Project displays the project summary task at the top of the Task Sheet. If necessary, double-click between column headings to display all values. Your screen should look similar to the following illustration.

These are some of the earned value fields available in Microsoft Project. For more information about any field, point to the column heading and in the Tool Tip that appears click the Help link.

Task Name	BCWS	BCWP	ACWP	SV	CV	EAC	E
0 Short Film Project	$53,169.44	$45,098.77	$49,285.63	($8,070.68)	($4,186.86)	$109,010.28	$100
1 Pre-Production	$28,749.32	$28,749.32	$29,296.13	$0.00	($546.81)	$29,296.13	$
23 Production	$24,420.13	$16,349.45	$19,989.50	($8,070.68)	($3,640.05)	$51,898.13	$
24 Scene 7	$4,900.00	$4,900.00	$5,415.25	$0.00	($515.25)	$5,415.25	
30 Scene 3	$5,179.00	$5,179.00	$6,603.50	$0.00	($1,424.50)	$6,603.50	
36 Scene 1	$6,756.25	$6,270.45	$7,970.75	($485.80)	($1,700.30)	$9,185.25	
37 Scene 1 sett	$2,082.00	$2,082.00	$3,470.00	$0.00	($1,388.00)	$3,470.00	
38 Scene 1 reh	$780.00	$780.00	$780.00	$0.00	$0.00	$780.00	
39 Scene 1 sho	$3,200.25	$3,200.25	$3,200.25	$0.00	$0.00	$3,200.25	
40 Scene 1 tear	$694.00	$208.20	$520.50	($485.80)	($312.30)	$1,735.00	
41 Scene 1-pro	$0.00	$0.00	$0.00	$0.00	$0.00	$0.00	
42 Scene 2	$2,209.88	$0.00	$0.00	($2,209.88)	$0.00	$2,209.88	
48 Scene 5	$5,375.00	$0.00	$0.00	($5,375.00)	$0.00	$6,003.00	
54 Scene 6	$0.00	$0.00	$0.00	$0.00	$0.00	$13,184.00	$
60 Scene 8	$0.00	$0.00	$0.00	$0.00	$0.00	$7,063.50	
66 Scene 4	$0.00	$0.00	$0.00	$0.00	$0.00	$2,233.75	
72 Post-Production	$0.00	$0.00	$0.00	$0.00	$0.00	$27,816.02	$

The project summary task shows you the complete project's earned value numbers. When displayed, it has a task ID of 0.

Here you can see most of the earned value numbers described at the beginning of this section. All earned value numbers are reported as dollars for easy comparison; negative amounts appear in parentheses.

tip

A quick way to view a task's earned value numbers in any task view is to display the Earned Value form. On the Tools menu, point to Customize and then click Forms. In the Customize Forms dialog box, select Earned Value and then click Apply. In the Customize Forms dialog box you can see the several built-in task and resource forms available. You can customize any form to include the specific fields you're most interested in. A shortcut for displaying most custom forms is to display the Custom Forms toolbar. On the View menu, point to Toolbars, and then click Custom Forms. For more information, ask the Office Assistant "How do I use custom forms?"

Next, you will view formulas that calculate CPI and SPI values. The Number1 and Number2 fields have been customized with formulas in this project file to save you time. However, you will view one of the formulas, to help you understand what they do.

8   On the Tools menu, point to Customize and click Fields.

The Customize Fields dialog box appears.

9   In the Type box, select Number from the drop-down list.

10   In the Field list, select CPI (Number1).

11   Under the Custom Attributes label, click the Formula button.

The Formula dialog box appears. Your screen should look similar to the following illustration:

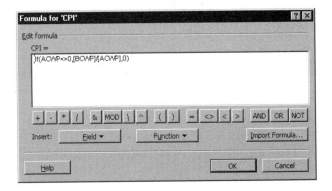

This formula calculates CPI for each task; CPI is simply BCWP divided by ACWP. (The formula actually has some additional content so it won't attempt the calculation when ACWP is zero—that is, for tasks that have no actual work yet.)

A similar formula has been provided for the Number2 field to calculate SPI. SPI is BCWP divided by BCWS.

12   Click Cancel to close the Formula dialog box, and then click Cancel again to close the Customize Fields dialog box.

To conclude this exercise, you will display the CPI and SPI columns in the Earned Value table.

13   Select the BCWS column heading.

14   On the Insert menu, click Column.

The Column Definition dialog box appears.

15   In the Field Name box, select SPI (Number2) from the drop-down list and click OK.

Microsoft Project displays the SPI column in the Earned Value table.

16   On the Insert menu, click Column.

The Column Definition dialog box appears.

17   In the Field Name box, select CPI (Number1) and click OK.

Microsoft Project displays the CPI column to the left of the SPI column. Your screen should look similar to the following illustration.

	Task Name	CPI	SPI	BCWS	BCWP	ACWP	SV	CV
0	☐ Short Film Project	0.92	0.85	$53,169.44	$45,098.77	$49,285.63	($8,070.68)	($4,186.86)
1	⊞ Pre-Production	0.98	1	$28,749.32	$28,749.32	$29,296.13	$0.00	($546.81)
23	☐ Production	0.82	0.67	$24,420.13	$16,349.45	$19,589.50	($8,070.68)	($3,640.05)
24	⊞ Scene 7	0.9	1	$4,900.00	$4,900.00	$5,415.25	$0.00	($515.25)
30	⊞ Scene 3	0.78	1	$5,179.00	$5,179.00	$6,603.50	$0.00	($1,424.50)
36	☐ Scene 1	0.79	0.93	$6,756.25	$6,270.45	$7,970.75	($485.80)	($1,700.30)
37	Scene 1 setup	0.6	1	$2,082.00	$2,082.00	$3,470.00	$0.00	($1,388.00)
38	Scene 1 rehears:	1	1	$780.00	$780.00	$780.00	$0.00	$0.00
39	Scene 1 shoot	1	1	$3,200.25	$3,200.25	$3,200.25	$0.00	$0.00
40	Scene 1 teardow	0.4	0.3	$694.00	$208.20	$520.50	($485.80)	($312.30)
41	Scene 1-process	0	0	$0.00	$0.00	$0.00	$0.00	$0.00
42	⊞ Scene 2	0	0	$2,209.88	$0.00	$0.00	($2,209.88)	$0.00
48	⊞ Scene 5	0	0	$5,375.00	$0.00	$0.00	($5,375.00)	$0.00
54	⊞ Scene 6	0	0	$0.00	$0.00	$0.00	$0.00	$0.00
60	⊞ Scene 8	0	0	$0.00	$0.00	$0.00	$0.00	$0.00
66	⊞ Scene 4	0	0	$0.00	$0.00	$0.00	$0.00	$0.00
72	⊞ Post-Production	0	0	$0.00	$0.00	$0.00	$0.00	$0.00

The CPI and SPI values tell us something about each task and phase in the project, and about the project as a whole:

- The project's CPI (as of the status date) is .92. One way you can interpret this is that for every dollar's worth of work we've paid for, only 92 cents' worth of work was actually accomplished.

- The project's SPI (as of the status date) is .85. One way you can interpret this is that for every dollar's worth of work we'd planned to accomplish, only 85 cents' worth was actually accomplished.

Let's all take a deep breath. Earned value analysis is one of the more complicated things you can do in Microsoft Project, but the information it provides on project status is invaluable. Earned value analysis also is a great example of one benefit of entering task and resource cost information in a project plan.

Lesson Wrap-Up

This lesson covered how to view and analyze several key aspects of project status, including cost and schedule variance and earned value analysis.

If you are going on to other lessons:

1   On the Standard toolbar, click Save to save changes made to Short Film Project 15.

2   On the File menu, click Close to close the file.

If you aren't continuing to other lessons:

●   On the File menu, click Exit.

Glossary

ACWP The actual cost of work performed. In earned value analysis, this is the actual costs of tasks that have been completed (or the portion completed of each) by the status date.

Baseline The original project plan saved for later comparison. The baseline includes the planned start and finish dates of tasks and assignments and their planned costs. Each Microsoft Project file can have only one baseline.

BCWP The budgeted cost of work performed. In earned value analysis, this is the budgeted cost of tasks that have been completed (or the portion completed of each) by the status date. BCWP also is called earned value, as it represents the value earned in the project by the status date.

Viewing and Reporting Status   15

BCWS The budgeted cost of work scheduled. In earned value analysis, this is the portion of the project's budget that is scheduled to have been spent by the status date.

Burdened labor rate A resource cost rate that reflects not only the resource's direct payroll cost, but some portion of the organization's indirect costs not directly relating to the resource's assignments on a project. Note that Microsoft Project doesn't support a burdened labor rate directly; if you want to use one, just enter it as a resources standard or overtime cost rate.

CPI The cost performance index. In earned value analysis, this is the ratio of budgeted to actual cost (CPI = BCWP/ACWP).

CV The cost variance. In earned value analysis, this is the difference between budgeted and actual cost (CV = BCWP − ACWP).

Earned value analysis A sophisticated form of project performance analysis that focuses on schedule and budget performance as compared to baseline plans.

Interim plan Tasks' start and finish values saved for later comparison. Each Microsoft Project file can have at most ten interim plans.

Project summary task The top-level task of any single project. The project summary task is automatically generated by Microsoft Project, and displayed through the View tab of the Options dialog box, which is available by selecting the Options command on the Tools menu. The Project Summary Task summarizes the duration, work, and costs of the entire project, and has a task ID of 0.

SPI The schedule performance index. In earned value analysis, this is the ratio of performed to scheduled work (SPI = BCWP/BCWS).

Stakeholders All people or organizations that might be affected by project activities (those who "have a stake" in its success). These also include those resources working on the project, as well as others (such as customers) external to the project work.

Status date The date you specify (not necessarily the current date) that determines how Microsoft Project calculates earned value numbers.

SV The schedule variance. In earned value analysis, this is the difference between current progress and the baseline plan (SV = BCWP − BCWS).

Variance Any deviation of the scheduled or actual project plan's schedule and budget information from the baseline plan.

Quick Reference

To compare scheduled and baseline task information

● On the View menu, click Tracking Gantt.

To display interim plans on a Gantt view

1 On the Format menu, click Bar Styles.

The Bar Styles dialog box appears.

2 Click the Insert Row button.

3 In the new cell directly below the Name column heading, type **Interim**.

4 In the same row, click the cell under the Show For…Tasks column heading and select Normal from the drop-down list.

5 Click the cell under the From column heading, and select one of the Start$n$ fields (Start1 through Start10), depending on the interim plan you want to display.

6 Click the cell under the To column heading, and then select one of the Finish$n$ fields (Finish1 through Finish10), depending on the interim plan you want to display.

7 Click the Bars tab in the lower portion of the Bar Styles dialog box, and select the shape, pattern, color, and other options you want the interim bars to have.

To view cost variance for tasks

1 On the View menu, click More Views.

The More Views dialog box appears.

2 In the Views list, select Task Sheet and click Apply.

3 On the View menu, point to Table and click Cost.

Task variance is contained in the Variance column.

To view cost variance for resources

1 On the View bar, click Resource Sheet.

2 On the View menu, point to Table and click Cost.

Resource variance is contained in the Variance column.

To set the project status date

1 On the Project menu, click Project Information.

2 In the Status Date box, type or select the date you want.

To display the Earned Value table

Resource
Sheet

1   On the View menu, point to Table and click More Tables.
The More Tables dialog box appears.

2   In the Tables list, select Earned Value and click Apply.

16

Identifying and Fixing Problems in Your Project

ESTIMATED TIME
30 min.

After completing this lesson, you will be able to:

✔ *Reschedule the remaining work for a task that has been interrupted.*

✔ *Edit work values for resource assignments, and replace resources assigned to a task.*

✔ *Assign overtime work to assignments, and assign additional resources to reduce task durations.*

Once work has started on a project, addressing **variance** is not really a one-time event but is instead an ongoing effort by the project manager. In this lesson, we'll focus on some of the many variance problems that can arise during a project as work progresses. We'll frame these problems around the **project triangle** introduced in Lesson 1.

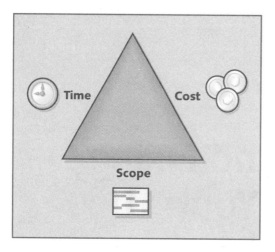

As noted in Lesson 1, **time**, **cost**, and **scope** are interconnected; changing one element can affect the other two. However, for purposes of identifying, analyzing, and addressing problems in project management, it's useful to fit problems into one of these three categories.

The specific issues we'll focus on in this lesson aren't necessarily the most common problems you'll face in your own projects. Because every project is unique, there's no way to anticipate what you'll run into. However, we've attempted to highlight the most pressing issues at the midpoint of the Short Film Project's duration and to apply solutions that may affect many of the problems that tend to surface in projects.

Practice files for the lesson

To complete this lesson, you will use a file named Short Film Project 16. Before you begin this lesson, open the Part 4 folder in the MS Project 2000 SBS Practice folder on your hard disk. Open the file 16A, and save it as Short Film Project 16 in the Part 4 folder.

Troubleshooting Time and Schedule Problems

Schedule variance is almost certainly going to appear in any complex project. Maintaining control over the schedule requires that the project manager (a) know when variance has occurred and to what extent and (b) take timely corrective action to stay on track.

PROJ2000-2-6
PROJ2000E-2-1

It's common for some corrective actions you take to cause new problems later in the schedule. If you've set up your project plan properly, you should be able to see such ripple effects. For example, in this exercise you delay work on a task because of an unanticipated event, but in doing so you further delay successor tasks and, ultimately, the project's finish date.

In this exercise, you report some work for the next task scheduled to start and troubleshoot a delay in work caused by a problem at the studio. You'll return to the project's finish date problem later in the lesson.

1   In the Task Name column, double-click the name of Task 55, "Scene 6 Setup."

The Task Information dialog box appears.

2   Click the General tab.

3   In the Percent Complete box, type or select **25** and then click OK.

Microsoft Project records progress for the task and displays a **progress bar** in a portion of the task's Gantt bar. Your screen should look similar to the following illustration.

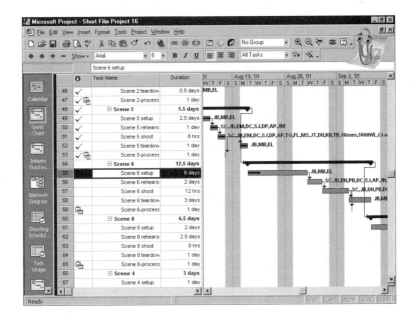

You've learned that on the evening of Wednesday, August 22, a water pipe burst in the studio where Scene 6 was to be shot. None of the project's equipment was damaged, but the cleanup will delay work until the following Monday, August 27. This effectively stops work on the production tasks for a few days. Next you'll reschedule uncompleted work so the project can start again on Monday.

4   On the Tools menu, point to Tracking and then click Update Project.

The Update Project dialog box appears.

5 Click Reschedule Uncompleted Work To Start After, and in the Date box select Sunday, August 26, 2001.

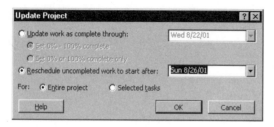

6 Click OK to close the Update Project dialog box.

Microsoft Project splits Task 55 so that the uncompleted portion of the task is delayed until Monday. Your screen should look similar to the following illustration.

Progress bars indicate the portion
of the task that has been completed.

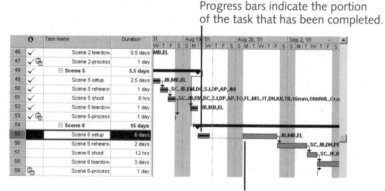

The task's remaining work has been rescheduled to start after August 26. The dotted line represents the resulting split in the task.

As you can see, although the duration of Task 55 remains at six days, its finish date and subsequent start dates for successor tasks have been pushed out. So although we've addressed a specific problem, in doing so we've created other problems in the remainder of the project. We'll address these next.

tip

You can disable the ability of Microsoft Project to reschedule uncompleted work on tasks that have any actual work. On the Tools menu, click the Options command. In the Options dialog box, click the Schedule tab and then clear the Split In-Progress Tasks box. For more information about this and other options on this tab of the Options dialog box, click the Help button that appears in the dialog box.

Troubleshooting Cost and Resource Problems

In projects where you've entered cost information for resources, you may find that to address many cost problems you must fine-tune resource and assignment details. Whether or not it's your intention, changing resource assignment details not only affects costs, but can also affect task durations.

After doing some research into the high cost variance of the electricians on the setup and teardown assignments, you learn that they're really needed for only a portion of the tasks' durations. After discussing the issue with the production manager, you agree that the electricians' assignments on the remaining setup and teardown tasks should be halved. While you're updating the project, you'll also handle the anticipated departure of another resource.

In this exercise, you adjust work values for resource assignments and replace one resource with another on upcoming assignments.

Resource
Usage

1   On the View bar, click Resource Usage.

The Resource Usage view appears.

2   On the View menu, point to Table: Entry and then click Usage.

The Usage table appears in the Resource Usage view.

3   In the Resource Name column, click the plus sign next to the name of Resource 12, "Electrician."

Microsoft Project displays the assignments for this resource.

4   In the Work column for "Scene 6 setup" type **24h** and then press the Enter key.

Microsoft Project adjusts the work of the electricians on this task to 24 hours.

5   Enter the following new work values for the electricians' remaining assignments:

For this assignment	Enter this work value
Scene 6 teardown	12h
Scene 8 setup	8h
Scene 8 teardown	4h
Scene 4 setup	4h
Scene 4 teardown	4h

When you're done, your screen should look similar to the following illustration.

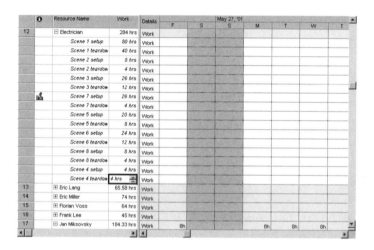

To conclude this exercise, you will update the project plan to reflect that a resource will be leaving the project early and his assignments will be taken over by another resource. Peter Kelly will be leaving the project just prior to the start of Task 83. You will replace Peter Kelly's assignment on this work and a later task with Kim Yoshida.

6   On the View bar, click Gantt Chart.

The Gantt Chart view replaces the Resource Usage view.

7   In the Task Name column, select the name of Task 83, "Clone dubbing master."

8   On the Standard toolbar, click the Go To Selected Task button.

9   While holding down the Ctrl key, select the name of Task 84, "Archive master film and audiotape."

10   On the Standard toolbar, click the Assign Resources button.

The Assign Resources dialog box appears.

11   In the Name column of the Assign Resources dialog box, select Peter Kelly and then click Replace.

12   In the Name column of the Replace Resource dialog box, select Kim Yoshida and then click OK.

Microsoft Project replaces Peter Kelly's assignment to these two tasks with Kim Yoshida.

13   Click Close to close the Assign Resources dialog box.

Your screen should look similar to the following illustration.

After replacing Peter Kelly with Kim Yoshida, her initials appear next to the Gantt Chart bars representing the tasks to which she has been assigned.

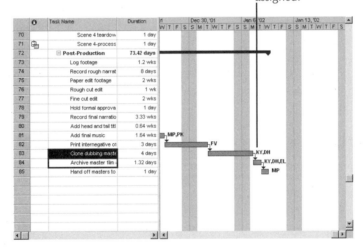

Troubleshooting Scope of Work Problems

PROJ2000E-2-2
PROJ2000E-2-8

You may recall from Lesson 1 that the project's scope includes all the work required—and only the work required—to successfully deliver the product of the project to its intended customer. Once project work has started, managing its scope usually requires making trade-offs: trading time for money, quality for time, and so on. You might have the goal of never making such trade-offs, but a more realistic goal might be to make the best-informed trade-offs possible.

In this exercise, you focus in on the project's finish date and make several trade-offs to ensure that the project will deliver its product within the time frame that its **sponsors** require.

1   On the Project menu, click Project Information.

The Project Information dialog box appears. As the schedule is now, if all the remaining work is completed as scheduled, the project will be completed on January 9, 2002. The sponsors of the project would like to see it completed before the new year, so you'll need to take steps to pull in the finish date.

2   Click Cancel to close the Project Information dialog box.

Because the project finish date is controlled by tasks on the critical path, you'll begin by viewing only those tasks.

3   On the Project menu, point to Filtered For: All Tasks and then click Critical.

Microsoft Project displays only the critical tasks. The remaining production tasks are already as compressed as they can be, so you'll focus on compressing the post-production tasks. To begin, you'll allow overtime work for several tasks, to shorten their durations.

4   In the Task Name column, select the name of Task 73, "Log footage," and scroll the Gantt Chart view so that task appears near the top of the view.

5   On the Standard toolbar, click the Go To Selected Task button.

6   On the Window menu, click Split.

The Task Form appears below the Gantt Chart view.

7   Click anywhere in the Task Form and then on the Format menu, point to Details and click Resource Work.

The Resource Work details appear in the Task Form.

8   In the Ovt. Work column for the resource named Editing Lab, type or select **10h**.

9   In the Ovt. Work column for the resource named Florian Voss, type or select **10h** and click OK in the upper right corner of the Task Form.

The overtime work values cause Microsoft Project to adjust the daily work assignments for these resources and to shorten the overall duration of the task. Your screen should look similar to the following illustration.

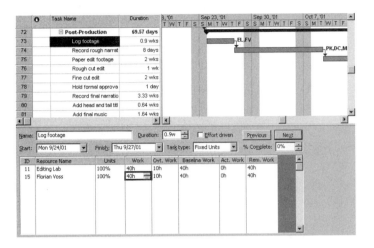

Note that each resource's total work on this task remains at 40 hours. Now, however, 10 of those 40 hours per resource will be scheduled as overtime. The same amount of work will be performed, but in a shorter time span. Microsoft Project will apply, if they have been set up, overtime cost rates to the overtime portion of the assignment.

10 In the Gantt Chart view, select the name of Task 74, "Record rough narration."

11 In the Task Form, enter 20 hours of overtime work for each of the three assigned resources and then click OK.

Microsoft Project schedules the overtime work and recalculates the task's duration. Your screen should look similar to the following illustration.

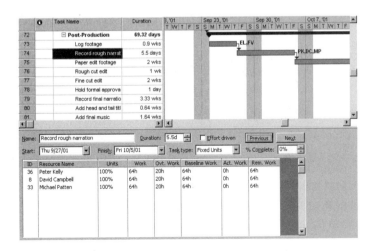

12   In the Gantt Chart view, select the name of Task 75, "Paper edit footage."

13   In the Task Form, enter 25 hours of overtime work for each of the four assigned resources and then click OK.

Microsoft Project schedules the overtime work and recalculates the task's duration. Your screen should look similar to the following illustration.

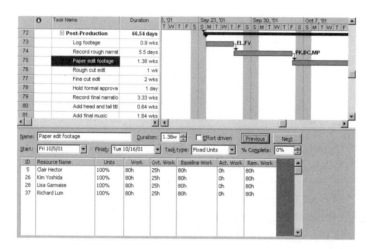

14   On the Project menu, click Project Information.

The Project Information dialog box appears. The adjustments you've made to the schedule have pulled in the project's finish date to 12/31/01. While that meets the target set by the project sponsors, given the overall performance to date you can expect some additional variance. In anticipation of this, you'll make further adjustments to the post-production tasks.

15   Click Cancel to close the Project Information dialog box.

Task 77, "Fine cut edit," has a long duration. After talking with the assigned resources, you all agree that assigning two more resources should reduce the duration of the task.

16   In the Gantt Chart view, select the name of Task 77, "Fine cut edit."

17   In the Task Form, select Effort Driven.

With **effort-driven scheduling** enabled, assigning more resources will reduce the task's duration. For more information about effort-driven scheduling, see Lesson 5.

18   In the Resource Name column of the Task Form, click the blank cell below the final assigned resource.

19   Click the down arrow and then select Doug Hampton.

20 In the cell below Doug Hampton, click the down arrow and then select John Thorson.

21 Click OK in the upper right corner of the Task Form to assign the resources.

Assigning these two resources has reduced the task's duration from two weeks to about a week and a half. It looks as though you'll still need to make some additional adjustments, however.

The longest-duration task left in the post-production phase is Task 79, "Record final narration." After you discuss this with the resources assigned, they agree that they can complete the task in two weeks without requiring overtime.

22 In the Gantt Chart view, select the name of Task 79, "Record final narration."

23 In the Duration box in the Task Form, type or select **2w** and click OK.

24 On the Project menu, click Project Information.

The Project Information dialog box appears.

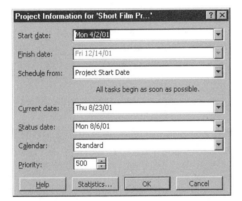

The project's finish date is now December 14, giving you about two weeks of buffer time before the new year. However, these final adjustments you've made have changed the final cost values as well.

25 Click Statistics.

The Project Statistics dialog box appears.

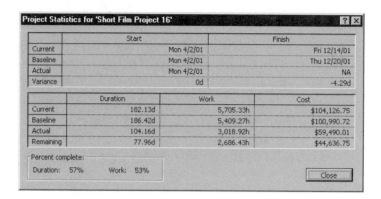

The current final cost calculation is around $104,000, although you know it's likely to go up.

26 Click Close to close the Project Statistics dialog box.

27 On the Window menu, click Remove Split.

You confer with the project sponsors, who agree that the additional cost is acceptable as long as you can deliver the final film masters to the distributors before the new year. Just over half the project's duration and work have elapsed. While producing the project deliverable within these constraints will be a challenge, you're both realistic and optimistic, and comfortable with your project management skills and your knowledge of Microsoft Project. Let's go!

Lesson Wrap-Up

This lesson covered how to apply a variety of remedies to time, cost, and scope problems. This lesson concludes the tutorial portion of this book.

● On the File menu, click Exit.

Glossary

Cost All the resources required to carry out a project, including the people and equipment who do the work and the materials consumed as the work is completed. Cost is one side of the project triangle model.

Effort-driven scheduling A scheduling method in which a task's work remains constant regardless of the number of resources assigned to it. As resources are added to a task, its duration decreases, but the work remains the same and is distributed among the assigned resources. Effort-driven scheduling is on by default in Microsoft Project, but it can be turned off for any task.

Identifying and Fixing Problems 16

Progress bar A graphical representation on a bar in the Gantt Chart view that shows how much of a task has been completed.

Project triangle A popular model of project management in which time, cost, and scope are represented as the three sides of a triangle. A change to one side will affect at least one of the other two sides. There are many variations on this model.

Scope The products or services to be provided by a project and the work required to deliver it. For project planning, it's useful to distinguish between product scope and project scope. Scope is one side of the project triangle model.

Sponsor An individual or organization that provides financial support and champions the project team within the larger organization.

Time The scheduled durations of individual tasks and the overall project; the schedule. Time is one side of the project triangle model.

Variance Any deviation of the scheduled or actual project plan's schedule and budget information from the baseline plan.

Quick Reference

To reschedule the remaining work for a task in progress

1   On the Tools menu, point to Tracking and then click Update Project.

2   Click Reschedule Uncompleted Work To Start After and then in the Date box type or select the date immediately after which you want work on the task to resume.

To edit resource assignments' work values

1   On the View bar, click Resource Usage.

2   In the Work column, edit the values you want.

To replace a resource assignment

1   On the View bar, click Gantt Chart.

2   In the Task Name column, select the task for which you want to replace a resource assignment.

3   On the Standard toolbar, click Assign Resources.

4   In the Name column of the Assign Resources dialog box, select the name of the resource you want to replace.

5   Click the Replace button.

6   In the Replace Resource dialog box, select the name of the replacement resource you want and then click OK to close the Replace Resource dialog box.

7   Click Close to close the Assign Resources dialog box.

To filter for critical tasks

●   On the Project menu, point to Filtered For: All Tasks and then click Critical.

To display the project finish date and other details

1   On the Project menu, click Project Information.

2   Click the Statistics button.

To enter overtime work values in the Task Form

Gantt
Chart

1   On the View bar, click Gantt Chart.

2   On the Window menu, click Split.

3   Click anywhere in the Task Form and then on the Format menu, point to Details and then click Resource Work.

4   In the Ovt. Work column for the resource to which you want to assign overtime work, enter the number of hours of overtime work you want.

PART

4

**ESTIMATED
TIME
10 min.**

Review & Practice

You will review and practice how to:

✔ *Record actual work, percent complete, and actual start dates for tasks.*

✔ *Compare baseline, scheduled, and actual plans, and view a project summary report.*

✔ *Change the scope of work to reduce overall project cost.*

To conclude this tutorial, you can practice the skills you learned in Part 4 by working through this Review & Practice section.

Scenario

Work on the music video for the band Fourth Coffee has commenced! You've been given the first actuals by the project team, and Leonard Zuvela, manager of the band, has asked for a status report. You also need to check the project's cost and schedule constraints, and if necessary take corrective action. The project must be completed no later than July 2, 2001, and the final budget must be below $30,000.

**Practice files
for the lesson**

To complete this section, you will use a file named Music Video Project 4. Before you begin this section, open the Part 4 folder in the MS Project 2000 SBS Practice folder on your hard disk. Open the file Part4A, and save it as Music Video Project 4 in the Part 4 folder.

Step 1: Record Actual Progress

For a demonstration of how to complete this step, double-click Part 4 Step 1 in the Multimedia folder on the Microsoft Project 2000 Step by Step CD-ROM.

The first tasks in the preproduction phase of the project have been completed. Things have gotten off to a bad start, however, and some of the tasks took longer than planned to complete.

1 Using the Update Tasks button on the Tracking toolbar, record that Task 2, "Develop script breakdown," started as scheduled, and was completed with a 9-day duration.

2 Record that Task 3, "Develop choreography," was completed as scheduled.

3 Record that Task 5, "Rehearsal," started one working day later than currently scheduled, had a 4-day duration, and is 100% complete.

You must complete the exercises in steps 1 through 3 sequentially.

For more information about	See
Recording actual work with the Tracking toolbar	Lesson 14
Recording the actual start date of a task	Lesson 14
Recording actual duration of a task	Lesson 14

Step 2: Check the Project's Status

For a demonstration, double-click Part 4 Step 2 in the Multimedia folder.

Leonard Zuvela has asked to see the progress made so far and would like a "big picture" summary of the project. Although you know the currently projected cost for the project is over the target of $30,000, you have been unable to get the key resources to agree on where to make cuts in the post-production phase. On the bright side, the projected finish date is well before the target deadline of July 2, 2001.

1 Switch to a Gantt Chart view that displays both baseline and scheduled task bars.

2 Display the Project Summary report (an Overview report) in the Print Preview window.

For more information about	See
Viewing baseline and scheduled details	Lesson 15
Reports	Lesson 15

For a demonstration, double-click Part 4 Step 3 in the Multimedia folder.

Step 3: Identify and Troubleshoot Variance

The schedule variance is acceptable to the project sponsors, but you're concerned about the high cost variance. You've developed a prioritized list of scope cuts to reduce the final project cost.

1   Check the project's current total cost.

2   Record that Task 6, "Shoot," is 100% complete.

3   Reduce the duration of Task 8, "Fine cut edit," to 3 days.

4   Reduce the work of the Producer on Task 8, "Fine cut edit," to 12 hours.

5   Reduce the work of the Director on Task 9, "Add final music," to 4 hours.

6   Check the project's current total cost and verify that it is less than $30,000.

7   Check the project's current finish date and verify it is prior to July 2, 2001.

For more information about	See
Viewing project statistics	Lesson 16
Changing a project's planned duration	Lesson 14
Changing a resource's work value on an assignment	Lesson 16

Finish the Review & Practice

If you are not finished using Microsoft Project:

1   On the Standard toolbar, click Save to save changes made to Music Video Project 4.

2   On the File menu, click Close to close the file.

If you are finished using Microsoft Project for now:

●   On the File menu, click Exit.

APPENDIX

A

If You're New to Windows or to Microsoft Project 2000

If you are new to Microsoft Windows or to Microsoft Project 2000, this appendix will show you the basics you need to get started. You'll get an overview of Windows and Microsoft Project features, and you'll learn how to use online Help to answer your questions.

If You Are New to Windows

Windows is an easy-to-use computer environment that helps you handle the daily work that you perform with your computer. You can use Windows 95, Windows 98, Windows NT Workstation version 4.0 Service Pack 4 or later, or Windows 2000 to run Microsoft Project 2000.

The way you use Windows and programs designed for these operating systems is similar. The programs look much alike, and you use similar menus to tell them what to do. If you're already familiar with Windows, skip to the section titled "If You Are New to Microsoft Project 2000"

Start Windows

Starting Windows is as easy as turning on your computer.

1   If your computer isn't on, turn it on now.

2   If you are using Windows NT or Windows 2000, press Ctrl+Alt+Del to display a dialog box asking for your user name and password. If you are using Windows 95 or Windows 98, you will see this dialog box if your computer is connected to a network.

3   Type your user name and password in the appropriate boxes, and click OK. If you don't know your user name or password, contact your system administrator for assistance.

Using the Mouse

Although you can use the keyboard for most actions, many actions are easier to do by using a mouse. The mouse controls a pointer on the screen. You move the pointer by sliding the mouse over a flat surface in the direction you want the pointer to move. If you run out of room to move the mouse, lift it up and put it down in a more comfortable location.

important

We assume that your mouse is set up so that the left button is the primary button and the right button is the secondary button. If your mouse is configured the opposite way, for left-handed use, use the right button when we tell you to use the left, and vice versa.

You'll use five basic mouse actions throughout this book.

When you are directed to	Do this
Point to an item	Move the mouse to place the pointer on the item.
Click an item	Point to the item on your screen, and quickly press and release the left mouse button.
Right-click an item	Point to the item on your screen, and quickly press and release the right mouse button. Clicking the right mouse button often displays a shortcut menu with a list of command choices that apply to that item.
Double-click an item	Point to the item, and quickly press and release the left mouse button twice.
Drag an item	Point to an item, and press and hold down the left mouse button as you move the pointer. Once the item is moved to the appropriate location, release the left mouse button.

Getting Help with Windows

When you're at work and you have a question, you might ask it of a coworker, or you might consult a reference book. To find out more about functions and features in Windows, you can use the online Help system. Using Windows Help is one of the quickest and most efficient ways to find your answer. You can access Windows Help from the Windows Start menu. For Help specific to a program, such as Microsoft Project 2000, most Windows programs also includes their own Help systems.

After the Help window opens, you can choose one of three ways to research your question. To find instructions about broad categories, you can look on the Contents tab; or you can search with the Index tab to find information about specific topics; or, finally, you can use the Search tab to look for Help files based on keywords that you provide.

In Windows 98 and 2000, on the Windows Help toolbar, click Web Help to automatically connect to Microsoft's Support Online Web site. Once connected, you can expand your search to include the Microsoft Knowledge Base, Troubleshooting Wizards, Newsgroups, and downloadable files.

If You Are New to Microsoft Project 2000

Microsoft Project 2000 is the latest version of Microsoft Project. It is designed to run on the Windows operating system. As did previous releases, Microsoft Project 2000 provides a rich feature set for planning, tracking and analyzing projects. For information about the major new features in Microsoft Project 2000, see "Finding Your Best Starting Point" at the beginning of this book. Also look for the "New in 2000" icons in the margin throughout this book.

One of the most significant new pieces of Microsoft Project 2000 is Microsoft Project Central. This is a Web-based companion product that enables a broad range of communication and reporting activities between the project manager and resources and other stakeholders. For more information about Microsoft Project Central, see Appendix D.

Microsoft Project is a powerful and at times complex application. Unlike other desktop applications you may use daily, the functions of Microsoft Project are closely tied to a specific vocation: project management. While you can master every aspect of Microsoft Word and still not become a great novelist, you can't use Microsoft Project to its fullest capacity without developing some project management expertise along the way.

You'll get considerable help in mastering Microsoft Project by using self-paced training material (such as this book), enrolling in more formal training, or through other means. For descriptions of some of the training and support options you may have available, see Appendix E, "What's Next?"

Getting Help with Microsoft Project

You can get assistance while working in Microsoft Project in a number of ways.

- For immediate help with almost any item you see in the Microsoft Project window, such as buttons and items in a Gantt Chart view, point at it with the mouse. After a moment, a ToolTip will appear. Some ToolTips, such as those for column headings, contain links to more complete Help.

- For help in some dialog boxes, click the Help button to get more complete Help about the options available in the dialog box.

- For help with a specific item in any dialog box, click the question mark button in the upper right corner of the dialog box, and then click on the item you want help with. A ToolTip appears.

- If you have a question about how to use or locate a feature in Microsoft Project, ask the Office Assistant. The more specific your question is, the better response you will get.

- For guided introductions to Microsoft Project, in the Welcome screen click Quick Preview or Tutorial. Or on the Help menu, point to Getting Started and then click the item you want.

- For a presentation of broad project management activities and how Microsoft Project supports them, see the Project Map. In the Welcome screen click Project Map. Or, on the Help menu, point to Getting Started and then click Project Map. Once you see the Project Map, select the project management phase or activity that you're interested in on the left, and then drill down for more details on the right.

- To see a variety of other items in Help, see the Reference topic: in the Welcome screen, click Reference, and in the Help topic that appears click the item you want.

APPENDIX

B

Matching the Exercises

Microsoft Project 2000 has many options that affect either how your screen appears or how certain features work. Some procedure steps, therefore, might not produce exactly the same result on your screen as appears in this book. If your results don't match those the lesson describes, you can use this appendix to determine whether the options you have selected are the same as the options used when preparing this book. You can follow the steps described to ensure that your results and screen appearance will exactly match what this book describes and shows.

important

Each computer system is configured with different hardware and software; therefore, your screen display of icons, folders, and menu options might not exactly match the illustrations in this book. These system differences should not interfere with your ability to perform the procedures in the book.

Change Screen Resolution

The illustrations in the procedures show a screen resolution of 800 by 600 pixels. If your screen resolution differs, you can change it to match the illustrations.

If your screen resolution differs

1   On the Windows Start menu, point to Settings, and click Control Panel.

2   Double-click the Display icon.

3   In the Display Properties dialog box, click the Settings tab.

4   In the Screen area, move the slider until "800 by 600 pixels" appears, and then click Apply.

If your monitor does not display properly at 800 by 600 pixels, click No, when prompted, to return to your previous settings.

> **tip**
>
> Your monitor and display adapter determine which screen resolutions you can use. If your computer is running in a controlled environment (such as using Windows Terminal Server), you might not be able to change your screen resolution at all.

Installing Microsoft Project Components

You can install Microsoft Project using one of several options. The procedures in this book assume that Microsoft Project was installed using the default options. If the default options were not used, some features described in the procedures might not be available to you, or they might be installed when you activate them (by selecting a menu option, for example).

If you seem to be missing entire components of Microsoft Project that are referenced in the procedures, rerun the setup program or consult with whoever installed Microsoft Project on your computer.

Using the Default Microsoft Project Settings

Microsoft Project makes it easy for you to change what you see on the screen to better suit your needs. The following instructions explain how to adjust some of the most common elements you see in Microsoft Project.

If No Toolbars Are Visible

If no toolbars are visible near the top of the Microsoft Project window, they might have been hidden. You can redisplay the toolbars you need for the lessons.

● On the View menu, point to Toolbars, and then click the toolbars you want. Most of the procedures require the Standard and Formatting toolbars.

If Menu Options Are Not Visible

The option you want might be temporarily hidden; if it is, you need to expand the menu.

● Point to the arrow or chevron at the bottom of the menu.

  The menu expands to display all options.

> **tip**
> You can also double-click the menu name to expand it.

If You Want To Turn Off Collapsing Menus

You can turn off the collapsing menu behavior if you want. If you turn this option off, menus always display all their options.

1 On the Tools menu, click Customize, and then click Toolbars.

2 In the Customize dialog box, click the Options tab.

3 Deselect the Show Full Menus After A Short Delay check box.

If the View Bar Does Not Appear on the Left Edge of the Microsoft Project Window

Many procedures refer to clicking buttons on the View Bar. If this bar is not visible, you can display it.

● On the View menu, click View Bar.

If the Office Assistant Is Not Visible

Some procedures refer to the Office Assistant, through which you search online Help. If the Office Assistant is not visible, you can display it.

● On the Help menu, click Microsoft Project Help.

> **tip**
> You can also change which Office Assistant character you see and other options. Right-click the Office Assistant, choose Options, and choose the options you want.

If Online Help Automatically Appears When You Start Microsoft Project

By default, Microsoft Project Help appears in a window adjacent to the Microsoft Project window when you start Microsoft Project. If you do not want to see the Help window, you can minimize it.

- In the Help window's title bar, click the Minimize button.

> **tip**
> We recommend you minimize, rather than close, Help, so that it appears more quickly if you need it.

If you prefer, you can turn off the automatic display of Help when Microsoft Project starts.

1   On the Tools menu, click Options, and then click the General tab.

2   Deselect the Display Help On Startup check box.

After the automatic display is turned off, you can still use Help through the Office Assistant or by clicking the Contents And Index command on the Help menu.

C

Customizing Microsoft Project

This appendix describes some of the common ways you can customize Microsoft Project to fit your own preferences. Some of the customization options in Microsoft Project are similar to those you see in other Microsoft Office family applications like Microsoft Word or Microsoft Excel. Some customization options even apply to all Microsoft Office family applications, regardless of the specific application in which you set them. Other options are unique to Microsoft Project.

Customizing the Microsoft Project Environment

As with other Microsoft Office family applications, you have several choices about how to work with Microsoft Project. In fact, some of the preferences you set automatically apply in the other Microsoft Office family applications and vice versa.

PROJ2000-1-2
PROJ2000E-6-3
PROJ2000E-6-8

tip

Many personal preference settings reside in the Options dialog box, which opens when you click the Options command on the Tools menu. To view Help about the items on each tab of this dialog box, click the Help button. To view Help about individual items in the dialog box, click the question mark button in the upper right corner of the dialog box, and then click the item you want to know more about.

To View Accessibility Options

Microsoft Project includes several features that may assist people with limited vision or dexterity or with other limitations in working in the application. These options are in various places throughout the application. The best place to look for information about such options is in Help.

1   Click the Office Assistant, or view the Answer Wizard tab of Help.

2   In the What Would You Like To Do box, type **Accessibility for people with disabilities** and then click Search.

3   View the topic "Accessibility for people with disabilities" or one of the other topics that appear.

To Set the Default Folder for Saving Files

You can specify the folder you wish to open by default in the Open and Save As dialog boxes by selecting the Options commandon the File menu. This is a good idea if you tend to keep most or all of your Microsoft Project files in one location.

1   On the Tools menu, click Options.

The Options dialog box appears.

2   Click the Save tab.

3   Under the File Locations label, select the specific type of file you want to specify a default location for and then click Modify.

The Modify Location dialog box appears.

4   Select the folder location you want and click OK.

5   Click OK again to close the Options dialog box.

To Save Files Automatically at a Preset Time Interval

You can set up Microsoft Project to save the active file or all open files automatically at the time interval you specify.

1   On the Tools menu, click Options.

The Options dialog box appears.

2   Click the Save tab.

3   Under the Auto Save label, select the Save Every box and then specify the time interval you want.

4   Select any other options you want under Auto Save and then click OK to close the Options dialog box.

To Hide the Office Assistant

You can show or hide the Office Assistant. When the Office Assistant is hidden, you can still access all Help contents by clicking Contents And Index on the Help menu.

●   To hide the Office Assistant temporarily, on the Help menu, click Hide The Office Assistant.

1   To turn off the Office Assistant, click the Office Assistant so that its balloon appears.

2   In the balloon, click Options.

   The Office Assistant dialog box appears.

3   Click the Options tab.

4   Clear the Use The Office Assistant box and then click OK.

5   To show the Office Assistant, on the Help menu, click Show The Office Assistant.

tip
Showing or hiding the Office Assistant in Microsoft Project affects all Office family applications, and vice-versa.

To Turn Off Personalized Menus and Toolbars

If you prefer to display the full-length menus rather than the shorter menus that adjust to feature the commands you use most frequently, you can turn off this feature.

1   On the Tools menu, point to Customize and then click Toolbars.

2   Click the Options tab.

3   Clear the Menus Show Recently Used Commands First box.

tip
Turning on or off personalized menus in Microsoft Project affects all Office family applications and vice-versa.

Working with the Organizer

The Organizer is the feature you use to share customized elements among Microsoft Project files. The complete list of elements you can copy between files with the Organizer is indicated by the names of the tabs in the Organizer dialog box.

PROJ2000-3-5
PROJ2000-5-1
PROJ2000E-4-3
PROJ2000E-6-9

The names of the tabs indicate the many types of items you can copy between Microsoft Project files using the Organizer dialog box.

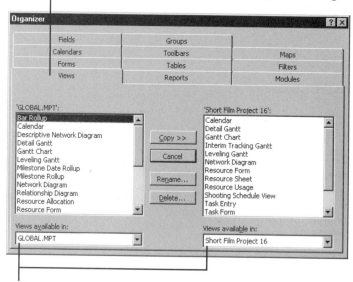

The two files between which you copy items appear here. In this example, the Organizer is set up to copy items between Global.mpt and Short Film Project 16.mpp.

To display the Organizer dialog box, on the Tools menu, click Organizer.

You can use the Organizer to copy items from and to the global template, named Global.mpt. The global template provides the default view, tables, and other elements to all new files you create in Microsoft Project. You can copy elements from the global template to any open project file or between two open project files.

tip

If you've customized a built-in view, table, form, or other element in a Microsoft Project file and wish to restore it to its original state, copy it from the Global template in the Organizer dialog box.

To Customize a File with the Organizer

1   Open the Microsoft Project file that contains the elements you want to copy to another file.

2   Open the Microsoft Project file (or create a new one) to which you want to copy elements from the first file.

3   On the Tools menu, click Organizer.

The Organizer dialog box appears.

4   Click the tab that describes the element you want.

5   On the left side of the Organizer dialog box, in the Available In box, select the name of the file from which you want to copy elements.

6   In the file list box on the left side of the Organizer dialog box, select the specific element you want, and then click Copy. The Copy button should contain two chevrons pointing to the right.

Microsoft Project copies the element to the file listed in the right side of the dialog box.

To Customize the Global Template

1   Open the Microsoft Project file that contains the customized element you want to add to Global.mpt, the global template.

2   On the Tools menu, click Organizer.

The Organizer dialog box appears.

3   Click the tab that describes the element you want.

4   In the box on the right side of the dialog box, select the specific element you want and then click Copy. The Copy button should contain two chevrons pointing to the left.

Microsoft Project copies the element to the global template.

Automating Repetitive Work with a Macro

PROJ2000E-7-3

Many activities you perform in Microsoft Project are repetitive. To save time, you can record a macro that captures keystrokes and mouse actions. The macro is recorded in Visual Basic for Applications (VBA), the built-in macro programming language of the Microsoft Office family of desktop applications. You can do sophisticated things with VBA, but if you prefer, you can record and play back simple macros without ever directly seeing or working with VBA code.

The macros you create are stored in the Global template by default, so they are available to you whenever Microsoft Project is running. The file for which you originally created the macro need not be open to run the macro in other files. If you wish, however, you can use the Organizer to copy the macro from the global template to another file to give it to a friend, for example. For more information, see "Working with the Organizer," above.

> **tip**
>
> VBA is a rich and well-documented programming language. If you'd like to take a closer look at VBA in Microsoft Project, on the Tools menu, click Macro and then select Visual Basic Editor. In the Microsoft Visual Basic window, on the Help menu, click Microsoft Visual Basic Help. To return to Microsoft Project, on the File menu, click Close And Return To Microsoft Project.

To Record a Macro

1   On the Tools menu, click Macro and then select Record New Macro.

The Record Macro dialog box appears.

2   In the Macro Name box, type the name you want. The name must begin with a letter and cannot contain spaces.

> **tip**
>
> To improve the readability of the macro name, use an underscore (_) in place of a space. For example, rather than naming a macro "FormatDuration" you can name it "Format_Duration."

3   If you wish to run the macro with a keyboard shortcut, in the Shortcut Key box type the letter you want.

You can't use a Ctrl+ key combination already reserved by Microsoft Project, however, so combinations like Ctrl+F and Ctrl+G are out. When you click OK to close the dialog box, Microsoft Project alerts you if you need to choose a different key combination.

4   In the Store Macro In box, select Global File to store the macro in the Global template so it will be available whenever Microsoft Project is running, or select This Project to store the macro in the active project file for exclusive use there.

5   In the Description box, enter whatever descriptive information will help remind you or others of the macro's purpose.

6   If necessary, adjust the Row References and the Column References settings
    (For most macros, you'll want to leave the default settings.)

7   Click OK.

    Perform the actions you want recorded in the macro. Microsoft Project does
    not literally record and play back every mouse movement like a video cam-
    era, but only records the results of the keystrokes and mouse actions you
    make. Don't feel rushed to complete the recording of the macro.

8   When you've finished recording the actions you want recorded, on the Tools
    menu, click Macros and then select Stop Recorder.

To Run a Macro

Do one of the following:

On the Tools menu, click Macro and then select Macros.

    The Macros dialog box appears.

- In the Macro Name box, select the macro you want to run and then click
  Run.

—Or—

- Press the shortcut key combination you assigned to the macro.

tip
To stop a macro while it is running, press Ctrl+Break.

APPENDIX

D

Introducing the Workgroup Features of Microsoft Project

For many project managers, communicating project details is one of the most important, time-consuming tasks they perform. Many project teams enjoy computer-based collaboration systems such as local area networks (LANs), e-mail, and access to intranets and the World Wide Web, but critical project information may seem "locked up" in Microsoft Project files under the control of the project manager. In Lesson 11 you used some of the features of Microsoft Project to publish project details in HTML format for viewing on an intranet or on the Web. In addition to publishing information out of Microsoft Project, you can also use workgroup features to bring information into Microsoft Project. Taking full advantage of the workgroup features of Microsoft Project allows the entire project team and other interested stakeholders to communicate online in performing essential tasks such as building project plans, tracking progress, reporting status, and viewing a wide range of project details.

This appendix introduces the two major ways of communicating project information among the project manager, resources, and other stakeholders. They are

- Using Microsoft Project with e-mail-based communication using a MAPI-compliant e-mail system such as Microsoft Outlook, Microsoft Outlook Express, or Lotus Notes. This approach is limited to reporting task assignments, status, and updates.

■ Using Web-based collaboration with the Microsoft Project companion product, Microsoft Project Central. Project Central offers a broad range of collaborative planning and tracking capabilities for all stakeholders in a project.

The specific workgroup solution that's best for you depends on your project team's network infrastructure, technical resources, and information needs. E-mail-based collaboration has relatively few setup requirements, but it is limited in what it can do for the project manager and resources. Project Central requires more setup but offers far more capabilities and benefits.

The one thing both workgroup solutions have in common is that they let the project manager maintain total control over the Microsoft Project data file. You control what information flows into and out of the data file.

Setting Up Workgroup Features in Microsoft Project

Both the e-mail-based and the Project Central workgroup solutions require you to configure Microsoft Project to use them.

To Enable Workgroup Communication in Microsoft Project

1   Open the Microsoft Project file for which you want to enable workgroup communication.

2   On the Tools menu, click Options.

3   Click the Workgroup tab.

4   In the Default Workgroup Messages For box, select Email for e-mail-based communication.

    Or

    Select Web for Project Central–based communication, and then enter the URL for the Project Central Server.

5   Click OK to close the Options dialog box.

    The option you choose will be the default workgroup communication method used for the resources who have assignments in the open Microsoft Project file, though different resources working on the same projects can use different workgroup communication methods. For example, you may have some resources with intranet access who use Microsoft Project Central, and others who use e-mail-based communication.

    Additional setup work is required for both e-mail-based and Project Central–based workgroup communication. For more information, see the following online documents included with Microsoft Project:

- For e-mail-based communication, see the section "Install the Workgroup Message Handler" in the online document C:\Program Files\Microsoft Office\Office\1033\Prjsetup.htm (assuming you installed Microsoft Project to the default location).

- For Web-based communication, see Pjcntrl\Help\1033\Svrsetup.htm on the Microsoft Project Step by Step 2000 CD-ROM.

Using E-mail-based Collaboration with Microsoft Project

PROJ2000-2-3

The e-mail-based communication feature of Microsoft Project is designed primarily to accomplish two things:

- Allow the project manager to send task assignments, updates, and status requests to assigned resources.

- Allow the assigned resources to accept task assignments and send task status reports to the project manager.

The primary benefit for the project manager in using e-mail-based workgroup communication is that the resources themselves supply the actual work details that are saved in the Microsoft Project file upon your approval. This is extremely useful, for two reasons. First, it gives you detailed and presumably accurate status of tasks in progress, although you may need to evaluate the accuracy of the resources' actuals, depending on your situation. Second, it captures in the Microsoft Project file detailed actuals that you can use later to analyze work patterns and develop standard task duration metrics, and for other purposes.

This section describes common activities that both the project manager and the assigned resources can accomplish using e-mail-based communication features. These are organized in the most likely order in which the project manager and the resources would accomplish these activities, and they identify who does what.

Project Manager: Notify Resources of Task Assignments

1 In Microsoft Project, assign resources to tasks.

2 Select the task or tasks for which you want to send assignment notifications.

3 On the Tools menu, click Workgroup and then select TeamAssign.

> **tip**
> If you display the Workgroup toolbar, you can also click the TeamAssign button.

Microsoft Project displays a Workgroup Mail dialog box.

4   In the Workgroup Mail dialog box, select All Tasks or Selected Tasks, and then click OK.

The TeamAssign dialog box opens.

5   In the Subject box and message portion of the dialog box, customize the default content as you wish.

6   Click Send.

Microsoft Project sends an e-mail message with the TeamAssign details to the assigned resources .

Resource: Accept a Task Assignment Request

1   In your e-mail application, open the TeamAssign message from the project manager.

2   In the TeamAssign message that appears, click Reply.

3   In the Message box, type any message you want the project manager to see.

4   To accept the assignment, click Send.

Or

To reject the assignment, in the Accept? column click No, and then click Send.

> **tip**
> If you are running Microsoft Outlook, tasks you accept are added to your Outlook Task list. Tracking these tasks' percent complete or marking as complete in the Outlook Task list is recorded in status reports you send to the project manager.

Project Manager: Request the Resource's Assignment Status

1   Select the task or tasks for which you want to request the status.

2   On the Tools menu, click Workgroup and then select TeamStatus.

> ## tip
> If you display the Workgroup toolbar, you can also click the TeamStatus button.

Microsoft Project displays the Workgroup Mail dialog box.

3   Select All Tasks or Selected Tasks, and then click OK.

The TeamStatus dialog box appears.

4   In the Subject box and the message portion of the dialog box, customize the default content as you wish.

5   Click Send.

Microsoft Project sends an e-mail message to the assigned resources with the TeamStatus request attached.

Resource: Send Assignment Status to the Project Manager

1   In your e-mail application, open the TeamStatus message from the project manager.

2   In the TeamStatus message that appears, enter the remaining work, daily actual work, and comments you want to make for the tasks listed.

3   Click Send.

Your status is sent to the project manager.

> ## tip
> In Microsoft Outlook, you can generate an unsolicited TeamStatus report to submit to the Project Manager. Open the Tasks folder, and then on the Actions menu, click New TeamStatus Report.

Project Manager: Update the Microsoft Project File with the Resource's TeamStatus Response

1   In your e-mail application, open the TeamStatus response message from the resource.

2   Review the actual values reported by the resource. If they meet with your approval, click Update Project.

Microsoft Project updates the file with the actuals from the resource. Any comments from the resource appear as task notes.

Using Web-based Collaboration with Microsoft Project Central

Microsoft Project Central is a companion product that works with Microsoft Project to allow a broad range of workgroup collaboration. Project Central consists of two major components:

- The server component, which runs on a Windows NT Server 4.0 or in Windows 2000 running Microsoft Internet Information Server. This component controls a database of Project Central information which, upon your approval, is synchronized with Microsoft Project files.

- The client component, which runs in Microsoft Internet Explorer (or the Browser Module included with Project Central) on the desktops of the project manager, the resources, and other stakeholders you've enabled to connect to the Project Central server component and to specific projects.

Together, Microsoft Project and the Project Central client and server components provide a complete Web-based communication and collaboration tool for project teams and stakeholders. Some of the most important activities that Project Central facilitates include allowing

- Project managers to publish project and portfolio (multiproject) status and other details in one central location.

- Resources to view personal task assignments and Gantt Charts, report actual work and other status, and, if enabled by the project manager, create new tasks and delegate tasks to other resources.

- Other stakeholders such as resource managers, upper management, and customers to view whatever project details they are most interested in and the project manager has made available.

- All involved in a project or portfolio of projects to use one standard tool to communicate project information.

The following sections describe some of the activities carried out by the three main users of Project Central: the project manager, the administrator, and the resource.

Project Manager Activities in Project Central

As with Microsoft Project, one key theme of Project Central is that the project manager controls the overall project plan and approves all updates between the Microsoft Project file and the Project Central server database. This section describes some of the common activities of the project manager in Project Central.

**PROJ2000-3-9,
PROJ2000E-6-1**

For a demonstration of common activities performed by the project manager, in the Multimedia folder on the Microsoft Project 2000 Step by Step CD-ROM, double-click Project Central Project Manager.AVI

Before you start any of the following activities, connect to the Project Central logon page and log on as a user who's been assigned the Manager role. When you do, a home page similar to the following illustration appears.

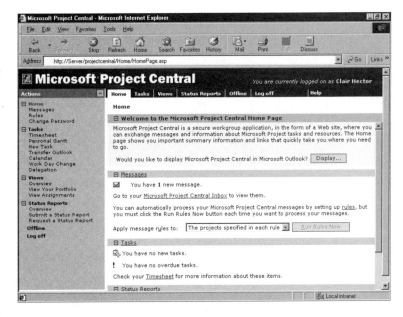

To Update Microsoft Project Central from Microsoft Project

As you make changes to the Microsoft Project file for which you've enabled Project Central Web communication, you should update Project Central with the latest project information from time to time. It's a good idea to do this at least as frequently as your project's status-reporting period.

1   In Microsoft Project, open the Microsoft Project file for which you've enabled Project Central Web communication.

2   On the Tools menu, click Workgroup, and then click Update Project to Web Server.

Microsoft Project updates the Project Central server database with the latest high-level details from the Microsoft Project file.

> ## tip
> You can choose to update the Project Central server database automatically every time you save the Microsoft Project file to which it is connected. On the Tools menu click Options, and then click the Workgroup tab. Click the Update Project Information to Microsoft Project Central Server On Every Save box.

To Set Up Status Reports

You can use Project Central as your team's main overall team status-reporting tool. Once you set up a status report design, it is ready for the resources you specified to submit their status at the time interval you specified.

1   In Project Central, on the Status Reports menu, click Request A Status Report.

The Request a Status Report page appears.

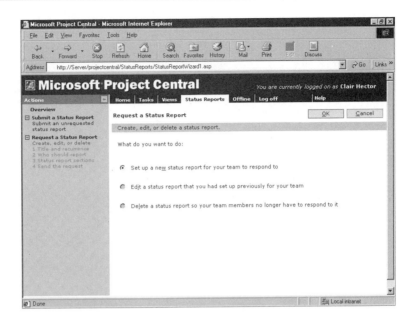

2   Click Set Up A New Status Report For Your Team To Respond To, and then click OK.

The first step of the Request A Status Report wizard appears.

3   Choose the options you want, and then click Next. On the subsequent pages of the wizard, follow the instructions on your screen.

To Set Up Auto-Accept Rules

To save time, you can set up rules that automatically accept certain types of requests from resources in Project Central. For example, you can set up rules to allow certain resources to create new tasks and have those reflected in the Microsoft Project file without your explicit approval, or automatically to approve requests to delegate tasks.

1   On the Home menu, click Rules.

The Rules page appears.

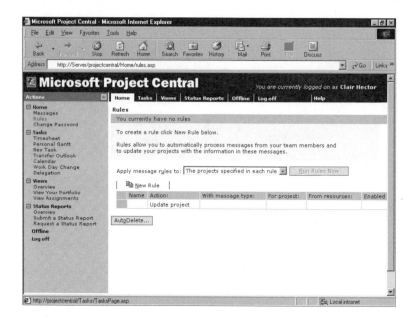

2 Click New Rule.

Step 1 of the Rules wizard appears.

3 Choose the options you want, and click Next. On the subsequent pages of the wizard, follow the instructions on your screen.

Administrator Activities in Project Central

PROJ2000E-2-3
PROJ2000E-6-4
PROJ2000E-6-5
PROJ2000E-6-6
PROJ2000E-6-7

This section describes common administrative activities the project manager or administrator perform in Project Central. Although Project Central distinguishes between the roles of project manager and administrator, you may in fact find yourself serving as both. The main difference between the two is that when you are logged on as an administrator, the Admin menu and its commands are available; when you are logged on as a project manager, they are not.

Before you start any of the following activities, connect to the Project Central logon page and log on as a user who's been assigned the administrator role. When you do, a home page appears.

Create Users and Permissions in Project Central

As an administrator, you control who has Project Central accounts and can view Project Central information. Initially, the resources and project managers from the Microsoft Project files you have connected to the Project Central server appear as users in Project Central, but you can add other users—such as customers or upper management—who are not resources in your projects.

For a demonstration of common activities performed by the administrator, in the Multimedia folder on the Microsoft Project 2000 Step by Step CD-ROM, double-click Project Central Administrator.AVI.

1 On the Admin menu, click Users.

The User List page appears.

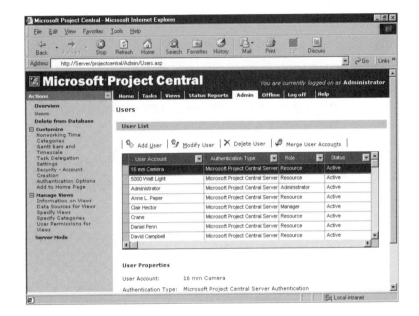

2 Click Add User.

The Add User page appears.

3 Under Add A New User, enter the authentication type, user account name, e-mail address, and other information.

---

tip

If a user is accessing Project Central over a network that requires Windows NT authentication, choose this option. It is more secure than the Microsoft Project Central Server authentication. In the next section, you will specify the overall authentication scheme used by Project Central.

---

4 Click Save Changes.

Set Security Options in Project Central

This activity requires setting the Project Central server to single-user mode. Before you do this, make sure nobody else is using Project Central.

1   On the Admin menu, click Server Mode.

Project Central displays the Server Mode page.

2   Click Single User, and then click Save Changes.

3   On the Admin menu, click Overview.

Project Central displays the Administration Overview page.

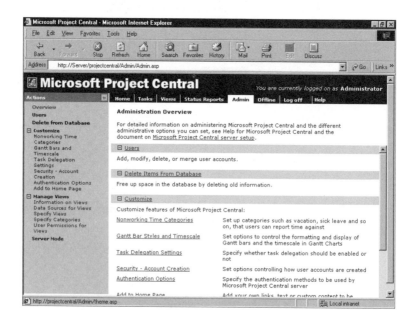

tip

You can also see some of the other customization options available here. You might want to explore these options while you have the Project Central server in single-user mode.

4   Under Customize, click Authentication Options.

Project Central displays the Authentication Options page.

5   Select the authentication and password options you want to apply to all users who will attempt to access this Project Central server, and then click Save Changes.

6   On the Admin menu, click Server Mode.

    Project Central displays the Server Mode page.

7   Click Normal, and then click Save Changes.

Format Gantt Charts in Project Central

Similar to the Gantt Chart formatting capabilities in Microsoft Project, you can format the Gantt Charts available in Project Central.

1   On the Admin menu, click Customize.

    The Administration Overview page appears.

tip

You can also see some of the other formatting and customizing options available here.

2   Under Customize, click Gantt Bar Styles And Timescale.

    The Gantt Bar Styles And Timescale page appears.

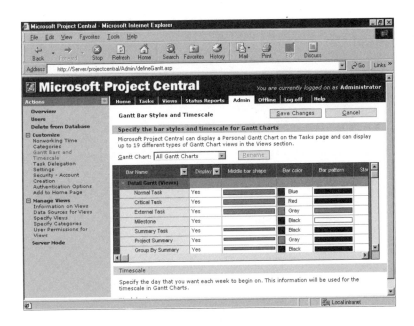

3   In the Gantt Chart box, select the specific Gantt Chart you want to customize.

4   Below that, select the formatting options you want.

5   Click Save Changes.

Create and Manage Views

As in Microsoft Project, you can create custom views in Project Central. You can also make views available exclusively to a specific category of user. The categories are described in the next procedure.

1   On the Admin menu, click Manage Views.

   The Information On Views page appears.

tip

The Information On Views page recommends that you read Svrsetup.htm prior to setting up views. In general, you should be familiar with the content of Svrsetup.htm prior to using any of the commands on the Admin menu.

2   In the Actions bar on the left side of the Project Central window, under Manage Views, click Specify Views.

   The Specify Views page appears.

3   To create a new view, click New View and then follow the instructions on your screen.

   Or

   To modify an existing view, click Modify View and then follow the instructions on your screen.

Create and Manage User Categories

You can assign Project Central users to one of four predefined categories:

- Team member (the default category to which all new Project Central users are assigned)
- Project manager
- Resource manager
- Executive

You can also create your own categories of users. For members of each category, you control the specific projects they have access to, as well as what views and other details such as resource assignments they can see.

1   On the Admin menu, click Manage Views.

The Information On Views page appears.

2   In the Actions bar on the left side of the Project Central window, under Manage Views, click Specify Categories.

The Specify Categories page appears.

3   To create a new category, click New Category and choose the options you want.

Or

To modify an existing category, select it in the list and then click Modify Category, and choose the options you want.

Enable Resources to Delegate Tasks Using Project Central

Task delegation in Project Central allows one resource to assign, or delegate, a task to another resource. By default, task delegation is enabled.

1   On the Admin menu, click Overview.

Project Central displays the Administration Overview page.

2   Under Customize, click Task Delegation Settings.

Project Central displays the Task Delegation Settings page. The default setting is Enable Task Delegation.

3   If this is not what you want, click Disable Task Delegation, and then click Save Changes.

Resource Activities in Project Central

PROJ2000-2-1

For resources and other stakeholders involved in a project, Project Central can serve as their single tool both for getting information from the project and for submitting information to the project (each subject to the project manager's approval). Project Central can replace or augment a variety of communication methods such as e-mail, paper-based status reports, timesheets, and the ubiquitous Gantt Chart on the bulletin board.

This section describes some of the common resource activities in Project Central. Before a resource can do any of these activities, however, he or she must be authorized to do so and be set up as valid users in Project Central by a project manager or administrator.

*For a demon-
stration of
common ac-
tivities per-
formed by
resources, in
the Multime-
dia folder on
the Microsoft
Project 2000
Step by Step
CD-ROM,
double-click
Project Central
Resource.AVI.*

Before you start any of the following activities, connect to the Project Central logon page and log on as a resource. When you do, a home page similar to the following illustration appears.

View Your Personal Gantt Chart

A personal Gantt Chart is a handy way to see just your own assignments in a familiar Gantt Chart format. The Personal Gantt Chart view in Project Central offers filtering, grouping, and other options to control how much detail you see in the Gantt Chart.

1   On the Tasks menu, click Personal Gantt.

    Project Central displays the Gantt View page.

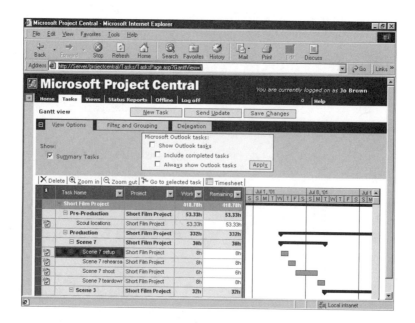

Also note the Filter and Grouping and Delegation tabs.

2   To see a specific task's Gantt bar, select it from the task list and then click Go To Selected Task.

View Your Timesheet and Send Updated Actuals to the Project Manager

The timesheet in Project Central gives you one central place for reporting actual work on assigned tasks, as well as past or upcoming nonworking time such as vacation days. After you submit actual work, the project manager evaluates it and, if he or she approves, updates the Microsoft Project file with your actuals.

1   On the Tasks menu, click Timesheet.

       The Timesheet page appears.

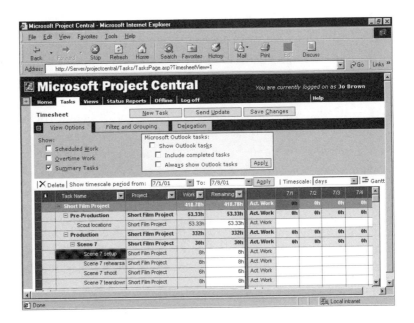

2   To record actual work on tasks, first select the task name. Then, in the timescaled grid on the right, enter the actual work values for the days you want. If the days for which you want to report work are not visible, change the Show Timescale Period From/To dates.

3   To submit the actuals to the project manager, click Send Update.

Create a New Task

If resources create new tasks in Project Central, these tasks can later be updated to the Microsoft Project file at the project manager's discretion.

Allowing resources to create new tasks in Project Central can serve two important purposes:

■   Allow resources to document tasks that were not in the initial project plan. This can help account for more of the work required to execute the project, which may be significantly more work than was initially identified in the Microsoft Project plan.

■ Record lower-level work that may be associated with a summary task in the Microsoft Project file. This ability allows for bottom-up project planning where the project manager can plan at the summary level and leave it to the resources to fill in the required subtasks.

1   On the Tasks menu, click New Task.

   The New Task page appears.

2   In the Project box, select the specific project to which this task should be associated. If the project you have in mind is not listed, contact the project manager.

3   Under What Outline Level Do You Want To Create The New Task In, select the option you want.

4   Under Task Information, fill in the details of the task.

5   Click Create Task.

Delegate Tasks to Another Resource

If the Project Central administrator has enabled task delegation for the active project, any resource can delegate, or reassign, a task in Project Central. When a resource delegates a task, he or she must specify the following:

■ To whom the task is to be delegated.

■ To whom the actuals should be sent—to them or directly to the project manager.

■ Whether the delegated task and its subsequent actuals should appear on their own timesheet.

The project manager must approve task delegations before updating the Microsoft Project file.

1   On the Tasks menu, click Delegation.

   The Timesheet page appears.

2   On the task list, select the task you wish to delegate.

3   Click Delegate Tasks.

   The Delegate Tasks wizard appears.

4   Follow the instructions on your screen.

Import Your Nonworking Time from Microsoft Outlook

If you use the Calendar module in Microsoft Outlook, you can import information about events marked as "Busy" or "Out of Office" so that those same blocks of time are reported as nonworking time to the project manager or on your timesheet. This is an effective way to keep your scheduled working availability synchronized with your real schedule. By doing so you control the time period in which nonworking time will be reported (for example, next week or next month) and the minimum duration of the events to be reported (for instance, don't report events shorter than two hours). Then, of all the events that meet the criteria you specify, you can still choose not to report some if you wish.

1 On the Tasks menu, click Transfer Calendar Entries From Microsoft Outlook. The first step of the Transfer Calendar Entries From Microsoft Outlook wizard appears.

2 Follow the instructions on your screen.

E

What's Next?

If you've completed most or all of the lessons in this book, you're well on your way to mastering Microsoft Project. However, one book can only get you so far. To help further your Microsoft Project and project management knowledge, here are a few sources available to you.

Joining a Microsoft Project Learning Community

If there's one thing we can say about Microsoft Project users, it's that they love to talk about the program and their work with it, and to share ideas with others. Whether you work in a large organization or independently, you're likely to find a community of Microsoft Project users nearby.

If you're in a large organization, especially one with a strong project management focus, you might find an internal Microsoft Project user group or support group there. Such groups often meet informally to provide peer training and support, to critique project plans, and to share best practices. If there isn't such a group in your organization, you might well start one.

In the public realm, there are many Microsoft Project user groups around the world. These groups typically meet on a regular basis to share tips and tricks about Microsoft Project. For example, in the Puget Sound area of the American Northwest where the authors live and work, there's an active Microsoft Project user group that meets most months for informal idea-sharing and for formal presentations by industry experts. Joining a user group is a great way to broaden your exposure to Microsoft Project usage; it also can be a great source for informal product support, training, and career networking.

Here are a few places where you can investigate Microsoft Project user groups and related resources:

- Msproject.com is an independent clearinghouse of information about Microsoft Project. The website contains links to a variety of resources that would interest any Microsoft Project user. Find it on the Web at http://www.msproject.com/

- The Microsoft Project Users Group (MPUG) offers both free and subscription-based information about a variety of Microsoft Project and project management resources, as well as a directory of Microsoft Project user groups around the world. Find it on the Web at http://www.mpug.org/

- The official Microsoft Project website on microsoft.com includes a variety of sales literature, product specifications, and links to other resources. Find it on the Web at http://www.microsoft.com/office/project/

- The official Microsoft Project newsgroup offers help and discussions with other users of Microsoft Project, including Microsoft Most Valuable Professionals (MVPs). You can use any newsreader software to access this newsgroup. To view or subscribe to this newsgroup, point your newsreader to news://msnews.microsoft.com/microsoft.public.project

Becoming Microsoft Project MOUS Certified

The Microsoft Office User Specialist (MOUS) program has offered users of Office programs a path to formal certification for several years. Now Microsoft Project 2000 has been added to the program. Becoming MOUS certified requires you to demonstrate your knowledge of the program at either a "core" or an "expert" level.

MOUS certification is strongly focused on Microsoft Project functionality, and can be a great complement to broader project management training. It's a great way to officially demonstrate and advertise your Microsoft Project knowledge to peers, clients, and employers. You can learn more about Microsoft Project 2000 MOUS certification on the Web at http://www.mous.net/

Joining a Project Management Learning Community

Probably more than most other desktop programs, Microsoft Project requires you to be involved in a specific formal activity: project management.   Project management can be an exciting mix of technical, organizational, and social challenges. The Project Management Institute (PMI) is the leading organization of professional project management. PMI focuses on setting project management standards, developing and offering educational programs, and certifying Project Management Professionals (PMPs).

PMI's *A Guide to the Project Management Body of Knowledge* (*PMBOK*) describes generally accepted project management practices, knowledge areas, and terminology. In addition, PMI publishes the journals *Project Management Journal* and *PM Network*. You can learn more about PMI on the Web at http://www.pmi.org/

Based in the United Kingdom, The Association for Project Management (APM) publishes the *APM Body of Knowledge*. The APM provides project management training as well as certification. You can learn more about APM on the Web at http://www.apmgroup.co.uk/

Two websites or "portals" that might interest you are Project Connections and GanttHead.com. You can find these subscription-based sites at the following Web addresses:

- http://www.projectconnections.com/
- http://www.gantthead.com/

Both sites offer a wide variety of training, discussion forums, and industry-specific metrics and best practices for project management.

Final Words

There are, of course, many worthwhile commercial and nonprofit organizations dedicated to Microsoft Project and project management besides those we've described here. Microsoft Project enjoys a leading position in the diverse, sometimes contentious, but always interesting world of project management. Wherever you are in your own Microsoft Project and project management knowledge and career development, you can find a great variety of supporting organizations and peers today. Good luck!

Index

Note: Page numbers in *italic* reference non-text material

U

V

W

About the Authors

Carl S. Chatfield

Carl is a documentation manager in the Microsoft Project User Assistance team at Microsoft. He joined the Project team shortly after Microsoft Project 98 shipped and prior to that worked in the Microsoft Excel and Microsoft Office teams.

Carl is a graduate of the master's program in Technical Communication at the University of Washington and has been certified as a Project Management Professional (PMP) by the Project Management Institute. He lives in Redmond, Washington.

Timothy D. Johnson

Tim is a support professional in the Microsoft Project Support group at Microsoft. He has supported customers in the use of Microsoft Project since version 3.0. He lives in Issaquah, Washington.

The manuscript for this book was copyedited and submitted to Microsoft Press in electronic form by Publishing Synthesis, Ltd. (www.pubsyn.com). Text files were prepared using Microsoft Word. Pages were composed by Publishing Synthesis, Ltd. using Adobe PageMaker 6.52 for Windows, with text in Sabon and display type in Syntax. Composed pages were delivered to the printer as electronic prepress files.

Cover Graphic Design by
Girvin | Branding & Design

Interior Designer
James D. Kramer

Illustrator
Michael Kloepfer

MICROSOFT LICENSE AGREEMENT
Book Companion CD

IMPORTANT—READ CAREFULLY: This Microsoft End-User License Agreement ("EULA") is a legal agreement between you (either an individual or an entity) and Microsoft Corporation for the Microsoft product identified above, which includes computer software and may include associated media, printed materials, and "online" or electronic documentation ("SOFTWARE PRODUCT"). Any component included within the SOFTWARE PRODUCT that is accompanied by a separate End-User License Agreement shall be governed by such agreement and not the terms set forth below. By installing, copying, or otherwise using the SOFTWARE PRODUCT, you agree to be bound by the terms of this EULA. If you do not agree to the terms of this EULA, you are not authorized to install, copy, or otherwise use the SOFTWARE PRODUCT; you may, however, return the SOFTWARE PRODUCT, along with all printed materials and other items that form a part of the Microsoft product that includes the SOFTWARE PRODUCT, to the place you obtained them for a full refund.

SOFTWARE PRODUCT LICENSE

The SOFTWARE PRODUCT is protected by United States copyright laws and international copyright treaties, as well as other intellectual property laws and treaties. The SOFTWARE PRODUCT is licensed, not sold.

1. **GRANT OF LICENSE.** This EULA grants you the following rights:

   a. **Software Product.** You may install and use one copy of the SOFTWARE PRODUCT on a single computer. The primary user of the computer on which the SOFTWARE PRODUCT is installed may make a second copy for his or her exclusive use on a portable computer.

   b. **Storage/Network Use.** You may also store or install a copy of the SOFTWARE PRODUCT on a storage device, such as a network server, used only to install or run the SOFTWARE PRODUCT on your other computers over an internal network; however, you must acquire and dedicate a license for each separate computer on which the SOFTWARE PRODUCT is installed or run from the storage device. A license for the SOFTWARE PRODUCT may not be shared or used concurrently on different computers.

   c. **License Pak.** If you have acquired this EULA in a Microsoft License Pak, you may make the number of additional copies of the computer software portion of the SOFTWARE PRODUCT authorized on the printed copy of this EULA, and you may use each copy in the manner specified above. You are also entitled to make a corresponding number of secondary copies for portable computer use as specified above.

   d. **Sample Code.** Solely with respect to portions, if any, of the SOFTWARE PRODUCT that are identified within the SOFTWARE PRODUCT as sample code (the "SAMPLE CODE"):

      i. **Use and Modification.** Microsoft grants you the right to use and modify the source code version of the SAMPLE CODE, *provided* you comply with subsection (d)(iii) below. You may not distribute the SAMPLE CODE, or any modified version of the SAMPLE CODE, in source code form.

      ii. **Redistributable Files.** Provided you comply with subsection (d)(iii) below, Microsoft grants you a nonexclusive, royalty-free right to reproduce and distribute the object code version of the SAMPLE CODE and of any modified SAMPLE CODE, other than SAMPLE CODE, or any modified version thereof, designated as not redistributable in the Readme file that forms a part of the SOFTWARE PRODUCT (the "Non-Redistributable Sample Code"). All SAMPLE CODE other than the Non-Redistributable Sample Code is collectively referred to as the "REDISTRIBUTABLES."

      iii. **Redistribution Requirements.** If you redistribute the REDISTRIBUTABLES, you agree to: (i) distribute the REDISTRIBUTABLES in object code form only in conjunction with and as a part of your software application product; (ii) not use Microsoft's name, logo, or trademarks to market your software application product; (iii) include a valid copyright notice on your software application product; (iv) indemnify, hold harmless, and defend Microsoft from and against any claims or lawsuits, including attorney's fees, that arise or result from the use or distribution of your software application product; and (v) not permit further distribution of the REDISTRIBUTABLES by your end user. Contact Microsoft for the applicable royalties due and other licensing terms for all other uses and/or distribution of the REDISTRIBUTABLES.

2. **DESCRIPTION OF OTHER RIGHTS AND LIMITATIONS.**

   - **Limitations on Reverse Engineering, Decompilation, and Disassembly.** You may not reverse engineer, decompile, or disassemble the SOFTWARE PRODUCT, except and only to the extent that such activity is expressly permitted by applicable law notwithstanding this limitation.

   - **Separation of Components.** The SOFTWARE PRODUCT is licensed as a single product. Its component parts may not be separated for use on more than one computer.

   - **Rental.** You may not rent, lease, or lend the SOFTWARE PRODUCT.

   - **Support Services.** Microsoft may, but is not obligated to, provide you with support services related to the SOFTWARE PRODUCT ("Support Services"). Use of Support Services is governed by the Microsoft policies and programs described in the user manual, in "online" documentation, and/or in other Microsoft-provided materials. Any supplemental software code provided to you as part of the Support Services shall be considered part of the SOFTWARE PRODUCT and subject to the terms and conditions of this EULA. With respect to technical information you provide to Microsoft as part of the Support Services, Microsoft may use such information for its business purposes, including for product support and development. Microsoft will not utilize such technical information in a form that personally identifies you.

- **Software Transfer.** You may permanently transfer all of your rights under this EULA, provided you retain no copies, you transfer all of the SOFTWARE PRODUCT (including all component parts, the media and printed materials, any upgrades, this EULA, and, if applicable, the Certificate of Authenticity), **and** the recipient agrees to the terms of this EULA.

- **Termination.** Without prejudice to any other rights, Microsoft may terminate this EULA if you fail to comply with the terms and conditions of this EULA. In such event, you must destroy all copies of the SOFTWARE PRODUCT and all of its component parts.

3. **COPYRIGHT.** All title and copyrights in and to the SOFTWARE PRODUCT (including but not limited to any images, photographs, animations, video, audio, music, text, SAMPLE CODE, REDISTRIBUTABLES, and "applets" incorporated into the SOFTWARE PRODUCT) and any copies of the SOFTWARE PRODUCT are owned by Microsoft or its suppliers. The SOFTWARE PRODUCT is protected by copyright laws and international treaty provisions. Therefore, you must treat the SOFTWARE PRODUCT like any other copyrighted material **except** that you may install the SOFTWARE PRODUCT on a single computer provided you keep the original solely for backup or archival purposes. You may not copy the printed materials accompanying the SOFTWARE PRODUCT.

4. **U.S. GOVERNMENT RESTRICTED RIGHTS.** The SOFTWARE PRODUCT and documentation are provided with RESTRICTED RIGHTS. Use, duplication, or disclosure by the Government is subject to restrictions as set forth in subparagraph (c)(1)(ii) of the Rights in Technical Data and Computer Software clause at DFARS 252.227-7013 or subparagraphs (c)(1) and (2) of the Commercial Computer Software—Restricted Rights at 48 CFR 52.227-19, as applicable. Manufacturer is Microsoft Corporation/One Microsoft Way/Redmond, WA 98052-6399.

5. **EXPORT RESTRICTIONS.** You agree that you will not export or re-export the SOFTWARE PRODUCT, any part thereof, or any process or service that is the direct product of the SOFTWARE PRODUCT (the foregoing collectively referred to as the "Restricted Components"), to any country, person, entity, or end user subject to U.S. export restrictions. You specifically agree not to export or re-export any of the Restricted Components (i) to any country to which the U.S. has embargoed or restricted the export of goods or services, which currently include, but are not necessarily limited to, Cuba, Iran, Iraq, Libya, North Korea, Sudan, and Syria, or to any national of any such country, wherever located, who intends to transmit or transport the Restricted Components back to such country; (ii) to any end user who you know or have reason to know will utilize the Restricted Components in the design, development, or production of nuclear, chemical, or biological weapons; or (iii) to any end user who has been prohibited from participating in U.S. export transactions by any federal agency of the U.S. government. You warrant and represent that neither the BXA nor any other U.S. federal agency has suspended, revoked, or denied your export privileges.

DISCLAIMER OF WARRANTY

NO WARRANTIES OR CONDITIONS. MICROSOFT EXPRESSLY DISCLAIMS ANY WARRANTY OR CONDITION FOR THE SOFTWARE PRODUCT. THE SOFTWARE PRODUCT AND ANY RELATED DOCUMENTATION ARE PROVIDED "AS IS" WITHOUT WARRANTY OR CONDITION OF ANY KIND, EITHER EXPRESS OR IMPLIED, INCLUDING, WITHOUT LIMITATION, THE IMPLIED WARRANTIES OF MERCHANTABILITY, FITNESS FOR A PARTICULAR PURPOSE, OR NONINFRINGEMENT. THE ENTIRE RISK ARISING OUT OF USE OR PERFORMANCE OF THE SOFTWARE PRODUCT REMAINS WITH YOU.

LIMITATION OF LIABILITY. TO THE MAXIMUM EXTENT PERMITTED BY APPLICABLE LAW, IN NO EVENT SHALL MICROSOFT OR ITS SUPPLIERS BE LIABLE FOR ANY SPECIAL, INCIDENTAL, INDIRECT, OR CONSEQUENTIAL DAMAGES WHATSOEVER (INCLUDING, WITHOUT LIMITATION, DAMAGES FOR LOSS OF BUSINESS PROFITS, BUSINESS INTERRUPTION, LOSS OF BUSINESS INFORMATION, OR ANY OTHER PECUNIARY LOSS) ARISING OUT OF THE USE OF OR INABILITY TO USE THE SOFTWARE PRODUCT OR THE PROVISION OF OR FAILURE TO PROVIDE SUPPORT SERVICES, EVEN IF MICROSOFT HAS BEEN ADVISED OF THE POSSIBILITY OF SUCH DAMAGES. IN ANY CASE, MICROSOFT'S ENTIRE LIABILITY UNDER ANY PROVISION OF THIS EULA SHALL BE LIMITED TO THE GREATER OF THE AMOUNT ACTUALLY PAID BY YOU FOR THE SOFTWARE PRODUCT OR US$5.00; PROVIDED, HOWEVER, IF YOU HAVE ENTERED INTO A MICROSOFT SUPPORT SERVICES AGREEMENT, MICROSOFT'S ENTIRE LIABILITY REGARDING SUPPORT SERVICES SHALL BE GOVERNED BY THE TERMS OF THAT AGREEMENT. BECAUSE SOME STATES AND JURISDICTIONS DO NOT ALLOW THE EXCLUSION OR LIMITATION OF LIABILITY, THE ABOVE LIMITATION MAY NOT APPLY TO YOU.

MISCELLANEOUS

This EULA is governed by the laws of the State of Washington USA, except and only to the extent that applicable law mandates governing law of a different jurisdiction.

Should you have any questions concerning this EULA, or if you desire to contact Microsoft for any reason, please contact the Microsoft subsidiary serving your country, or write: Microsoft Sales Information Center/One Microsoft Way/Redmond, WA 98052-6399.

Proof of Purchase

0-7356-0920-9

Do not send this card with your registration.
Use this card as proof of purchase if participating in a promotion or
rebate offer on *Microsoft® Project 2000 Step by Step*. Card must be used in conjunction with
other proof(s) of payment such as your dated sales receipt—see offer details.

Microsoft® Project 2000 Step by Step

_____
WHERE DID YOU PURCHASE THIS PRODUCT?

_____
CUSTOMER NAME

Microsoft®
mspress.microsoft.com

Microsoft Press, PO Box 97017, Redmond, WA 98073-9830

OWNER REGISTRATION CARD   **Register Today!**   0-7356-0920-9

Return the bottom portion of this card to register today.

Microsoft® Project 2000 Step by Step

_____   _____   _____
FIRST NAME   **MIDDLE INITIAL**   **LAST NAME**

_____
INSTITUTION OR COMPANY NAME

_____
ADDRESS

_____

_____   _____   _____
CITY   **STATE**   **ZIP**

_____   ( )
E-MAIL ADDRESS   **PHONE NUMBER**

U.S. and Canada addresses only. Fill in information above and mail postage-free.
Please mail only the bottom half of this page.

For information about Microsoft Press®

products, visit our Web site at

mspress.microsoft.com